WOMEN NOVELISTS AND THE ETHICS OF DESIRE, 1684–1814

Joseph Highmore, 1692–1780, *Mr. B. Finds Pamela Writing*. From *Four Scenes from Samuel Richardson's Pamela*, 1743–44 © Tate, London 2007

Women Novelists and the Ethics of Desire, 1684–1814
In the Voice of Our Biblical Mothers

ELIZABETH KRAFT
University of Georgia, USA

ASHGATE

Published by
Ashgate Publishing Limited
Wey Court East
Union Road
Farnham
Surrey GU9 7PT
England

Ashgate Publishing Company
Suite 420
101 Cherry Street
Burlington, VT 05401-4405
USA

Ashgate website: http://www.ashgate.com

British Library Cataloguing in Publication Data
Kraft, Elizabeth
Women Novelists and the Ethics of Desire, 1634–1814: In the Voice of our Biblical Mothers
1. English fiction – Women authors – History and criticism. 2. English fiction – 18th century – History and criticism. 3. English fiction – Early modern, 1500–1700 – History and criticism. 4. English fiction – 19th century – History and criticism. 5. Women in literature. 6. Desire in literature. 7. Ethics in literature 8. Desire – Moral and ethical aspects
I. Title
823.5'099287

Library of Congress Cataloging-in-Publication Data
Kraft, Elizabeth.
Women Novelists and the Ethics of Desire, 1684–1814: In the Voice of our Biblical Mothers / by Elizabeth Kraft.
    p.   cm.
1. English fiction – Women authors – History and criticism. 2. English fiction – 18th century – History and criticism. 3. English fiction – Early modern, 1500–1700 – History and criticism. 4. English fiction – 19th century – History and criticism. 5. Women in literature. 6. Desire in literature. 7. Ethics in literature. 8. Desire – Moral and ethical aspects. I. Title.
PR858.W6K73 2008
823'.5099287–dc22   2007035237

ISBN 978-0-7546-6280-8

Reprinted 2009

Mixed Sources
Product group from well-managed forests and other controlled sources
www.fsc.org Cert no. SA-COC-1565
© 1996 Forest Stewardship Council
FSC

Printed and bound in Great Britain by
MPG Books Ltd, Bodmin, Cornwall.

Contents

Acknowledgments

The writing of any book, I suppose, is a journey. The writing of this book has been a particularly interesting one for me in that it took place during a time of personal transition and redefinition when the constants in my life seemed fewer than the changes. Throughout the entire process, however, I was aware of some permanent undergirding commitments, including a love of text, a love of learning, a love of teaching, and an appreciation for support and kindness shown at any time, in any way.

Among the kind supporters I wish to acknowledge are the following. They bear no responsibility for anything you will read in the ensuing pages—unless, of course, I credit them there. For the most part, the kindnesses they have shown have been personal—sometimes inconsistent, sometimes temporary—but at some point each of the people I name did step forward with an encouraging word or a bit of practical advice. They are: Melvyn New, George Dynin, Nancy Felson, Judith Shaw, Betty Jean Craige, Mark Boren, Kate Montweiler, Nicole Reynolds, Crystal Landrum, Julie Barfield, Patricia Hamilton, Jeanine Casler, Jennifer Wilson, Kay Weeks, Darlene Ciraulo, Matt Kozusko, Douglas Anderson, Bill Free, Marya Free, Bill McCarthy, Paula Feldman, Tricia Lootens, Rachel Uziel, Janice Simon, Barbara McCaskill, Marlyse Baptista, Elissa Henken, Marilyn Gootman, Gary Grossman, Phillip Gerson, Martine Brownley, John Sitter, Paul Hunter, Kristina Straub, Katarzyna Jerzak, Anne Williams, Susan Rosenbaum, Roxanne Eberle, Chloe Wigston Smith, Sujata Iyengar, and Richard Menke.

I am grateful, as well, to the acquisitions editors at Ashgate—Ann Donahue and Erika Gaffney—for their own generosity of spirit and for the equally generous and erudite anonymous reader they commissioned to evaluate my manuscript. The seriousness and thoroughness with which this reader responded and guided me were instrumental in helping me shape the final argument. I felt I was working with a collaborator after the first reader's report.

Early in my career at the University of Georgia, I received a Sarah Moss Fellowship that allowed me to spend three months in London to complete a course of reading at the British Library in women's fiction of the eighteenth century. My 1985 PhD was awarded just at the moment that the field began to pay attention to neglected texts written by women during the age of Dryden, Pope, Swift, and Johnson. In 1989, the reassessment and recovery of women's texts was in full swing, and my successful grant proposal asked the University of Georgia to help me "catch up." Subsequent years found me teaching eighteenth-century women's fiction, editing their works, directing dissertations on the topic. The Sarah Moss Fellowship provided the seed money for what turned out to be a career-long preoccupation, and I am proud to acknowledge my debt here.

More recently, the University of Georgia Research Foundation three times awarded me financial support for this particular project. I am very grateful to the various committees who would have been justified, to my mind, had they lost patience with me. But they did not, and I appreciate their confidence in me.

I would also like to thank three rabbinic advisers on whom I relied for parts of this study: Scott Saulson, Ronald Gerson, and Ronald Brauner. All are my teachers, and all have provided insight into various texts I discuss herein. They might disagree with what I did with that insight, but I am indebted to them for providing it!

I thank my colleague and friend Joel Black who listened to me describe an enterprise I had abandoned and who encouraged me to reconsider. His words gave me some confidence in myself when I most needed it. Without his generous responsiveness, this book would still be a stack of papers on my desk.

I dedicate the book to the women in my life—my mother, Mary, my aunts, my grandmothers, my sister, Susan, my niece, Nicole, and her three daughters, my longtime "girlfriends," Franne Entelis and Sylvia Leary, my women students, my female colleagues, my friends and sisters at CCI, the women who have inspired me by their public lives, the women who have inspired me by their private behavior and personal commitments to family and friends. To all women who refuse to be quiet, all women who insist on speaking in their own voices and doing their own thing whether it's conventional, unconventional, original, traditional, expected, or way out there—I extend appreciation and bid you keep talking and doing, changing and growing...like Sarah, Rebekah, Leah, Rachel, Hagar, Deborah, Ruth, Aphra, Delarivier, Eliza, Frances, Dorothy, another Sarah, Charlotte, Elizabeth and all the others ... from then until now and beyond.

Introduction

In the Voice of a Woman

This study, like all such works, began with a simple question: what did women writers of the Restoration and eighteenth century in England have to say about female heterosexual desire? By the end, of course, my original query had multiplied into a series of complex concerns. One way to trace the development of the argument that will follow would be to record the history of the mutation of my simple question. How did I move from interest in women's expressions of sexual desire to the relationship between desire and philosophical materialism, desire and pastoral motifs, desire and the use of language, desire and national identity? How do materialism, pastoralism, nationalism, and sexual desire come to occupy the same textual space in the late seventeenth century? Is this joint occupation of textual territory contested? Do ideas remain fused through the period or does fiction written by women eventually separate strands that were once interwoven—and, if so, at what cost to the representation of desire? Efforts to answer those questions began to resonate with emphases of recent studies of Restoration and eighteenth-century literature as well as with the foci of certain works in the emerging field of ethical criticism and theory. And, eventually, my investigations took me back to the texts that ethical theorists examine—biblical narratives that focus on heterosexual desire.

This book is, in part, a meditation on female desire that sees and, indeed seeks, connections between the women writers of the early modern period in England and the women who populate some of the best known narratives of western culture. The older texts are not mined as source material, but are invoked as records that speak to perennial concerns, especially about love, sexual desire, and spiritual longing. The texts are evidence of presences and voices that have come to inhabit our collective consciousnesses, and perhaps consciences as well, whether we know it or not. Drawn on by ethicists to talk about woman's "voice," these texts serve this study in a similar way—that is, to outline the shape of female subjectivity, to stand as guideposts to the central concerns and rewards attendant on expression, presence, and being. The juxtaposition of these disparate texts is ethically illuminating in that it clarifies the project pursued by women writers of the long eighteenth century—a project focused on the examination and articulation of desire.

As such, this study challenges some of the received notions regarding the representation of women and desire that have dominated the field of cultural studies for the past few decades. The 1980s taught us to analyze structures of power, to recognize that power defines and in a very real sense defies the notion of social relationship, even (or perhaps especially) the relationship between men and women. Posited against an ideal of existential freedom, cultural analyses of this period alerted us to the variety and insidiousness of women's oppression. We came to accept as theorem the theory that women are and have long been victims of patriarchal power, that their own formulation and articulation of desire of any kind—sexual, political, material—is and has long been impossible. What we take to be their voices are merely the echoes of language spoken by men; what we mistake for their desires are merely versions of what they have been taught by men to want. This synopsis is an oversimplification of complex, subtle, and often very persuasive arguments, but in broad outline it does capture the intellectual position on heterosexual desire that prevailed for over two decades. And though it is being challenged now in increasing emphases on the way women's communities (present and past) provide alternative, empowering means of self-identification and self-construction, this thesis remains in place, underwriting still some analyses of gender relations and exchange between the sexes.[1] I was told quite bluntly by an anonymous reader of an essay having to do with the subject I am introducing here that "'woman' (not to mention 'woman's desire') is a male construct, a projection in which women do not exist at all." While such a view has force and value as a premise of deconstructive analysis, in terms of ethical inquiry, it will not do. Women can and do take responsibility for their own desires; they can and do recognize otherness. They can and do occupy the subject position in their own discourse; they can and do construct themselves.[2]

It is undeniable, however, that the analyzable artifacts of the past, including the written word, provide merely traces of woman's desire—her agency and subjectivity—not its full articulation. Even in works written by women, we see the force of cultural formulae, standards, and practices—formulae, standards and practices that define women as objects of desire, not subjects, that position them as the other by which man defines himself rather than the self posited against the male (or some other) other. Since the 1970s feminist theory and criticism has been interrogating various aspects of the literary representation and construction of woman. By now we recognize the dangers of essentializing gender and universalizing historically contingent assumptions about sexuality. But what we have not thoroughly assimilated

---

1   For a notable exception, see Lynne Segal, *Straight Sex: Rethinking the Politics of Pleasure* (Berkeley, 1994) who recognizes that "desire flows through binaries in all directions at once, all of the time" (161). She is cited by Alan Sinfield whose "Lesbian and Gay Taxonomies," *Critical Inquiry* 29 (2002): 120–38, proposes a series of definitional categories not based on power or conventional gender roles. Both Segal and Sinfield acknowledge the importance of the work of Michel Foucault, but they also move beyond it. On this topic see Joel Black's analysis of Foucault's "mistaken belief . . . that he could treat sexuality as a separate discursive phenomenon apart from an ethics of the self, on the one hand, and an erotics of the imagination, on the other." "Taking the Sex Out of Sexuality," in David H. J. Larmour, Paul Allen Miller, and Charles Platter (eds), *Rethinking Sexuality: Foucault and Classical Antiquity* (Princeton, 1998), p. 59.

2   A fact often ignored in theoretical discourses, as Amy Richlin has argued with regard to Foucault's *History of Sexuality*: Even in ancient literature, there is a corpus of women's writing, and consequently, as Richlin puts it, "if we want to inquire into what they thought about the desiring subject, we have only to look." "Foucault's *History of Sexuality*: A Useful Theory for Women?" in Larmour, Miller, and Platter (eds), *Rethinking Sexuality*, p. 153. See also Lin Foxhall's essay in the same volume, "Pandora Unbound: A Feminist Critique of Foucault's *History of Sexuality*," wherein Foxhall notes that "reality, hard to get at, is usually more complicated than ideology" (132).

into our various critiques of gender and sexuality is the degree to which writers of the past themselves were skeptical about essential and universal definitions. Much of the literary effort of English women writers of the long eighteenth century in particular was centered on the examination of the power, force, and meaning of sexual desire. As the works I will discuss illustrate, these women writers tended to see such desire in terms of historical moments, individuated histories, contingent narrative circumstances. The "fact" of woman's desire may be an assumption these writers do not question, but the operations and consequences of that desire are far from predictable either in terms of narrative content or moral purpose.

There are three limitations placed on this inquiry that require some explanation: First, the limit of nation; second, the limit of epoch; and, third, and probably most problematic, the limited focus on heterosexual as opposed to same-sex desire. These limits are all focal choices that will sometimes blur, but they are restrictions that I have consciously adopted for clear reasons. I will explain these limitations in the order I have listed them. I begin with nation. It is, of course, conventional in the discipline of literary studies to demarcate our intellectual inquiries by national boundaries, a tendency that has prevailed for many generations, self-perpetuated and self-sustained by institutional structures that unnaturally separate French, German, Asian, Spanish, Italian, English, African, and so forth studies into "departments," thus naturalizing the compartmentalization of knowledge and "fields." Convention notwithstanding, a study devoted to seventeenth- and eighteenth-century literary expressions of female desire that does not treat French writers such as Mesdames des Sevigne, Stael, Graffigny, and Lafayette or Messieurs La Clos, Marivaux, Rousseau, and de Sade for that matter seems intellectually suspect from the broadest point of view. To this charge, I will say that the absence of these writers is more perceived than real. While I focus on women novelists who wrote in English and lived primarily in England, I take into account the fact that most were as well read in the works of their French contemporaries as in the works of their English peers. I treat seriously their serious engagement with French and Italian romances in particular; and I often elaborate the correspondences between the narratives of these women with those of their European contemporaries or predecessors.[3]

Nevertheless, my focus is decidedly English because of the unique contribution England made in the seventeenth and eighteenth centuries to an international debate about political and sexual power. Discussions about sexual desire in this country during this period are grounded in the questions and questionings about natural law that were opened up in England by the cataclysmic events of the 1640s. Just as the following century and a half would witness a resolution of the large issues about governance and political power brought to the fore by the Civil War, the execution

---

3   For the reverse argument, i.e. that English literature was well known in Europe, in this case by German readers, see Bernhard Fabian, "English Books and Their German Readers" which tracks the increasing production of translations from mid-century on. In Paul Korshin (ed.) *The Widening Circle: Essays on the Circulation of Literature in Eighteenth-Century Europe* (Philadelphia, 1976), pp. 119–96. For the novelistic culture shared by French and English women novelists, see April Alliston, *Virtue's Faults: Correspondences in Eighteenth-Century British and French Women's Fiction* (Stanford, 1996), pp. 19, 250 n.32.

of the King, and the settlements of 1689 and 1701, it would also witness a related development in the evolution of gender construction and definitions of sexuality. The period of time with which this study begins is characterized by an openness of mind and expression, a fluidity of sexual self-definition, and a combination of playfulness and serious inquiry about desire that mark it as a unique time in English cultural history and confer upon it a unique place in European thought and expression as well. The period is also distinguished in England by the emergence of that literary phenomenon, Aphra Behn, who took desire as her central subject and who explored it with energy, precision, and courage both in her art and, at least by her own account, in her life as well. That voice profoundly guided her immediate successors, Delarivier Manley and Eliza Haywood, who self-consciously struggled to retain the subject as an appropriate one for women writers. The emergence of three prolific and influential women writers happened in England in this period—and nowhere else in Europe. This fact makes the time and the place a central point of concern for anyone interested in the history of female sexuality and the ethics of desire.

All of these women, however, also recognized the fact of same-sex desire, and it might be argued that to focus my own discussion on heterosexual desire is to limit my inquiry in ways the writers themselves would find mystifying. Certainly throughout the period women expressed passion for one another in words seemingly inflected by sexual appetite. Sometimes, as in the case of Behn and Manley in particular, the expressions of same-sex desire are quite explicit. Notably, especially in Behn's work, homosexual passion, both male and female, is represented as normative.[4] Indeed, as the libertine creed accepted the body's urges as natural and rejected culturally imposed restraints, it would follow that a writer philosophically committed to libertinism would represent same-sex passion without regarding it as a threat to social stability or individual sexual integrity. In fact, Behn's works suggest that recognition and celebration of same-sex passion are requisite for both a healthy social order and a full human experience.

Later writers, however, approach the topic of homosexual passion much more cautiously (and much more conventionally in terms of attitudes that would come to prevail) than Behn does. Of her immediate successors, Manley casts lesbian physical love in the range of the "unnatural"; and Haywood treats the subject in the covert, inexplicit, negatively salacious way that becomes the fictional, indeed the cultural, norm for centuries to follow.[5] For Manley, such negativity does not

---

4   Behn depicts female-female desire explicitly in her poem "To the Fair Clarinda, who made Love to me, imagin'd more than Woman." See Elizabeth Wahl's discussion of this poem as "one of the few instances in which a woman writer openly depicts female-female desire" (60). *Invisible Relations: Representations of Female Intimacy in the Age of Enlightenment* (Stanford, 1999), pp. 55–60.

5   See Wahl on the suspect nature of female friendship, or "*tendre amité*" in *The New Atalantis*, and in the court of Queen Anne, as well, pp. 117–29. Many critics have commented on Haywood's subversive narrative strategies. See, in particular, Stuart Shea, "Subversive Didacticism in Eliza Haywood's *Betsy Thoughtless*," *Studies in English Literature* 42 (2002): 559–75; Deborah J. Nestor, "Virtue Rarely Rewarded: Ideological Subversion and Narrative Form in Haywood's Later Fiction," *Studies in English Literature* 34 (1994): 579–98; and David Oakleaf, "The Eloquence of Blood in Eliza Haywood's *Lasselia*," *Studies in English*

represent a rejection of the libertine code so much as it speaks to cultural discomfort with the political power of certain individual women during the early eighteenth century. In the sixteenth century, a strong female English monarch had controlled her court and her country by surrounding herself with male advisers whose prominence and power she both manipulated and respected. Elizabeth's eighteenth-century successor, Queen Anne, conducted state affairs in a court dominated by powerful women. Her closest advisers were female: first, Sarah Churchill and, later, Abigail Masham. The fact that Masham supplanted Churchill because the queen and the Duchess of Marlborough quarreled over the naming of appointees to the cabinet will in itself suggest that these friendships had enormous political significance and were therefore of extraordinary political concern.

Manley was a satirist, a Tory, and as such she deployed a set of metaphors and characters designed to discredit the Whigs, in particular the Duke and Duchess of Marlborough, with a greater emphasis on the Duchess, Sarah Churchill, than the Duke. Same-sex love is part of Manley's satirical lexicon, a vocabulary developed to describe a society in a state of decay, dominated by ungoverned passions that impede the creation of a just, wise nation.[6] In her world, same-sex desire is no more and no less unsavory than adultery, incest, rape, or coercion, but that it is part of that pantheon and clearly denominated a social and political ill suggests a construction quite different from Behn's view that same-sex desire is as incidental, occasional, and normative as opposite sex desire.

With Haywood and the writers who follow her, the topic becomes if not less important, at least more submerged, and the struggle to define female subjectivity in a heterosexual world seems the significant task at hand. It is through stories of erotic desire for the male other that these later novelists explore the possibilities of fulfillment for women in the contemporary world. They take the structure and preoccupations of romance narratives and feminize them in several important ways. For example, the later novelists substitute the male paragon for the unattainable romance heroine, and they strive to discover the means by which women could actively pursue desire for this object of their longings. This rehabilitation of romance is not a mere inversion of the formula, however, for the novelists realize that their female characters must be worthy objects of desire. The novelists' own desire to write narratives featuring women whose actions are significant and meaningful, then, is constantly thwarted or at least hampered by narrative demands that the admirable female character remain passive and aloof, unsullied by involvement in a morally complicated world.

I believe that the central concern of all significant narrative is to explore and articulate the ethics of human behavior.[7] Literature is focused on the ramifications of

---

Literature 39 (1999): 483–98. Alexander Pettit specifically discusses Haywood's distance from Behn and Manley in her use of domestic spaces, a trope for her treatment of transgressiveness in general. See his "Adventures in Pornographic Places: Eliza Haywood's *Tea Table* and the Decentering of Moral Argument," *Papers on Language and Literature* 38 (2002): 244–69.

6   On the Tory use of family as a satirical motif, see Heinz-Joachim Müllenbrock, *The Culture of Contention: A Rhetorical Analysis of the Public Controversy about the Ending of the War of the Spanish Succession, 1710–1713* (München, 1997), pp. 60–1.

7   Pertinent here is Adam Zachary Newton's observation: "Cutting athwart the mediatory role of reason, narrative situations create an immediacy and force, framing relations of

good or bad choices; plots from *Hamlet* to *Persuasion* to "Bartleby the Scrivener" demonstrate that not choosing is also a choice. The ethical being cannot be placidly inactive and remain an ethical being. One central contention of this study, then, is that female novelists of the long eighteenth century recognized the ethical danger posed to women by the cultural privileging of the passive female object of desire. They would not have phrased their concerns in such language, of course, but their narratives are defined by the tension that arises when an ethical sensibility confronts social barriers to just and deliberate action.

As the writers of the great romance narratives—Ariosto and Tasso—realized, ethical behavior is not so much complicated by erotic desire as it is fueled by such desire. Ethical theorists of our own time, Emmanuel Levinas, Luce Irigaray, Jacques Derrida, Michel Foucault, concur. The ethical behavior of women, however, is a subject that even they do not fully explore, inasmuch as the culture they address and describe does not—even now—provide women a full range of opportunity for ethical decision or erotic self-definition, particularly heterosexual self-definition. In England in the late seventeenth century, however, cultural conventions of all kinds were scrutinized; the time was ripe for change, and women writers felt and reflected in their works the energies of revolutionary thought. The eighteenth century witnessed the re-establishing and redefinition of masculine power that in many ways narrowed rather than expanded the possibilities for women; nevertheless, even in this period, the literary market provided an opportunity for women to discover voices with which they could articulate desire, explore ethical choice, and challenge—overtly or subversively—the roles assigned them by the society in which they lived. It would be late in the eighteenth century, in the ferment of change inspired by another revolution, that Mary Wollstonecraft would fully examine the relationship between erotic desire and political, ethical female agency. But she is the product of a novel-reading feminine culture, and her feminist sensibility was no doubt nurtured by some of the very narratives discussed in the following pages. *A Vindication of the Rights of Woman* can be seen as a watershed, not a break from the feminine past but a bursting of that past into the future.

Assertion of rights, personhood, desire are predicated on the ability to speak from the subject position. When female protagonists come to inhabit realistic fiction, they necessarily take on subjectivity; they naturally speak out. Significantly, however, they also retain the sense of themselves as objects of male desire. Charlotte Lennox's *Female Quixote* elaborates this paradox by focusing the realistic plot on a young female subject who is deluded into thinking herself the object of desire. Arabella's desire is to be the center of her own story, and she achieves that desire, not by inhabiting the role of romance heroine, but by becoming a realistic protagonist in pursuit of dreams, a protagonist whose actions and reactions precipitate actions and reactions and whose longing creates a narrative pattern of flight, pursuit, satisfaction, or disappointment. In reality, cultural convention discouraged the eighteenth-century woman from actually living or attempting to live out the narrative of her own

---

provocation, call, and response that bind narrator and listener, author and character, or reader and text. . . . In this sense, prose fiction translates the interactive problematic of ethics into literary forms." *Narrative Ethics* (Cambridge, 1995), p. 13.

desires. Paradoxically, however, in realistic narrative, women readers were treated to possibilities or at least fantasies of their own centrality. The heroine of the realistic novel is no less the object of romantic longing and the purpose toward which action is directed than is her romance counterpart; but, in a significant departure from romance narrative, the realistic novel presents objects of desire as subjects who desire as well.

The love between men and women and the pleasures and pains to be found therein became a dominant concern of the novel as a genre in the eighteenth century and continued to be a preoccupation well into the nineteenth century—though not without resistance. In 1810, in a retrospective essay that surveys the young genre, by then arrived at the state of stability necessary for such a synthetic summary, Anna Letitia Barbauld devotes a lengthy paragraph to the focus of narrative fiction on erotic desire and the delusional dangers that result from such an emphasis. "Love is a passion particularly exaggerated in novels," she begins. "It forms the chief interest of, by far, the greater part of them. In order to increase this interest, a false idea is given of the importance of the passion. It occupies the serious hours of life; events all hinge upon it; every thing gives way to its influence, and no length of time wears it out." And there are problems attendant on such a focus, as Barbauld explains: "When a young lady, having imbibed these notions, comes into the world, she finds that the formidable passion acts a very subordinate part on the great theatre of the world; that its vivid sensations are mostly limited to a very early period." In fact, this tendency to form false expectations seems so serious to Barbauld that she elaborates extensively on behalf of the deluded young lady:

> She will find but few minds susceptible of [love's] more delicate influences. Where it is really felt, she will see it continually overcome by duty, by prudence, or merely by a regard for the show and splendour of life; and that in fact it has a very small share in the transactions of the busy world, and is often little consulted even in choosing a partner for life. In civilized life both men and women acquire so early a command over their passions, that the strongest of them are taught to give way to circumstances, and a moderate liking will appear apathy itself, to one accustomed to see the passion painted in its most glowing colours. Least of all will a course of novels prepare a young lady for the neglect and tedium of life which she is perhaps doomed to encounter. If the novels she reads are virtuous, she has learned to arm herself with proper reserve against the ardour of her lover; she has been instructed how to behave with the utmost propriety when run away with, like *Miss Byron*, or locked up by a cruel parent, like *Clarissa*; but she is not prepared for indifference and neglect. Though young and beautiful, she may see her youth and beauty pass away without conquests, and the monotony of her life will be apt to appear more insipid when contrasted with scenes of perpetual courtship and passion.[8]

In this wry critique of the psychological dangers of novel-reading, Barbauld confirms the power of narrative to give voice and shape to desire. While Lennox couches her observation in the form of satire, she tacitly advances the notion that there is a type of narrative that will not spawn delusory hope, that will channel

---

8   "On the Origin and Progress of Novel-Writing," in *Anna Letitia Barbauld: Selected Poetry and Prose*, ed. William McCarthy and Elizabeth Kraft, Broadview Literary Texts (Peterborough, Ontario, 2002), pp. 411–2.

desire to more appropriate ends. Barbauld, in effect, denies that such is the case. In doing so, she asserts what literary critics and scholars often want to obscure, the link between romance and the novel, fantasies of centrality, whether of subjectivity or significance, that speak to the deepest cultural and psychological needs of an ever-growing readership.

Nearly two centuries have passed since Barbauld gave voice to her concern, and despite generations of commentary pointing out that "realistic fiction" is not realistic, that love is not the central business of life, that there is no "man on a white horse" out there ready to rescue the "woman in distress" that many feel themselves to be at some point, narrative fiction continues to provide quotidian fantasies particularly geared to a heterosexual female readership. Sophisticated, informed critical readers today will agree that the best fiction is no longer focused exclusively or even predominantly on heterosexual love. Many novels treat difficult themes of loss, discomfort, despair, regret, and triumph stemming from cultural conflicts, historical wounds, personal deficiencies or challenges; these narratives, in fact, tend to be more highly regarded today than novels that explore the joys and sorrows associated with the pursuit of romantic happiness. But any trip to a local bookstore is enough to instruct us that the market for romance in the guise of realistic fiction is a thriving one. It is pointless to deny that love is and will always be—if not the central concern of life—a fundamental concern of narrative fiction.

In fact, as Nancy Armstrong argues in *Desire and Domestic Fiction*, throughout the eighteenth and nineteenth centuries, the novel existed solely to articulate desire, to define for both men and women the nature and end of heterosexual attraction. Such novelistic preoccupation was manifestation of a larger cultural emphasis on social contract "which creates what it seems to organize."[9] In "describing" the ideal woman, in other words, novels, conduct books, educational tracts, and other literature of the period were aimed toward making women "desire to be what a prosperous man desires."[10] The literature scripted male desire in defining this feminine ideal, creating a gender difference that, Armstrong demonstrates, is essential to the political and economic power of the middle class. In her view, the female protagonist of eighteenth- and nineteenth-century novels such as *Pamela, Evelina*, and *Jane Eyre* stands for the emergence of middle-class individualism as a force antagonistic to aristocratic power. The casting of class struggle in sexual terms was politically expedient as "[n]ovels rewarding self assertion on the part of those in an inferior position undoubtedly provided the middle-class readership with a fable for their own emergence."[11] The eighteenth- and nineteenth-century female protagonists, in other words, are the embodiment of middle-class desire, desire that is not really sexual, but economic and political, sexualized, but neither driven nor satisfied by the longings or needs of the physical body.[12]

---

9   *Desire and Domestic Fiction: A Political History of the Novel* (New York and Oxford, 1987), p. 33.

10   Ibid., p. 59.

11   Ibid. p. 51.

12   Ibid. Armstrong, of course, draws heavily on the theories of Foucault who explores the difference between sex and sexuality, regarding the second as a construct that emerged in

More than their nineteenth-century counterparts, however, female protagonists of the eighteenth-century novel, as Armstrong puts it, "understand social experience as a series of sexual encounters."[13] That such sexual encounters for Moll Flanders, Roxana, Pamela, and Clarissa are entwined with the social and economic class conflict of eighteenth-century England is Armstrong's point, and a point well taken. But there is an entire body of fiction written by women, chronicling women's experience in terms of sexual desire, that precedes Defoe and Richardson. This fiction is largely concerned with sexual behavior within the aristocracy, between men and women of the same class. Power, politics, and wealth are central to the depictions of these relationships as well, but not in the same way that they will be when the paradigm shifts to idealize the morally superior, socially inferior woman who desires "nothing more than economic dependency upon the man who valued her for her qualities of mind."[14]

The earlier body of fiction is the subject of Ros Ballaster's 1992 *Seductive Forms*, a study focused, as is the first part of this book, on the fiction of Aphra Behn, Delarivier Manley, and Eliza Haywood. Ballaster agrees with Armstrong that "the development of the figure of the domestic woman in fiction and its attendant ideal of feminine sensibility is indeed instrumental in the production of bourgeois hegemony."[15] She insists, however, on a distinction between fiction of the mid-to-late eighteenth century and the fiction produced by women prior to 1740. Prose narratives by Behn, Manley, and Haywood do not participate in the definition of the bourgeois ideal. Instead, these works articulate political distinctions and stake a claim for women's authority to write, to think, to judge, and to act. The narratives also explore and exploit the woman's and the woman writer's ability to seduce. In Ballaster's words: "Behn, Manley, and Haywood reveal themselves to be far from subjected by the imposition of an emergent philosophy of 'separate spheres.'"[16] Instead, these writers are concerned primarily with "exploring alternatives that offer models for the female victim to come to 'mastery' of or resistance to the fictional text" itself.[17]

The following discussion begins by focusing on this earlier fiction in which the social equality of the protagonists allows a concentration on the ethics of desire as opposed to the politics of sexuality. The first three chapters examine themes central to ethical inquiry, particularly the recovering of the woman's voice and perspective in expressions of desire. Aphra Behn, Delarivier Manley, and Eliza Haywood, early in her career as a writer of narrative fiction, acknowledge frankly the fact of female heterosexual desire. Their fictions are largely centered on the examination of the force of this desire, its significance, its potential for good and for ill, its emotional, political, linguistic dimensions. Their configurations of such desire draw on romance

---

the eighteenth century with the articulation of gender difference.

13   Ibid., p. 29.

14   Ibid., p. 49.

15   *Seductive Forms: Women's Amatory Fiction from 1684 to 1740* (Oxford, 1992), p. 10.

16   Ibid., p. 29.

17   Ibid., p. 30.

conventions, but are not, in the end, part of the romance tradition. Neither do they provide the material from which mid-century novelists will draw. Instead, Behn, Manley, and Haywood outline plots and themes from which later novelists will draw away in the manner Armstrong describes. The domestic ideal will replace and repress the sexual ambitiousness and independence of earlier female protagonists, creating a different kind of sexual difference than the ethical difference asserted and examined by early women novelists.[18]

Yet, as the remaining chapters of this study will demonstrate, the suppressing of female erotic desire in the creation of the feminine ideal is neither smooth nor seamless in the world of the novel. Women writers such as Sarah Fielding, Frances Burney, Charlotte Smith, and Elizabeth Inchbald struggle in their efforts to encode feminine ideals that deny their female protagonists voices and desires of their own. Their novels reveal the difficulty with which they agree, as it were, to repress desire, to channel it into the larger cultural project of establishing middle-class political power. Certainly, their fictions did contribute to that project, but their absence from the canon, and, until recently, all but the vaguest cultural memory, is a testament to the fact that they did not do so as well as other novels did. Of Burney's works, *Evelina* only has enjoyed significant canonical status. Of Fielding's, Inchbald's, and Smith's, none at all. Burney's later novels and the novels of Inchbald and Smith illustrate just what was suppressed in the defining of the feminine and the literary ideal. Retrospectively, from the vantage point of the roiling emotional power of the Brontes and George Eliot, and from the paradigmatic formal perspective of Jane Austen, the fictions of Fielding, Inchbald, Burney, and Smith seem aesthetically flawed and emotionally thin. But by approaching them from the opposite chronological direction we see the depth and difficulty (formal and emotional) of their struggle to repress expressions of female desire in deference to the emergent domestic ideal.

The first part of this study, then, stands along with Ballaster's *Seductive Forms* as part of the "prehistory" of the bourgeois novel that came to dominance during the mid-eighteenth century and held sway through the following century as well. As my argument continues, however, it will reveal the influence of another scholar, Margaret Anne Doody who, along with Ballaster, has significantly transformed our thinking about women, desire, and the novel. The emphasis of both Doody and Ballaster on the continuity rather than the disjunction between romance narratives and the novel is an important one inasmuch as, first, it allows us to see and comment on formal features and thematic preoccupations that exist in early novels written (primarily by women) to a readership whose taste has been formed by romance. Instead of dismissing such novels because they do not reflect what came to be the generic contours of the form, we are encouraged by Ballaster and Doody to apply new critical paradigms that draw on a richer, more complex understanding of the development of the novel.

---

18   See also Margaret Doody's interesting gloss on another sense of "domestic"—as "nationally inturned." The novel, as it developed in the eighteenth century in England, she proposes, was most striking for its "ability to *exclude*." *The True Story of the Novel* (New Brunswick, 1996), p. 292.

When I turn to the works of Sarah Fielding, Elizabeth Inchbald, Frances Burney, and Charlotte Smith, therefore, I will not be exploring the rise of the domestic feminine ideal. I could do so, for, as I note above, the novels of these women participate in the larger cultural project described by Armstrong. Certainly each novelist creates models of feminine domesticity that define and delineate desire, but each novelist also reveals resistance to the emergent ideal. That resistance is what interests me, as it seems to me to be the location for ethical inquiry that continues along the lines established by Behn, Manley, and Haywood. As Doody puts it, if "the heart of public discipline is the tranquil marriage in which women behave themselves and acknowledge no desire," to know desire (or Eros, in her terminology) is "to know more about ourselves."[19] Such knowledge is the foundation of ethics, for "to respect ourselves and Eros is to begin to wish to refrain from the enslavement and abuse of others."[20] The following study takes seriously the linkage between desire and ethics, drawing on these earlier studies and participating in the discussions begun by Armstrong, Ballaster, Doody, and others. The unique contribution I hope to make is in tying together the works of the early and late female novelists of the long eighteenth century through ethical paradigms that speak to their (and our) continuing concerns with female voice, presence, and longing. I admire but do not try to emulate Doody's sweep; I respect but beg to differ with Armstrong's privileging of the domestic; I most identify with Ballaster's project and the terms in which she conceives and executes it, but I wish to extend the inquiry beyond the half-century point that she uses as her temporal boundary. My most significant departure from and addition to the growing body of literature on women novelists of this period, however, is my decision to bring them into dialogue with women of the biblical past. In doing so, I am asserting that while Aphra Behn and her near contemporaries wrote in and to a specific historical moment, the works they produced speak to all times their own, of course, and ours as well.

---

19   Ibid., p. 262.
20   Ibid.

Chapter 1

Matriarchal Desire and Ethical Relation

The novelists we will examine in the following pages of this book are the matriarchs of British fiction. As such, they bear comparison to the matriarchs of biblical narrative, mothers of a primarily patriarchal world whose voices have been obscured by time and tradition. Like the biblical matriarchs, the women novelists have left traces of their existences and echoes of their voices. Their sounds, their words, and even their silences document longings and desires which are both temporal and eternal, both sensual and spiritual, both ethical and beyond ethics. To hear and understand, we have to be open to their otherness, responsive to their demands, accepting of our own obligation to listen and to attend. Most importantly, we need to admit the possibility that these women of the past can teach us something we do not already know.

Our tendency to adopt evolutionary models of analysis works against this demand. Luce Irigaray, for example, asserts that "new models of sexual identity" are necessary in order for woman to discover "her humanity and her transcendency."[1] Is that true? What about the old models? What about the matriarchs? Some would answer that they offer no model for sexual identity because they have none, being, as they are, the creations of men or speaking, like ventriloquists' dummies, in the voices of men. But is that generalization not a bit too glib? The mothers of the novel actually did write their narratives, and the voices and actions of the mothers of the Bible are set down in the texts side by side with the voices and actions of the fathers. If time and tradition have subjugated these women, it is not necessarily because subjugation was foreordained. The presences are there. Derrida would call them "traces," perhaps. I would suggest they are stronger than that. We have failed to see and hear these women because we have expected, and to some degree projected, their absence and silence. There are women in the texts, both biblical and early modern, who speak in distinct women's voices. When we hear their words as the words of men, we are misunderstanding them, for they are speaking as women.

To hear them as such, of course, requires that we admit sexual difference, and perhaps it is the hazard attendant on such an admission that has hampered us as critics of literature and culture. After all, the essentializing of difference, whether in terms of race, class, gender, or sexuality itself has been responsible for a wide variety of human wrongs, from mere slights to grave injustices to unspeakable acts of cruelty.[2]

---

1   *Elemental Passions*, trans. Joanne Collie and Judith Still (New York, 1992), pp. 3, 4.

2   See Thomas Laquer for the argument that in the early modern period "distinct sexual anatomy was adduced to support or deny all manner of claims in a variety of specific social, economic, political, cultural, or erotic contexts." *Making Sex: Body and Gender From the Greeks to Freud* (Cambridge, MA, 1990), p. 152. In general, as Roxann Wheeler notes, binary opposition "simplifies complex situations and phenomena." *The Complexion of Race:*

Socially conscious critics and commentators have quite understandably, and quite responsibly, tried to ameliorate the potential for wrong by emphasizing similarity and points of connection. Paradoxically, however, the notion of difference—or otherness—is also crucial to an understanding of ethics. As explained by philosopher and talmudic scholar Emmanuel Levinas, the essential ethical act is the opening of oneself to the demands of the other to momentarily escape the self, not in possession of the other, but in transcendent participation in the divine or the infinite.[3]

"Ethics used to be a coercive, customary manner of ensuring the cohesiveness of a particular group through the repetition of a code," explains Julia Kristeva.[4] The term, in other words, signaled the assumption of hegemonic values and the assertion of cultural stability. "Now, however," she continues "the issue of ethics crops up wherever a code (mores, social contract) must be shattered in order to give way to the free play of negativity, need, desire, pleasure, and jouissance, before being put together again."[5] The mid twentieth century was such a time, and it was in the atmosphere of great social change and worldwide paradigm shifts that Levinas began to raise ethics to the level of "first philosophy." [6] The late seventeenth century was also a time of political and societal revolution which prompted the writers with whom I am concerned to examine—with less discipline but with as much creative intensity as Levinas brings to bear—the implications of their own philosophical precepts.

Ethical thought insists on individual responsibility for the construction of the self whatever the conditions imposed by culture or society, so in addition to acknowledging the demands of the other, the ethical person is always, on some level, a subject—never solely an object, never exclusively a victim, never a mere expression of someone else's ideology or power. According to Levinasian ethics, the self, not society, is responsible for its fate and its behavior toward the other. This point troubles some of Levinas's critics. As Lawrence Buell has noted, the primary charge against ethical criticism is its failure to take into account the historical circumstances and political realities that impede the individual subjectivity necessary for ethical action.[7] Without the ability to realize a self, it is impossible to recognize obligation

---

Categories of Difference in Eighteenth-Century British Culture (Philadelphia, 2000), p. 40. Irigaray's project is the rehabilitation and reification of binary difference. See *Essential Passions*, p. 3.

3   Levinas, as Stephen H. Webb has put it, "raises the ethical to the sphere of [the] religious." "The Rhetoric of Ethics as Excess: A Christian Theological Response to Emmanuel Levinas," *Modern Theology* 15 (1999): 3.

4   Kristeva, *Desire in Language: A Semiotic Approach to Literature and Art*, ed. Leon S. Roudiez, trans. Thomas Gora, Alice Jardine, and Leon S. Roudiez (New York, 1980), p. 23.

5   Ibid., p. 23.

6   The idea suffuses Levinas's work. See, in particular, "Ethics as First Philosophy," trans. Seán Hand and Michael Temple, in Seán Hand (ed.) *The Levinas Reader* (Oxford, 1989), pp. 75–87 and *Totality and Infinity: An Essay on Exteriority*, trans. Alphonso Lingis (Pittsburgh, 1969), pp. 42–8 and 194–219.

7   Buell, "Introduction: In Pursuit of Ethics," *PMLA* 114 (1999): 14. See also Gerald Doppelt, "Can Traditional Ethical Theory Meet the Challenge of Feminism, Multiculturalism, and Environmentalism," *The Journal of Ethics* 6 (2002): 383–405.

to an other, be that other nature, man, woman, or God. Still, ethically speaking, whatever one's circumstances, there may be occasion for the self to meet the other on terms of equality, freedom, and openness. The ethical being will remain alert to the possibility of such face-to-face encounters for it is through such meetings that one participates in the essence of the divine or, put another way, is transported, temporarily, into the presence of God.

Levinas is not silent on the social and political inequities that problematize the ethical being. He locates the distinction between the ethical and the unethical in their opposite approaches to desire which emerge from opposite notions of what it means to be a "subject." In Levinas's formulation, there is a crucial discrimination to be made between a desire that is *aroused* by the ever-exterior other and a desire that demands to be *satisfied* by the other through possession and power, in essence an erasure of alterity. We experience "the infinite in the finite" according to Levinas, through a desire "which the desirable arouses rather than satisfies."[8] The desirable is the other whose relationship to the I Levinas explains through the notion of "face"— which "signifies . . . an exteriority that does not call for power or possession, an exteriority that is not reducible . . . to the interiority of memory, and yet maintains the I who welcomes it."[9] The face-to-face encounter between I and other takes place in the present and is not to be expressed by totalizing formulae. It is an incidental meeting that gives rise, in the present moment, to "the idea of infinity." The transient and transcendent joining of two separate beings is, in Levinas's terminology, a "society" or a union without possession, the opposite indeed of possession which makes a "totality" of one out of two beings.[10] The ethical relationship begins with the face-to-face encounter that leads to the caress—an exploration of the otherness of the other, touch that "transcends the sensible," touch that "is not an intentionality of disclosure but of search: a movement unto the invisible."[11]

My own acquaintance with the thought and work of Emmanuel Levinas dates back only a few years. I first read *Totality and Infinity* around the year 2000 or 2001, having come to the book through one of Levinas's most stringent feminist critics, Luce Irigaray. The final chapter of *An Ethics of Sexual Difference* offers a "reading" of *Totality and Infinity* in which Irigaray takes Levinas to task. Levinas's emphasis on generation (the birth of the son) and transcendence (the movement toward God) results in "separating [the woman] off into the subterranean, the submarine," according to Irigaray. "What of her own call to the divine," she asks.[12] What of it? I wondered. So, I went to the source, and I discovered that indeed Levinas has "little to say," in answer to Irigaray's question.[13] Women function in Levinas's reading of biblical texts as means of transcendence, certainly not objects, but also not the important faces in face-to-face encounters. Abraham's relationship with Sarah is

---

8   *Totality and Infinity*, p. 50.

9   Ibid., p. 50.

10   Ibid., pp. 50, 104.

11   Ibid., pp. 257–8.

12   *An Ethics of Sexual Difference*, trans. Carolyn Burke and Gillian C. Gill (Ithaca, 1984), pp. 195, 196.

13   Ibid., p. 196.

far less significant to Levinas than the patriarch's response to Isaac. Indeed it is the akedah, the binding, and the near-sacrifice of Abraham's son, that, for Levinas, occasions the first ethical act in recorded history. What stopped Abraham's knife in its passage to the body of his son bound on the altar? The scripture says simply "God." But how are we to understand this intervention? For Levinas, the face of Isaac is the means by which Abraham experiences the presence of God.[14]

It is Abraham's radical realization of Isaac's complete otherness that provides the path to the divine. Irigaray, it seems to me, does misunderstand Levinas when she sees the son as merely a reflection or extension of the father. Levinas's point is exactly the opposite. Abraham is privileged in Levinas's ethical landscape precisely because he recognized difference in a relation that most regard as sameness. Putting philosophy aside for a moment, and thinking in terms of common human behavior and emotion, Abraham's discovery of "otherness" in the father/son relation seems nothing short of miraculous. What then becomes mystifying is the tendency of husbands and fathers to regard wives and daughters as extensions of their own identity. Here, unlike the father/son relation, difference is evident because it is physiological. Yet, Irigaray's contention that we lack an ethics of sexual difference seems undeniable. From this reading and these meditations, I began to wonder: what did the matriarchs have to say?

Sarah Laughed

When God established the covenant between himself and Abram, he demanded much and promised much. He was explicit in both his demands and his promises. God begins by appearing to Abram and identifying himself: "'I am El Shaddai,'" he asserts, and he will go on in the course of the conversation that follows to re-name Abram and his wife Sarai to indicate their new status as progenitors of the covenanted people chosen by this God (Genesis 17: 1).[15] The establishing of the covenant, in this face-to-face encounter thereby takes on the flavor of an ethical exchange. God demands that Abram "Walk in My ways and be blameless," and in exchange, he promises "I will establish My covenant between Me and you, and I will make you exceedingly numerous" (Genesis 17: 1–2). It turns out that the covenant

---

14 In *Fear and Trembling*, Søren Kierkegaard offers a reading of Genesis 22, Abraham's near sacrifice of his son Isaac at the command of God, as a story of faith that suspends the teleology of ethics. Abraham's absolute devotion to his God causes him, according to Kierkegaard, to behave unethically toward his son precisely because "Abraham's action ... is purely a private undertaking," an act of faith. *Fear and Trembling: Dialectical Lyric by Johannes de silentio*, trans. Alastair Hannay (London, 1985), p. 88. The paradox of faith, according to Kierkegaard, "determines . . . [one's] relation to the universal through his relation to the absolute, not his relation to the absolute through his relation to the universal" (97–8). Levinas's reading of the same story suggests another conclusion. To use terms echoic of Kierkegaard, Abraham's relation to the particular *is* his relation to the absolute.

15 Quotations from biblical texts are, unless otherwise noted, from *Jewish Publication Society Hebrew-English Tanakh: The Traditional Hebrew Text and the New JPS Translation* (Philadelphia, 1999).

entails that Abraham "shall be the father of a multitude of nations" (Genesis 17: 4). In fact, Abram's new name signifies "father of a multitude."[16]

From the moment of his bestowing on Abram the name Abraham until the point in the chapter at which he departs, a span covered by 16 verses, El Shaddai harps on the theme of generation. He tells Abraham "I will make you exceedingly fertile" (Genesis 17: 6); nations and kings "shall come forth from you" (Genesis 17: 6). "I will maintain My covenant between Me and you, and your offspring to come" (Genesis 17: 7). And "I assign the land you sojourn in to you and your offspring to come, all the land of Canaan, as an everlasting holding" (Genesis 17: 8). The land is a sign of God's favor, but God requires a sign from his people as well, and the sign again points to generation: "You shall circumcise the flesh of your foreskin, and that shall be the sign of the covenant between Me and you" (Genesis 17: 11). As God expounds upon this commandment, again he emphasizes Abraham's numerous offspring: "throughout the generations, every male among you shall be circumcised at the age of eight days" (Genesis 17: 12).

Up until this point, Abraham seems to be simply listening. He does not react to the demands or to the promises, taking even the edict of circumcision in stride. Although he and Sarah have had no children, Abraham has a son, Ishmael, whom he fathered by Hagar, Sarah's handmaid, at Sarah's insistence. Sarah's selfless dedication to preserving her husband's seed had been repaid by haughtiness on Hagar's part—an attitude for which Sarah chided Abraham ("The wrong done me is your fault! I myself put my maid in your bosom; now that she sees that she is pregnant, I am lowered in her esteem" [Genesis 16: 5]), but domestic tension notwithstanding, Abraham seemed proud of and dedicated to his son. So he no doubt had confidence in Ishmael's eventual ability to begin fathering those generations that the Lord was speaking of. In fact, significantly, at the time of this conversation, Ishmael was exactly thirteen years old, the age at which Jewish boys would become men when such rites and rituals were established in the culture and tradition. Abraham's complacent silence speaks of awe and reverence for his God, but it also attests to his sense of his and his son's own abilities and strengths.

The next thing God says, however, shakes Abraham's self-possession: "As for your wife Sarai, you shall not call her Sarai, but her name shall be Sarah. I will bless her; indeed, I will give you a son by her. I will bless her so that she shall give rise to nations; rulers of peoples shall issue from her" (Genesis 17: 16). This pronouncement turns out to be too much for Abraham. In verse 3, after El Shaddai had named himself and started speaking of a covenant, Abraham had thrown himself on his face, in awe. In verse 17, in response to this revelation of how the generations were to be produced, Abraham again throws himself on his face, but this time, as he does so, he laughs and says "to himself": "Can a child be born to a man a hundred years old, or can Sarah bear a child at ninety?" (Genesis 17: 17) El Shaddai does not seem to understand the ways of men and women, so Abraham offers a suggestion: "O that Ishmael might live by Your favor!" (Genesis 17: 18) While God agrees that Ishmael will be a great man and "exceedingly numerous, . . . father of twelve

---

16 *Jewish Study Bible Featuring the Jewish Publication Society Tanakh Translation*, ed. Adele Berlin and Marc Zvi Brettler (Oxford, 1985): Gen. 17: 4 and 5n.

chieftains," it is Sarah's child, who will be called Isaac (signifying "laughter"), with whom and through whom for generations to come God will maintain "an everlasting covenant" (Genesis 17: 19). God's last words reiterate this promise: "My covenant I will maintain with Isaac, whom Sarah shall bear to you at this season next year" (Genesis 17: 21).

Abraham and Sarah do not have a relationship of mutual subjectivity. As many commentators point out in analysis of their story, Abraham, at various points in their history together, treats Sarah as a possession, a means for his own survival, little more than a domestic servant, a nuisance or an inconvenience or a fact of life (depending on her mood and her demands on him). When she complains of Hagar's behavior, for instance, Abraham gives in: "Your maid is in your hands. Deal with her as you think right" (Genesis 16: 6), hardly an ethical response given Sarah's anger and Hagar's pregnancy.[17] Sarah may be right when she blames Abraham for the maidservant's haughtiness, or, she may be wrong.[18] Whatever the case, Abraham is not interested enough in making peace between the women of his household to take responsibility for the situation. The patriarch who always answers God with the words "here I am" is inclined to answer his wife with words or actions to the effect of "that's your problem." So, it is no surprise that while Abraham enacts to the letter the commandment to circumcise himself and all the men of his tribe, he neglects to inform Sarah that she has a year to prepare for the birth of their son. In fact, the Lord himself has to reappear in order to bring Sarah into the covenant. And that is precisely what happens in Chapter 18 of Genesis; Sarah is specifically drawn into a face-to-face encounter with God in which her own place within the covenant is established and honored.

Genesis 18 begins with a statement of another of God's appearances before Abraham, this time in the plains of Mamre. Abraham is sitting in the entrance of his tent; it is very hot. He looks up to see three men and, following the laws of

---

17   As Tikva Frymer-Kensky notes, the phrase "'do to her what is good in your eyes' . . .is the verbal equivalent of washing one's hands." *Reading the Women of the Bible: A New Interpretation of their Stories* (New York, 2002), p. 229.

18   Tradition has it both ways—Jewish misrashim "finding fault with Hagar"; Islamic tradition, taking the opposite view. Renowned Jewish commentator Nehama Leibowitz interestingly blames Sarah, not for insensitivity but for over-enthusiastically undertaking "a mission" requiring "high standards" she could not maintain. Thus she "descend[s] from the pinnacle of altruism and selflessness into much deeper depths than would ordinarily have been the case." *New Studies in Bereshit (Genesis)*, trans. Aryeh Newman (Israel, n.d.), p. 156. Frymer-Kensky notes that "readers today tend to be angry at Sarai, to castigate her for being insensitive to the plight of someone for whom she should have felt both compassion and solidarity." *Reading the Women of the Bible*, p. 226. For the New Testament view of Hagar as a (negative) reflection on Jewish enslavement to the Law, see Ruth Mellinkoff "Sarah and Hagar: Laughter and Tears," in Michelle P. Brown and Scott McKendrick (eds), *Illuminating the Book: Makers and Interpreters. Essays in Honor of Janet Backhouse*, The British Library Studies in Medieval Culture (London and Toronto, 1998), p. 38. On the resistance of Islam to "Hagarism" see Patricia Crone and Michael Cook, *Hagarism: The Making of the Islamic World* (Cambridge, UK, 1977), pp. 8–9. Hagar will feature again in this study as an ethical paradigm on her own count. See Chapter 6, pp. 132–7, 144.

hospitality for which he is renown, he jumps up to invite the men in for water and rest.[19] Of course, part of a nomadic man's hospitality always rests on the women of his tent, and Abraham is no exception. He tells Sarah to bake bread while he himself kills and prepares a calf for the men to eat in the shade of a tree outside the tent. As they complete the meal the men ask Abraham, "Where is your wife Sarah?" "There, in the tent," Abraham answers (Gen. 18: 9). Then one of the men speaks singly: "I will return to you next year, and your wife Sarah shall have a son!" (Gen. 18: 10)

Sarah is listening at the entrance of the tent, and she begins to laugh "to herself"— as Abraham had done before (Genesis 18: 12). She laughs, however, for a slightly different reason than her husband did. What amuses her is the thought that she is to "have enjoyment—with my husband so old" (Genesis 18: 12). While she is pondering this circumstance with, perhaps, glee, the Lord addresses Abraham and asks "Why did Sarah laugh, saying, 'Shall I in truth bear a child, old as I am?'" (Genesis 18: 13) We realize, of course, that she did not say what the Lord says she said. Some rabbinic commentary points to this discrepancy as an example of God's kindness as Sarah's actual words reflect on Abraham and his possible inability to provide pleasure or, by implication, seed.[20] Other commentators point out that it is generation of the son, not the pleasure of the female lover, that is important to God, an interpretation that would seem to be supported by the fact that God addresses Abraham to find out why Sarah laughs. Yet, even that detail is subject to another reading. Abraham and Sarah, who have not been lovers recently and whose marriage has not been one of reciprocity and mutuality heretofore, have actually responded to the Lord's announcement in precisely the same way—if for different reasons. They have laughed—and their shared amusement, glee, joy, surprise are to be commemorated forever in the name of their son. They meet in laughter for pleasure and generation.

Significantly, the episode ends with the Lord's reiteration of his plan to return "at the same season next year, and Sarah shall have a son" (Genesis 18: 14). At this announcement, Sarah sobers considerably, and she says, afraid, "I did not laugh" (Genesis 18: 15). God then addresses her directly: "You did laugh." Commentators have been harsh with Sarah for her laughter, taking God's words here as apparent chastisement for her belief that there are things "too wondrous for the Lord" (Genesis 18: 14). But I see this remark as an honor to Sarah. God has heard her laughter

---

19 Abraham here addresses the men as "my lords," but the episode begins when "the Lord appeared to him" in Genesis 18:1. As W. Gunther Plaut comments: "The Hebrew sentences are couched alternately in the singular and plural, suggesting the fusion of two literary traditions" Genesis 18: 3n. *The Torah: A Modern Commentary*, ed. W. Gunther Plaut (New York, 1981). The *Jewish Study Bible* includes a further observation: "The relationship of the Lord to the men is unclear. Perhaps, as in some Canaanite literature, we are to imagine a deity accompanied by his two attendants" (Genesis 18: 1–2n.). On the angel as "a representation of divine presence in human affairs," see Richard Elliott Friedman *Commentary on the Torah* (New York, 2001), Genesis 18: 3n, and *The Hidden Face of God* (New York, 1995), pp. 10–11.

20 "'Great is peace,' remarks a rabbi in the Talmud about this point, 'for even the Holy One (blessed be He) made a change on account of it,' sparing the couple the discord that might have come had Abraham known Sarah's true thought." Cited in *Jewish Study Bible*, Gen. 18: 13n.

which, we remember, is "to herself"—private, perhaps even silent laughter—and we (and she) can assume he has read her thoughts as well. She will not only bear a child, but she will have enjoyment in conceiving that child. God's gift to Sarah is the gift of laughter and joy in love.[21]

After Isaac's birth, the attention of both Abraham and Sarah is focused on their son, not on one another, but something happened in the laughter shared between husband and wife, for not only was Isaac engendered but Sarah, in a sense, was herself born as an individual person with voice and subjectivity that extends beyond her role as a wife or even as a mother. She came into existence on her own account in her face-to-face encounter with God. Her comment at the birth of Isaac attests to her own sense of laughter as her special dispensation, significant also to the community as a whole: "God has brought me laughter; everyone who hears will laugh with me" (Genesis 21: 6). Sarah's empowerment extends to a moral certainty about actions she must take to preserve the community of which she is the matriarch by virtue of Isaac's birth, particularly the imperative she feels at the feast given in honor of Isaac's weaning, an absolute assurance that she must demand the exile of Hagar and Ishmael. Again, it is a moment of derision that provokes Sarah. She sees Ishmael mocking the ceremony, and she says to Abraham: "Cast out that slave-woman and her son: for the son of that slave shall not share in the inheritance with my son Isaac" (Genesis 21: 10). Abraham, who loves both of his sons, is reluctant this time to give Sarah sway over the fates of Hagar and Ishmael. Instead of shrugging his shoulders and telling Sarah to do as she will, he struggles with the demand she has placed on him, a fact that also attests to a change in their relationship since the conception and birth of Isaac. As Abraham worries about what to do in light of Sarah's demands, the Lord intervenes and provides directive that underscores Abraham's evident inclination to regard Sarah in a different light than he had done for most of their marriage. God says to Abraham: "whatever Sarah tells you, do as she says, for it is through Isaac that offspring shall be continued for you" (Genesis 21: 12). God promises both Abraham and Hagar that the seed of Ishmael shall also be great, but it is Sarah's voice, her words, her vision, that he endorses, and he does so precisely because her voice speaks to his design, his own focus on Isaac as the bearer of the covenant he has established. Isaac is the laughter that all will hear, the source of community, the point at which the particular gives rise to the universal which attests to relation to the absolute.[22] Sarah's laughter of love and pleasure, it turns out, is also the laughter of faith.

---

21   My reading is perhaps influenced by Mario Brelich's interpretation of Sarah's rejuvenation in preparation for the sexual pleasure she is to experience. See his philosophical novel *The Holy Embrace*, trans. John Shepley (Chicago, 1994), pp. 185–210.

22   For a discussion of Sarah's spirituality as a spirituality rooted in particulars, see Jerome Gellman, *Abraham! Abraham! Kierkegaard and the Hasidim on the Binding of Isaac* (London, 2003), pp. 100–2.

The Woman at the Well

The limitation of Levinas's theory of the other, according to both Irigaray and Jacques Derrida (and, though less adamantly, to Catherine Chalier, as well) resides in his failure to accord the female other true otherness. She is the object of male erotic desire and the means of transcendence through the birth of a son for Levinas. The erotic caress, for Levinas, leads to fecundity which produces the son, through whom the male "I" becomes an other and thereby transcends his own essence or identity. In this process the female beloved is left behind. In Irigaray's words:

> Although he takes pleasure in caressing, he abandons the feminine other, leaves her to sink, in particular into the darkness of a pseudoanimality, in order to return to his responsibilities in the world of men-amongst-themselves. For him, the feminine does not stand for an other to be respected in her human freedom and human identity. The feminine other is left without her own specific face. On this point, his philosophy falls radically short of ethics. To go beyond the face of metaphysics would mean precisely to leave the woman her face, and even to assist her to discover it and to keep it. Levinas scarcely unveils the disfigurements brought about by ontotheology. His phenomenology of the caress is still implicated in it.[23]

Derrida is not as harsh, but his insight is the same. In the voice of a woman, he challenges the notion that only a son and not a daughter can represent the kind of transcendence Levinas seeks; in the voice of a woman he complains about the erasure of female desire and points to its traces in the very words Levinas uses to explain "responsibility for the other"—words from the Song of Songs which—though Levinas himself does not acknowledge as much—speak of her desire.[24]

In the voice of this woman Derrida ends his essay with a wail of protest (printed in all capital letters) at the erasure of the female in a concept of otherness that does not acknowledge the primacy of sexual difference. His point, like Irigaray's, is that to ignore the notion of sexual difference, to conceive of sexual otherness as less than primary and fundamental, is by definition to subordinate woman to the totality that is man. Derrida's words are clearer than mine: "To desexualize the link to the wholly-other, . . . to make sexuality secondary with respect to a wholly-other that in itself would not be sexually marked . . . is always to make sexual difference secondary *as* femininity."[25]

The corrective to Levinasian ethics on this point, according to Derrida, Irigaray, and Chalier, is to acknowledge an ethical responsibility for woman beyond her role as bearer of sons. It is to laugh with Sarah, to listen to her voice, to acknowledge her pleasure and her joy as well as her maternity. These philosophers, therefore, return to what we could call, following Robert Alter, the biblical betrothal narrative or "type-scene," the beginning of the erotic relationship.[26] According to Levinas, the

---

23 "Questions to Emmanuel Levinas: On the Divinity of Love," in Robert Bernasconi and Simon Critchley (eds), *Re-reading Levinas* (Bloomington, 1991), pp. 113–14.

24 "At this very moment in this work here I am," in Bernasconi and Critchley (eds), *Re-reading Levinas*, pp. 18–19.

25 Ibid., p. 43.

26 *The Art of Biblical Narrative* (New York, 1981), pp. 47–62.

emblematic moment of ethical response to the other is the phrase: "Here I am."[27] This is Abraham's repeated response in Genesis 22 as he follows God's commandment, first, to sacrifice his child and then to stay his hand. It is the response of Isaiah to a vision of the Lord in which he hears the voice of the Lord ask "Whom shall I send, and who will go for us?" "Here am I; send me," answers the prophet. "Here I am means send me," asserts Levinas.[28] The phrase represents a "responsibility for the other, going against intentionality and the will, . . . [which] signifies not the disclosure of a given and its reception, but the exposure of me to the other, prior to every decision."[29] It is Abraham's response; it is Isaiah's response; but it is also Rebekah's response—and this, according to Derrida and Chalier and (implicitly, though not specifically) Irigaray, is the point that Levinas has missed.[30]

My concern is with the depiction of eighteenth-century women characters who say "Here I am; send me" and who are thereby responsive to the demands of the other, by women novelists who themselves desire and who speak their own desires, either directly or in the voices of their characters. I am arguing that works that we have historically regarded as salacious, titillating, amoral, and often immoral are at their core ethical—and ethical precisely because of the presence of female subjectivity, desire, and pleasure. The novelists depict a world in which a woman's willingness to love, and to express that love sexually, is regarded as wrong, outside the boundaries of taste and morality. In fact, the connotations of "libertine," the philosophical stance out of which much ethical thought about sexuality grew, are almost exclusively pejorative. We associate the term with moral decadence, sensual excess, and atheism. Catherine Cusset has summarized the evolution of the term thus:

> The word appears for the first time in French in a translation of the New Testament in 1477 and reappears eighty years later, in 1545, in the title of Calvin's treatise *Contre la Secte phantastique et furieuse des libertins qui se nomment spirituels*. During the sixteenth century, 'libertine' and 'atheist' became synonymous. The concept slowly evolved from heresy and atheism to debauchery. By the end of the eighteenth century, the word *libertinage* came to mean a way of living and of thinking that evoked sexual freedom, seduction, and frivolity. It has kept that sense today: a libertine is a man, or a woman, 'leading a dissolute life.'[31]

Cusset is speaking of French libertinism and French literature, but her remarks are pertinent, for certainly the English, from the beginning, associated the pursuit

---

27   *Otherwise Than Being or Beyond Essence*, trans. Alphonso Lingis, Martinus Nijhoff Philosophy Texts, vol. 3 (The Hague, 1981), p. 142.

28   Ibid., p. 199 n.11. Levinas cites Isaiah 6: 8.

29   Ibid., p. 141.

30   Chalier's response to Levinas focuses directly on the story of Rebekah's betrothal while Derrida's (like Irigaray's), as we have already seen, draws primarily on the Song of Songs. See Chalier's "Ethics and the Feminine" in *Re-reading Levinas*, pp. 127–8. However, the conclusion of Derrida's essay alludes powerfully to the betrothal narratives with its final word: "BOIS." "At this very moment," p. 47.

31   "Editor's Preface: The Lesson of Libertinage," *Yale French Studies*, special issue on *Libertinage and Modernity* 94 (1998): 2 n.2.

of sensual (in particular sexual) pleasure with the French manners and mores that dominated the court of Charles II. In a sense, I suppose, it is pointless to try to "rehabilitate" a term that was never untainted; yet, admittedly, that is what I am trying to accomplish. For the denotative association of "libertine" and "liberty" is an important one. When the events of the late seventeenth century created the climate for re-examination of cultural practices and beliefs, they opened all avenues for exploration, thought, reconfiguration. An emphasis on the moment of sexual arousal, the recognition of mutual attraction, the desire for consummation does yield narratives of seduction, decadence, and dissolution typical of Behn, Manley, and Haywood.[32] But very different narrative trajectories are possible, and these possibilities ethically inform the narratives these women wrote. In other words, by accepting and depicting female responsiveness to the demands of the male other, Behn, Manley, and Haywood invoke the ethical ideal of reciprocity or double desire however short of the ideal their stories ultimately fall.

All of these writers would have been familiar with the biblical narratives in which female lovers accept responsibility for the other through an arousal of desire.[33] Because of the pervasiveness of Christian practice in the late seventeenth and eighteenth centuries, the influence of biblical texts at this time was profound, if often unacknowledged. Again, I wish to remind readers, however, that the following discussion is not meant to argue influence or stand as a source study. Instead, I turn to the biblical narratives that provide models of double desire in order to elaborate what is ethically articulated therein. What does reciprocal, equal love look like? What are its narrative contours? How does it affect the individuals concerned? What does it mean? Why does it happen and to what end?

We got a glimpse of the phenomenon toward the end of the narrative of Abraham and Sarah, whose desire is rekindled in a shared moment of laughter and commemorated by the birth of a son and the establishment of a covenant with their God. But the face-to-face encounter between Abraham and Sarah is literally mediated by God. Abraham and Sarah do not see God in the face of the other; they see the other in the face of God. Their descendants will experience love more directly, as they come together without mediation in chiastic meetings that lead to (rather than result from) momentary transcendence into the infinite or the presence of God.

---

32 Cusset asserts that (in France) "No women wrote libertine novels: in the eighteenth century, women wrote sentimental novels, identifying with the victim and not the seducer." "Editor's Preface," 2 n.2. That is not true in England, as we shall see.

33 Such familiarity would have been fostered through works of literature based on the biblical texts, as well as knowledge of the texts themselves. Abraham Cowley's *Davideis*, for example, made the obscure Merab (who was betrothed to David, but who married, instead, Adriel) familiar enough for the playwright George Etherege to have Harriet allude to her in *The Man of Mode*: "like the haughty Merab, I 'Find much aversion in my stubborn mind,' which 'Is bred by being promised and designed'" (Act 3, scene 1 quoting Book 3 of *Davideis*). The source of knowledge for Aphra Behn's Hellena is not specified, but she, too, is thoroughly acquainted with biblical representations of women. She refers to Jeptha's daughter (Judges 11: 37–40) as evidence of "the old law [that] had no curse to a woman like dying a maid" (*The Rover*, Act 3, scene 2).

The first instance of such a love occurs in Genesis 24 and concerns the biblical matriarch Rebekah. It is a story of God's power, a story of family dynasty, a story of individual faith. It is a story of responsiveness to the other once removed, as it were; yet it is also a story of profound spiritual longing and intense sexual desire. And at the center of the narrative is a young woman at a well who is kind to a stranger, a hospitable young woman whose responsiveness is a sign of desirability and an indication of the awakening of her own desire.[34]

Abraham and his family are living among the Canaanites and Abraham is old. It is time for Isaac to marry, but Abraham does not want a Canaanite woman for his son's wife. He sends a servant, probably Eliezer, to his own country to find a wife, but the servant has reservations.[35] Maybe she won't want to follow him back to a strange land. Abraham is insistent: Isaac must not accompany the servant; the woman must leave her home and follow him. The servant prays for aid:

> O Lord, God of my master Abraham, grant me good fortune this day, and deal graciously with my master Abraham: Here I stand by the spring as the daughters of the townsmen come out to draw water; let the maiden to whom I say, 'Please lower your jar that I may drink,' and who replies, 'Drink, and I will also water your camels'—let her be the one whom you have decreed for Your servant Isaac. Thereby shall I know that You have dealt graciously with my master. (Genesis 24: 12–14)

And it happens just that way. Rebekah comes to the well; she responds to the request for a drink with the words "Drink my lord . . . I will also draw for your camels, until they finish drinking" (Genesis 24: 18–19). And the servant knows he has found the wife for Isaac. He accompanies her to her home where he is welcomed with a feast and where he informs Rebekah's family of the purpose of his journey and the miracle of finding the woman God intended for Isaac. The family is not opposed to the union, but they wish for Rebekah to delay her departure. Abraham's servant says no; she must accompany him now. Her family leaves the decision to her: "Will you go with this man?" She answers "I will" (Here I am; send me) (Genesis 24: 58).

For Chalier, Rebekah's gesture is "the disruption of being by goodness beyond maternity."[36] For Derrida it is an exchange that should force Levinas to recognize the seriasure of the feminine in an ethics that depends on her: "SHE DOESN'T SPEAK THE UNNAMEABLE YET YOU HEAR HER BETTER THAN ME AHEAD OF ME AT THIS VERY MOMENT WHERE NONETHELESS ON THE OTHER SIDE OF THE MONUMENTAL WORK I WEAVE MY VOICE SO AS TO BE EFFACED

---

34   Parts of the following discussion appeared first in my essay "Laurence Sterne and the Ethics of Sexual Difference: Chiasmic Narration and Double Desire," *Christianity and Literature*, 51 (2002): 363–85. Used with permission.

35   Chalier identifies the servant as Eliezer, as does traditional biblical commentary which cites the authority of Genesis 15: 2 in which Eliezer is identified as the steward of Abraham's house. "Ethics and the Feminine," p. 127. The servant in Genesis 24 is said to be the "senior servant of [Abraham's] household," which would suggest but does not unambiguously assert that the two are the same. Alter scrupulously refers to the servant in Genesis 24 as "the servant." *The Art of Biblical Narrative*, pp. 52–4. I follow Chalier and tradition.

36   Ibid., p. 128.

THIS TAKE IT HERE I AM EAT—GET NEARER—IN ORDER TO GIVE HIM/ HER—DRINK."[37] For Irigaray, more generally, the gesture would speak (like the traces of female desire in the Song of Songs) to the importance of carnality to a just notion of the divine or to a notion of a just divinity. After all, Rebekah is not merely good, she is desirable as well: "The maiden was very beautiful, a virgin whom no man had known" (Genesis 24: 16). Further, when she lifts her eyes to meet the lifted eyes of Isaac, when she sees the face of her future husband, she immediately gets off of her camel and veils herself, acts that speak of her own desire, of her own recognition of that desire (Genesis 24: 64–5). Irigaray's plaintive question to Levinas "why and how long ago did God withdraw from the act of carnal love?" suggests that it is not really the feminine that Levinasian ethics (and western culture in general) erases or buries or encrypts; it is the mutuality of the caress between beings wholly otherwise that we fail to acknowledge.[38] We recognize desire, but not the double desire that can exist only between lovers of the opposite sex.[39]

The ethical centrality of this erotic desire has been buried by our traditions, obscured by our laws, but it is recoverable in the foundational texts of our culture— as the provocative examination of biblical narrative by Levinas, Derrida, Chalier, and Irigaray suggests. Robert Alter has identified many narrative moments in the Hebrew Bible that allude to the general structural pattern set up in Genesis 24. In fact, significantly, he notes that this first occasion is the only one in which "the girl, not the stranger, draws water from the well."[40] Alter's reading of what he calls a "divergence from the convention"[41] focuses on the significance of Rebekah, for she "is to become the shrewdest and the most potent of the matriarchs, and so it is entirely appropriate that she should dominate her betrothal scene."[42] As Rebekah's betrothal is the originary narrative of the type-scene, however, we might more profitably view the reversal and the repetitions of this reversal as a Derridean seriasure—repetitions of the same which would obscure the presence of the other were it not for the disruption that "dislocates the Same toward the Relation."[43] The betrothal narrative may become the story of male desire, but Genesis 24 records the fact of female desire in the initial erotic encounter just as powerfully as it will be documented in

---

37 "At this very moment," p. 47.

38 "Questions to Emmanuel Levinas," p. 116.

39 I am writing from Irigaray's point of view here. While Levinas does not take love as his central subject, he does not ignore the topic in as thoroughgoing a fashion as Irigaray suggests, as is evidenced by his comment in "Enigma and Phenomenon": "Human sexuality is perhaps but . . .[the] expectation of an unknown, but known, face." In Adriaan T. Peperzak, Simon Critchley, and Robert Bernasconi (eds), *Emmanuel Levinas: Basic Philosophical Writings* (Bloomington, 1996), p. 73.

40 *The Art of Biblical Narrative*, p. 53. Other betrothal scenes discussed by Alter include that between Jacob and Rachel (Genesis 29), that between Moses and Zipporah (Exodus 2), that between Ruth and Boaz (Ruth 2), that between David and, first, Michal, then Abigail, then Bathsheba where marriages are preceded by bloodshed rather than the drink of water, and two aborted betrothal narratives—one involving Saul (1 Samuel 9) and one, Samson (Judges 14).

41 Ibid., p. 54.

42 Ibid.

43 Derrida, "At this very moment," p. 24.

the Song of Songs. After all, as Alter points out, the bridegroom is not even present in this instance of the betrothal type-scene; it is Rebekah's desire that forwards the action and determines the outcome.[44]

In the first occurrence of the betrothal narrative in Genesis 24, the central episode of the pattern is reiterated a significant three times: the servant articulates the narrative as a sign to be fulfilled; Rebekah comes to the well and the events unfold as he predicted; he recounts the episode to Rebekah's family at the feast to convince them of God's governance of the events. Further, the narrative's power is increased by the presence of a chiasmus at its center. This chiasmus is repeated three times, but here I quote from the actual meeting of the servant and Rebekah: "The servant ran toward her and said, 'Please, let me sip a little water from your jar.' 'Drink, my lord,' she said, and she quickly lowered her jar upon her hand and let him drink" (Genesis 24: 17–18). We can extract the chiasmus by paraphrasing: "Let me drink (sip) / Drink my lord." It is the exchange that precedes her further generosity—that for which she is not asked, the watering of the camels.[45]

Significantly, both Levinas and Irigaray figure the ethical exchange as a chiasmus. Levinas's invocation of the chiastic figure recalls the Greek χ. The lines of the figure represent two "readings," two voices: the point of crossing is really a moment of surrender, an admission of inadequacy or vulnerability, in which one voice demands of the other voice "interrupt me."[46] For Irigaray, chiastic meetings between beings wholly otherwise are better figured by the sign for infinity, the double loop: ∞. This kind of chiastic exchange represents the coming together, moving apart, coming together, moving apart of ever-repeatable intimacy. Irigaray prefers the double loop as a figural representation of the ethics of heterosexual love. In a sense, both figures speak to the same insight: the point of meeting is a point at which an individual's responsiveness to the demand of an other results in a merging that is both profound and temporary. The self does not become the other through this exchange, yet the self is radically altered. Simon Critchley has described the Levinasian chiasmus as

---

44   Alter, *Art of Biblical Narrative*, pp. 53–4. As Friedman puts it in glossing a later episode in Rebekah's life: "in matters of revelation, man is not more important than woman" to God. *Commentary on the Torah*, Gen. 25: 19n.

45   Obviously, I am playing a bit fast and loose with the use of "chiasmus" here. Chiastic structure is typical of much biblical narrative. This particular narrative does not include literal chiasmus of the sort we will note below in the Song of Songs. The Hebrew word for drink is "sh'tei." In Gen. 14, Eliezer's prayer, the "drink/drink" passage noted here is phrased "v'eshteh v'amrah sh'tei" which is the closest any of the four versions of the meeting comes to a chiastic phrasing of the moment. Yet the central exchange is a chiastic one in terms of the narrative actions as predicted, reported, and recounted—asking for drink, being given drink, drinking. For a discussion of chiasmus and narrative structure, see John W. Welch, "Introduction," in John W. Welch (ed.), *Chiasmus in Antiquity: Structures, Analyses, Exegesis* (Gerstenberg, 1981), pp. 9–16. As a structural principle, chiasmus, or "inverted parallelism," as Welch calls it, produces an "intensification . . . both by building to a climax at the center [of the structural unit] as well as by strengthening each element individually upon its chiastic repetition" (9, 10).

46   Observed by Simon Critchley in "'BOIS'—Derrida's Final Word on Levinas," in *Re-reading Levinas*, p. 186.

"a movement from the Same towards the other which never returns to the Same."[47] Irigaray's chiasmus signifies a movement "in which each can go toward the other and come back to itself."[48] The emphasis is slightly different, but the ethical point is the same. With regard to Rebekah, chiastic meeting results in a marriage without loss of identity or voice (I will not enter into an elaborate defense of this position, but if the reader is inclined to question it, I suggest that Rebekah's continued selfhood is evident in her behavior with regard to securing Jacob's birthright from her husband who favored Esau).[49] In Chalier's words, Rebekah's behavior at the well signifies her "ability to perceive the Other's demand as a demand that is meant for her."[50] That perception is chiastic as self and other meet without possession; it is signaled in this narrative, as it will be in others concerning both our biblical and our early modern matriarchs, by a rhetorical chiasmus that emphasizes the importance of the exchange.

L'dodi v'dodi Li

If, as Derrida and Irigaray assert, the Song of Songs provides cultural traces that point to a presence that is now an absence, difference that has been interpreted as sameness, what can we infer about that presence from the fragmentary evidence provided? What, who is the female lover, according to this text? She is one who speaks of her physical desire, her longing for "the kisses of [his] mouth" (Song 1: 2). She is "dark, but comely," one who has been excluded, punished, rejected—"my mother's sons quarreled with me, / They made me guard the vineyards"—but who nonetheless has a sense of her own worth: "Let me not be as one who strays / Beside the flocks of your fellows" (Song 1: 5–7). She objectifies her lover; she identifies him as her beloved and describes him by analogies to pleasing properties of the natural world:

My beloved to me is a bag of myrrh
Lodged between my breasts.
My beloved to me is a spray of henna blooms
From the vineyards of En-gedi. (Song 1: 13–15)

She is the object of her lover's desire "the rose of Sharon / A lily of the valleys" (Song 2: 1). She responds to her lover's demands: "My beloved spoke thus to me, / 'Arise, my darling; / My fair one, come away!'" (Song 2: 10). She is both, as Irigaray points out, lover and beloved and her beloved is also her lover: "My beloved is mine/ And I am his" (Song 2: 16). But such union is not possession; it is not identity, for she tells her lover "Set out, my beloved, / Swift as a gazelle / Or a young stag, / For the hills of spices!" (Song 2: 17). That image of freedom, lovely as it is, initiates

---

47   Ibid., p. 164.

48   *An Ethics of Sexual Difference*, p. 9.

49   As Friedman points out, in this regard Rebekah and Jacob exercise "control of their own destiny" in determining succession, unlike Abraham who allows God to choose. *Commentary on the Torah*, Gen. 17: 18n.

50   "Ethics and the Feminine," p. 127.

the cyclic rhythm of desire-possession-loss-desire-possession-loss that defines the remainder of the text, for it stands in contrast to the beginning of chapter 3: "Upon my couch at night / I sought the one I love— / I sought, but found him not" (Song 3: 1).[51]

The male lover in the Song of Songs pursues, possesses, and withdraws. The female lover pursues as well; she also possesses, but she does not withdraw. And there is another, perhaps more significant difference. While the lovers share the metaphors of nature in their description of the physical attraction they feel for one another, certain metaphors seem to belong to the female lover alone. Her pursuit is not the lithe, joyous canter of freedom on the side of a mountain as is her lover's. Her movements are associated with images of confinement, city streets on which she is not free to travel; gardens that are enclosed if abundant with vegetation. Her rapturous imagined repossession of her beloved removes him from nature, into "the house of my mother, / Of her who taught me— / I would let you drink of the spiced wine, / Of my pomegranate juice" (Song 8: 2).

The language of longing that the lovers speak is interchangeable, hers as intense as his. And this similarity is figured in their most usual epithet for one another: "my brother," "my friend" "my sister, my spouse."[52] As Irigaray points out, the Song of Songs "tells of the complexity of the nuptials between the two lovers (*l'amante et l'amant*), the two beloveds (*l'aimée et l'aimé*), who are born of different mothers and so do not belong to the same traditions, to the same genealogies, or to the same gods."[53] The assertion of kinship is, therefore, especially important in the context; as a metaphor for sexual relationship that preserves difference in the act of union, it is most fitting, as Restoration and eighteenth-century writers would also discover. In the Song of Songs, it seems a metaphor for chiastic love, "of the sensual delight (*volupté*) of the lovers who wed each other with all their senses, with their whole body, inviting to their encounters the most succulent fruits of the earth." [54] The tarnish of incest that will reside in the brother/sister metaphor for the women writers of the later period does not seem to inform the biblical text. Yet it is significant that the female lover speaks of friendship as well as kinship, signifying the demand for a kind of equality one does not hear in the voice of the male lover.

The last chapter of the Song of Songs acknowledges the pain of love, even as it continues to invoke the metaphor of kinship and the elements of the natural world to assert the enduring desire of the female speaker. Such pain does not quench the female lover's desire. "Passion is mighty as Sheol; / Its darts are darts of fire, / A blazing flame" (Song 8: 6). Yet "Vast floods cannot quench love, / Nor rivers drown

---

51 It is important to note in this text that the rhythm, while having a narrative component, is not driven by cause and effect toward a resolution of conflict. The pattern is repetitive, cyclical. The text is a song, and its power is lyric in nature, comprised of verse, refrain, and repetition.

52 With "my sister, my spouse," I quote the King James translation as more accurate than the JPS "my bride, my own." Ariel Bloch and Chana Bloch translate the phrase "my sister, my bride" and note the significance as a metaphor for "intimacy" as well as a term of affection. *The Song of Songs: A New Translation* (Berkeley, 1995), p. 175.

53 Irigaray, "Questions to Emmanuel Levinas," p. 110.

54 Ibid.

it" (Song 8: 7). As it began, the Song ends with the voice of the Shulamite woman, speaking her sexual entitlement ("I am a wall / My breasts are like towers") and her sexual desire ("O you who linger in the garden, / A lover is listening; / Let me hear your voice"). The very last verse continues the theme in the same voice: "Hurry, my beloved, / Swift as a gazelle or a young stag, / To the hills of spices!" (Song 8: 14) Her desire continues unabated, nurtured as it is by periodic separation, vibrant fantasies, joy in and with the other. We know her lover will return to her, and take her with him to the garden of delights.

The female speaker in the Song of Songs has a clear sense of what she wants from her lover. She repeats it twice: "His left hand was under my head / And his right hand caressed me."[55] This chiastic entwining is the familiar lovers' pose. It speaks of tenderness, ownership, and possession. It is the physical manifestation of the chiastic refrain "L'dodi v'dodi Li"—"I am my beloved's / And my beloved is mine" (Song 6: 3) This possessiveness is distinct from the possessiveness by which two identities become one in the act of love, however. The lovers retain their distinct voices; theirs is a mutual and reciprocal exchange, as is evident in almost any chapter of the Song. And theirs is a transcendent love, as well, as we see in the fifth chapter of the Song. Here, the voice of the male lover asserts possession and demands pleasure: "I have come to my garden, / My own, my bride; / I have plucked my myrrh and spice, / Eaten my honey and honeycomb, / Drunk my wine and my milk. / Eat, lovers, and drink: / Drink deep of love!" (Song 5: 1) His sensory fulfillment is clear, but so is his generosity. In spite of the preponderance of I's and my's, the speech ends with a gesture of transcendence. He expresses his desire; he demands his fulfillment; indeed, he states his satiation. But he is not content to gratify himself; he wishes to extend the pleasures of love to all.

When the female lover speaks, she emphasizes her responsiveness to the demands of her lover: "My beloved took his hand off the latch, / And my heart was stirred for him. / I rose to let in my beloved; / My hands dripped myrrh— / My fingers, flowing myrrh— / Upon the handles of the bolt" (Song 5: 4–5). When she finds upon "opening" to her beloved that he "had turned and gone," she begins to seek him, to call him, though she is beaten by the watchmen of the city, "bruised" and exposed: "the guards of the walls / Stripped me of my mantle" (Song 5: 7) Helpless herself, she sends word through other women to speak to her beloved, to raise his pity for her, to make him sense his "obligation": "I adjure you, O maidens of Jerusalem! / If you meet my beloved, tell him this: / That I am faint with love" (Song 5: 8). These words speak of a sexual longing so intense that it requires the metaphor of disease. This metaphor and the other predominant images associated specifically with the female lover—the city streets, the enclosed garden and the chambered house—suggest the particular nature of this female lover's desire even as images from the natural world, kinship metaphors, and demands of obligation link her inextricably with her male lover's desire.

The Song speaks, then, of mutual passion and of sexual difference and of transcendence through erotic love. The complex of metaphors draws attention to

---

55   Song 8: 3; in 2: 6 "his left hand is under my head and his right hand doth embrace me."

the particular restrictions placed on female desire—but these same metaphors also powerfully attest to the existence of that desire, and to its strength as well. The Song stands as a crucial document in the ethics of desire because it documents sexual longing, satisfaction, obligation, and demand, on the part of a woman and in the voice of a woman. What is ethically at stake in both the Song of Songs and in later literature that draws on the metaphorical heritage provided by this text (whether consciously or not) is the simple *acknowledgment* of female desire—that it exists and that it can and does coexist with sexual *difference*.

In moments of erotic exchange "both angel and body [are] found together." These are Irigaray's words describing what she calls the fundamental requirement of "a sexual or a carnal ethics."[56] A world based on such ethics does not now exist, Irigaray maintains; if it is to exist, it must reinscribe what has been erased: the fact of double desire. She recognizes mutual desire as an ethical necessity in the meeting between beings of irrefutable alterity; for mutual subjectivity (give me to drink) and mutual generosity (drink) are the necessary preconditions for building (or perhaps rebuilding) a world in which the divine is present in the carnal act. As it is the seriasure of female desire that has driven God from the erotic encounter (by denying otherness and insisting on the totality that is male desire), to reintroduce the divine, the female subject, the woman lover, must be reinscribed. In returning to the vision of erotic exchange central to these narratives, we begin to restore the female half of the double loop or to follow the trajectory of female identity that forms one half of the Greek χ. We begin to see in the exchange between lovers the possibility of transcendence, the movement toward the divine in the act and expression of desire.

The writers with whom the following study is concerned also place erotic exchange at the center of their narratives; they also hold as an ethical ideal the notion that such an exchange should occur between two subjects, not a subject and an object of desire. They sometimes employ chiasmus in their depictions of desire; they sometimes allude to the voices of the biblical women whose articulations of desire we have examined above. Most importantly, they speak—often in the voices of their female characters, sometimes in their own. While the world they speak of is not one in which the ethics of sexual difference, respect for and responsiveness to the otherness of an other, is easily or often realized, it is the ideal that underlies the fiction of each of the women novelists I discuss. For them, such an ideal is not a romance motif so much as it is a vision made possible by a society that is re-examining itself on every level. It is an ideal rooted in the foundational religious text of their culture—the Bible—but an ideal focused on ethical relations between human beings rather than on Christology or salvation mythologies. The writers hold the love between men and women, love given freely in response to the demands of the other, as a high, spiritual value. The end result of such love is not necessarily peace and happiness and placidity. The meeting between two beings of essential difference can result in the chiasmus of the sideways 8 (permanent, ever renewable, union) or the chiasmus of the χ (the meeting from which the two depart, bound on separate trajectories). The ethical meaning of responsibility and responsiveness is the same either way. If a woman is a subject rather than an object, she will have

---

56 *Ethics of Sexual Difference*, p. 17.

as much to say after she has opened herself to the demands of an unreliable other as she will after she has opened herself to the demands of a trustworthy other. Her subjectivity, her voice, her willingness to respond is the essence of her desire, an ethical desire that does not seek to possess or to own but rather to know the other on his own terms.

Bound by two periods of revolution, the period 1684–1814 is unique in British history as a period of rethinking, reshaping, and reformulating all categories of human social interaction. As the following chapters will demonstrate, the women novelists of this period, no less intensely than their male counterparts, explore the significance of a world in which each individual is called upon to act responsibly. What they emphasize that the male writers of the period often ignore is that to act responsibly is to be responsive to the demands of an other and to answer those demands as Sarah, Rebekah, and the female lover in the Song of Songs answered before them: "Here I am; send me."

Chapter 2

Men and Women in the Garden of Delight

Political theorizations of the female other have emphasized the construction of sexual difference in terms of power relations. To inhabit the role of the feminine is, politically speaking, to inhabit the lesser, the inferior role. A rethinking of the other in the ethical terms outlined in the preceding chapter makes it possible to see difference in "other" ways. When the question is not power over the other but response to the other, when the goal is not individual achievement but social bond, when the ultimate aim is transcendence rather than immanent eminence, the other becomes a privileged position from the point of view of the same—not absorbable into the identity of the same. The other awakens one to awareness of obligation. Response is an opening to the other's demand for recognition of the very difference that defines otherness. To respond to the other is not to transfer power, to capitulate, to lose some sort of contest. It cannot be thus because the response is momentary, transient, and equivocal. The same returns to himself or herself, different for the encounter, but not fully possessed of or by the other. The physical union between lovers who retain their separate identities in the act of love is a privileged version of this ethical relation. Heterosexual lovers who embody difference biologically are in some ways the best representatives of the ethical relationship. Cultural differences that have been grafted onto the biological beings of men and women, of course, make discussing heterosexual lovers in ethical terms fraught with problems. Yet, as these are just more acute versions of the same difficulty we encounter in separating the notion of power politics from ethical relation in any encounter between two beings, the heterosexual couple remains an important site for the exploration of ethical questions.

Restoration and eighteenth-century women writers thought so too. For Aphra Behn, Delarivier Manley, and Eliza Haywood in particular the fundamental obstacle to female happiness was the institution of marriage. Writing at a time when thinkers of both sexes were examining anew all the preconceived notions they had inherited from church and state, these women wrote about what they knew best from the position they inhabited in their own place and time. Fundamental to the fictional worlds of these writers is the acceptance of female as well as male subjectivity. Indeed, as William Warner has put it, their novels "teach readers, men as well as women, to articulate their desire."[1] These women, he argues, played a "crucial

---

1   "Formulating Fiction: Romancing the General Reader in Early Modern Britain," in Deidre Lynch and William B. Warner (eds), *Cultural Institutions of the Novel* (Durham, 1996), p. 284.

early role in the formation of an Enlightenment subjectivity."[2] While Warner's "subjectivity" is in the end a selfish individualism, and while certainly the novels of Behn, Manley, and Haywood chronicle debased versions of love (love as conquest, manipulation, control), their fictions also pay homage to the ideal of love, romantic love, as Janet Todd would have it, love as reciprocal, mutual, ethical exchange in the terms that I am employing.[3] And to do so, they traveled imaginatively to a place and time—a literary locale, not a real one—the pastoral wherein metaphors, images, set scenes, and themes allowed them to sing their own song of songs, as it were, about female desire.[4]

The most famous garden in all of literature, of course, is the garden of Eden, and, as the following discussion will demonstrate, as it was in Eden, it is in fiction: the garden of delight generally presages a fall from grace. It would be surprising if that were not the case; these writers wrote under the influence not only of the biblical narrative itself, but of its recent powerful retelling by John Milton in *Paradise Lost*. Nevertheless, Behn, Manley, and Haywood are willing to give credence to the garden as a scene of innocent sexual pleasure (even between illicit lovers) at least for the moment in which the pleasure is described and enjoyed (by characters and readers alike). These novelists do not endorse the Augustinian view, which by the time they were writing had become the general Christian view, that "spontaneous sexual desire is the proof of—and penalty for—universal original sin."[5] Indeed, these writers claim sexual impulse as a God-given gift that, like all gifts, can be misused and abused, but that also provides access, particularly for women, to various mysteries—mysteries of knowledge, of power, and of spirituality. We have seen in the previous chapter that in biblical texts concerning the relationship between God and the Hebrew people, the awakening of female sexual desire plays a crucial, legitimate role. While certainly Eve's advice prompts Adam to choose the wrong path in the third chapter of Genesis, in the twenty-first chapter of the same book, we have God's own voice

---

2   Ibid., p. 284.

3   Todd, "'The hot brute drudges on': Ambiguities of Desire in Aphra Behn's *Love-Letters Between a Nobleman and his Sister*," *Women's Writing* 1 (1994): 279. Todd discusses *Love-Letters* as a narrative of desire "for the aware self-preserving woman" who must come to terms with "the cruelty of male sexuality, the erotics of male violence and aggression and ... the male dream of rape" (279, 281). The narrative, Todd argues, regards "any transcendent entity," including love, with "complex skepticism" (289).

4   Behn seems to envision an edenic garden akin to Luce Irigaray's invocation of a similar garden world, which Gayatri Spivak has described as a place "where woman's sin does not make man's difficult access to knowledge possible." Spivak remains dubious about both the place ("It is hard for me to enter that garden") and what it is said to signify: i.e. the "impossible intimacy of the ethical." "French Feminism Revisited," in Judith Butler and Joan W. Scott (eds), *Feminists Theorize the Political* (London, 1992), pp. 79, 81. See also Heidi Hutner's description of the "golden age" deployed in Behn's *The Rover, Part II* as an ineffective strategy for female emancipation. "Revisioning the Female Body: Aphra Behn's *The Rover*, Parts I and II," in Heidi Hutner (ed.), *Re-reading Aphra Behn: History, Theory and Criticism* (Charlottesville, 1993), p. 117.

5   I quote from Elaine Pagels, *Adam, Eve and the Serpent* (New York, 1988), p. xviii.

enjoining Abraham to listen to what Sarah says, to heed her counsel.[6] If Eve doomed western women to silence and silencing by masculine power and prerogative, it is not because the Bible itself decreed that such be the case. It is without question that the structure of ancient Hebrew society was patriarchal, as was the structure of English society in the period under consideration here.[7] But that does not mean that women did not speak for themselves, in their own words and of their own desires. Indeed, the novels written by women in the late seventeenth and early eighteenth centuries in England reverberate with women's voices, not voices crying in the wilderness, but voices speaking and being heard in the garden of delight.

Ubi Sunt?

It is fitting, therefore, that in Aphra Behn's *Love Letters Between a Nobleman and his Sister*, it is not Genesis but the Song of Songs that occupies a pivotal position. Eve's powers of persuasion and Sarah's spirited self-possession speak to aspects of female subjectivity, it is true, but not the kind of subjectivity that interests Behn in her thinly veiled *chronicle scandaleuse* about Henrietta Berkeley and her brother-in-law, Lord Grey. Silvia's voice is, instead, inflected by the cadences of the frank and demanding Shulamite woman whose first words in the Song of Songs are "Oh, give me of the kisses of your mouth."[8] Silvia herself even acknowledges as much in the epistolary lament she pens as she leaves her father's house to join Philander in Paris, both in direct reference to the biblical text and in her words which are a variation on Song 3: 1 ("I sought the one I loved— / I sought, but found him not") and Song 5: 6 ("I sought, but found him not; I called, but he did not answer"):

> I sought thee every where, but like the languishing abandon'd Mistress in the *Canticles*,
> I sought thee, but I found thee not, no bed of Roses wou'd discover thee; I saw no print

---

6   According to Pagels, Jewish commentators used the edenic narrative to map out standards of "sexual practices ranging from abhorrence of public nakedness . . . to marital practices designed to facilitate reproduction" (xxi). Early Christian teachers followed suit, but as Christianity developed and expanded, the emphasis on original sin (and specifically original *sexual* sin) became "rooted in our cultural attitudes" (xxvii).

7   In fact, the incontestable patriarchy of Judeo-Christian Western society has led feminist scholars like Margaret Gibson to assert that "[g]ender ethics requires that women have their own genre/gender, genealogy, and their own project/projection of the divine." "Guiltless Credit and the Moral Economy of Salvation," *j-spot: Journal of Social and Political Thought*, online edition, 1, No. 3 (2001): 15; http://www.yorku.ca/jspot/3/mgibson.htm, accessed 11/28/2003. Obviously, my argument stops short of endorsing Gibson's view.

8   As Ariel Bloch and Chana Bloch observe: "The Shulamite's lively presence has been obscured by two millennia of translations and interpretations that, for the sake of propriety, have presented her as a sweet young thing, chaste and demure and properly bridal. In most translations (the King James Version is a notable exception), she wears a veil, a reading not supported by the Hebrew. . . . When we lift the veil from her face, the Shulamite is revealed as a passionate young woman, as spirited and assertive as Juliet." *The Song of Songs*, p. 5. The female lover is referred to once in the Song as a "Shulamite" (7: 1), a word of uncertain meaning. See Bloch and Bloch, p. 197n.

of thy dear shape, nor heard no amorous sigh that cou'd direct me—I ask'd the wood and springs, complain'd and call'd on thee through all the Groves, but they confess'd thee not; nothing but Echo's answer'd me, and when I cried *Philander*—cried—*Philander*, thus search'd I till the coming night and my increasing fears made me resolve for flight, which soon we did, and soon arriv'd at *Paris* . . .[9]

That Silvia invokes this passage in her transit from country to city is significant, for the pastoral has been necessary to this love affair which will not survive the complexities of urban existence—life "in the world." The anguished expression of loss and unfulfilled desire is appropriate. Philander too had quoted the Song of Songs earlier in a scene of similar longing: separated from Silvia and unable as yet to convince her to yield to his importunities, he writes, "I am sick of Love" (16). His allusion follows a description of a dream in which he tries to convince Silvia that "Honour appears not . . . in silent Groves and grotto's, dark Alcoves, and lonely recesses." In his dream, "my *Silvia* yielded! . . . and made me happier than a Triumphing God!" (15) In the privileged space of pastoral, even the act of incest seems compliant with "Divine Decrees" (16).

This doubled allusion to the biblical text serves to sanitize, indeed idealize, the initial impulses between Silvia and Philander. In the beginning of this narrative, Behn clearly wants the reader on her lovers' side, sympathetic to Silvia in particular, despite the public scandal they have caused. Through Silvia, Behn centers female desire in the narrative in the same way and to the same end that it is centered in the Song itself—not to chasten the woman but to acknowledge her. Like the Song of Songs, the pastoral love story of Silvia and Philander begins with the speech of a woman—not in her own voice as yet, but with firsthand testimony that she has a voice and that she uses that voice to express desire. In the letter which opens the narrative, Philander writes to Silvia: "I parted from you resolv'd to obey your impossible commands" (11). As he continues his letter, however, we begin to sense his confusion: what have her commands actually been? After all, she has spoken with words and "with sighs she wou'd in vain conceal" (11). In her answer to Philander, she clarifies the situation for him by noting "that I was not at all pleas'd with the Vows you made me, to endeavour to obey me, and I then even wisht you wou'd obstinately have deny'd obedience to my just commands" (12). If Silvia does not speak first in the epistolary exchange, it is nevertheless clear that her will and her desire (and thus her voice) are dictating at least some of the events of this unlawful romance. As Judith Kegan Gardiner has observed, Silvia "maintains her integrity through desire" the way later novelistic heroines will "achieve integrity through chastity."[10] In fact, her desire, increasingly the source of her power, is early on linked to her ability to speak, to write, to demand from her lover, in the manner of the Shulamite woman before her, exactly what she wants.

---

9   *Love Letters Between a Nobleman and his Sister,* in Janet Todd (ed.) *The Works of Aphra Behn* (7 vols, Columbus, 1995), vol. 2, pp. 101–2. Further references will be cited parenthetically in the text.

10   "The First English Novel: Aphra Behn's *Love Letters*, the Canon and Women's Tastes," *Tulsa Studies in Women's Literature* 8 (1989): 215.

As in the Song of Songs, desire is also associated with the pastoral setting in both conventional and unconventional ways. Conventionally, the pastoral is the domain of female power, and the garden is woman's natural habitat, the place where she presides physically, at some times, spiritually at others. The speaking woman in the pastoral domain is a less conventional indication of this power, however, than the "spoken about" woman.[11] In the classical canon, pastoral poems feature the complaints of shepherds attesting to the ability of woman to inflict emotional pain. Sometimes pastoral depictions of nature figure the feminine as an other to be tamed and controlled (as in the Garden of Eden) or tilled and harvested (as in Virgil's *Georgics*), a force to be reckoned with, and eventually subdued. The pastoral's recognition of feminine power, then, is neither simple nor simpleminded.

Indeed, as William Empson has pointed out, pastoral simplicity in general is an illusion; in all its manifestations, the pastoral is infused with deep contradictions. For all its charm, the pastoral serves not to soothe us but to convince us of the inadequacy of life. For all its rustic, youthful cast of characters, the pastoral often elevates these humble (feminine) presences in order to shore up the powerful (masculine) absences. For all its language of humility, the pastoral is often cunningly deceptive. And for all its elevation of sexual innocence and innocent sex, the pastoral often sublimates the sex drive into a love for nature that denies natural human desires by transmuting those desires into a longing for the natural world. In sum, Empson notes, the pastoral works by "putting the complex into the simple," or, as Annabel Patterson observes, the pastoral is the domain of the ideological where the prevailing political tensions of the day are both (imaginatively) evaded and exposed.[12]

In the pastoral setting of Part 1 of Behn's *Love Letters*, or indeed that of the Song of Songs itself, male and female collaborate in fantasies that explore such tensions, contradictions, and complexities. Theirs is a private world of sexual energy that is heightened by the imaginative playfulness they share. The lovers indulge in role-playing that intensifies their pleasure in one another through anticipatory rhetoric and elevated sentiment. In the Song, the Shulamite woman refers to her lover as her "king" (Song 1: 4), and she exults in images of beauty and splendor associated with nature and summoned as evidence of a power and wealth beyond what kingship could confer: "Our couch is in a bower; / Cedars are the beams of our house, / Cypresses the rafters" (Song 1: 16–17). Other passages speak directly of Solomon's wealth, his "palanquin [chariot] / Of wood from Lebanon" with "posts . . . of silver, / [a] back

---

11   This generalization applies to the classical pastoral. As Ann Messenger and Gail David have shown, during the early modern period, female-centered and female-authored pastoral featured women subjects and speakers. Messenger notes of Aphra Behn that "pastoral allowed her to say what she wanted to say. She wanted to write about love, love in general and her own experiences with it, and about politics." *Pastoral Tradition and the Female Talent: Studies in Augustan Poetry* (New York, 2001), p. 16. David traces the way women writers appropriated pastoral conventions to develop narratives of female heroism. *Female Heroism in the Pastoral* (New York, 1991).

12   William Empson, *Some Versions of Pastoral* (New York, 1974), p. 22. Empson's emphasis is on pastoral as proletarian art and dialectical process. Annabel Patterson focuses on the "history of Virgil's *Eclogues* in Western culture" in her *Pastoral and Ideology: Virgil to Valéry* (Berkeley, 1987), p. 7.

of gold, /. . . / Wearing the crown that his mother / Gave him on his wedding day, / On his day of bliss" (3: 9–10), a passage Ariel Bloch and Chana Bloch interpret as associated with the lovers' "play-acting outdoors: Solomon as the Shulamite's 'king,' their royal 'chambers,' their leafy 'bed.'"[13] Silvia and Philander are similarly playful. Children of wealth and privilege, they become lovers in a pastoral romance in order to imaginatively shed their responsibilities and heighten their sense of freedom and possibility. They also cast each other as deities of nature, the "Triumphing God" and "the young Goddess of the Grove" (15; 21). Like the lovers in the Song, Silvia and Philander envision each other in fantasies of worldly power. Philander wishes to "lay claim to *Silvia*, to take her without controul to shades or Palaces" (73). Silvia styles her "yielding" as the loss of a "dull Empire to Almighty Love" (29), and she, like Philander, tends to think in terms of the juxtaposition of retirement and royal prerogative: "I hate the noise of Equipage and Crowds, and would be more content to live with thee in some lone shaded Cottage, than be a Queen" (66). For Philander and Silvia, such fantasies bleed over easily into ideological justifications for rebellion. Seeing themselves as privileged gods, they come to feel themselves subject to no laws but the laws of nature. Having entertained the notion of absconding with Silvia to a palace, Philander is but a step or two from asserting his right to the palace as well as the girl. Finally, the association of illicit pastoral love with landed wealth blends the pastoral alternative with "the World" and its debaucheries. What Behn styles a place of retirement in which "modesty hides from the World" (4) in her dedicatory letter to Thomas Conlon becomes in the narrative proper not only a place of immodest behavior but also the locale of public scandal and urban gossip.[14]

To note the similarities between the treatment of pastoral in the Song and in Part 1 of *Love Letters*, therefore, is not to suggest that Behn's work records a love that bears much resemblance, finally, to the reciprocal, ethical passion described in the Song. Yet it is to say that Silvia is accorded voice and power in the beginning, raising the possibility of reciprocity, mutuality, and fulfillment in the garden of delight. It is also to note that in addition to being the domain in which she has voice, the pastoral is also the place in which she discovers the power of her body. In the Song, the encryption of the pastoral onto the female body is a particularly complex erotic strategy. To figure the body as a pastoral landscape is, in a sense, to reverse the ekphrastic impulse of objectification.[15] In the Song, the natural world comes together in the female body, thereby extending woman's subjectivity and increasing

---

13   Bloch and Bloch, p. 162.

14   Behn's comparison of the royalist Conlon, himself the subject of scandalous public talk, and Philander is complex and provocative. In general, though, this distinction holds: Conlon was involved in a scandal that caused him to retreat and retire to his country estate. Philander's scandal occurred on the estate of his in-laws and prompted a movement toward town.

15   As W. J. T. Mitchell puts it, "female otherness is an overdetermined feature in a genre that tends to describe an object of visual pleasure and fascination from a masculine perspective, often to an audience understood to be masculine as well." "Ekphrasis and the Other," in his *Picture Theory: Essays on Verbal and Visual Representation* (Chicago, 1994), 163. See also Richard F. Hardin, *Love in a Green Shade: Idyllic Romances Ancient to Modern* (Lincoln, 2000), pp. 21–2, for the centrality of ekphrasis to idyllic romances of all types.

her presence. Her hair "is like a flock of goats / Streaming down Mount Gilead"; her "teeth are like a flock of ewes / Climbing up from the washing pool; / All of them bear twins, / And not one loses her young"; her "brow / Gleams like a pomegranate split open"; and her breasts "are like two fawns / Twins of a gazelle" (Song 4: 1–5) She is a "garden locked"; a "sealed up spring"; a "fountain locked" (Song 4: 12). She is the pastoral landscape, neither in it nor of it but somehow one with it. Yet, such passages reveal certain anxieties, for granting the woman subjectivity, her body remains vulnerable in a way that the masculine body is not. The Shulamite's lover traverses the natural world, ranging far, retreating and returning, in command of the landscape, the entire terrain. She, on the other hand, is the natural world; she does not travel far but in her very physical self she embodies the adventure, mystery, challenge of discovery and desire. Yet in the urban environment, in Jerusalem, she is endangered, beaten, abused. Even in the rural setting, she is enclosed in a walled garden, in a room with a locked door, in her mother's house, in her brother's vineyard. The Shulamite woman's experience of the garden is the opposite of Eve's in that the Shulamite discovers sexual passion without transgression. For her, knowledge and love are legitimately intertwined. Even so, the garden is not one of unalloyed delight; it exists in a larger world, and its meaning is connected to that world, as is true of all such gardens.

That Silvia's body is not similarly described by her lover does not suggest that her body is less the point, or less meaningful to both her lover and the world at large, than is the Shulamite's body. In fact, Silvia knows exactly what the significance of her body is. That is why she styles her passion for Philander as a civil war between Love and "that Traytor Honour" who "heads the mutiners within," and as she continues to muse on her conflict, she indicates even more clearly what is at stake for England in the choice she will finally make: "I can't forget I'm Daughter to the great *Beralti*, and Sister to *Mertilla*, a yet unspotted Maid, fit to produce a race of Glorious Hero's" (25). Of course, like the Shulamite woman, she does forget, for Silvia's story, her song, is—at least in the beginning—a song of passion and not a song of power.

The same cannot be said of Philander, however, and it is largely due to his character and his concentration on power that the pastoral sequence of *Love Letters* differs fundamentally from the book famously called by Rabbi Akiba "the holiest of the holy."[16] The lovers in the Song of Songs love with abandon, without the control conferred by marriage or familial sanction. They even love incestuously, on a metaphorical level. But, more importantly, they savor their love, each exulting in the specificity of the other's physical self and reveling in descriptions that capture and convey unusual beauty, strength, and allure. In the example quoted above, the male lover describes the Shulamite's teeth as newly washed sheep "bearing twins," an odd, and oddly appealing, metaphor that suggests the whiteness, evenness, cleanness of his beloved's teeth, the beauty of her mouth. Later, the Shulamite describes her lover's cheeks as a "bed of spices," his hands as "rods of gold, / Studded with beryl," his belly as "a tablet of ivory, / Adorned with sapphires," metaphors that imply his beauty, value, ability to dazzle and attract (Song 5: 13–14). In contrast, Philander and Silvia employ empty, formulaic adjectives —"lovely," "charming"—rhetoric that is,

---

16 Mishna, Yadayim 3: 5; quoted by Bloch and Bloch, p. 28.

as Donald Wehrs has pointed out, as treacherous as it is predictable. In describing her "'bright hair and . . . lovely eyes,'" Wehrs explains, "Philander presents Silvia with a literary image to mirror."[17] Philander presents himself through a succession of literary types, including the "rural swains" of the pastoral tradition. To Wehrs, *Love Letters* "delineates the consequences of abandoning a conception of identity and language in which 'honour' constrains desire; those consequences take the form of a dissolution of all loyalties, scruples, and affections."[18]

In *Love Letters*, the idealism of the pastoral is placed in vexed contrast to prevailing ideologies of sexual and political power, not in order to discredit the ideal so much as to illustrate that (and how) antithetical values threaten it, and on its very soil. Wehrs blames individual ambition and the aggressive pursuit of sexual and political power for the dissolution of the bonds that provide "ethical, social, or intellectual" defense against the "whimsy" of unscrupulous others as "love gives way to pride" time and time again.[19] The significance of such dissolution is also suggested by the setting itself. The locale in which the Song of Songs takes place reveals a diverse population of property owners (the Shulamite's brothers own vineyards; she refers to her mother's home) and nomadic tribes (shepherds who graze their flocks and live in temporary dwellings). Likewise, the pastoral landscape of Behn's *Love Letters* also includes distinct groups of people as well as differentiated geographical domains, groups and domains which signify separate spheres of influence, power, danger, and possibility. But in *Love Letters*, the different people and the various places are all part of one overarching entity, the estate. Through repeated references to the topography of the Berkeley estate and its surrounding environs, Behn both establishes and obscures the questions of power that underlie the incestuous union of Lord Grey (Philander) and Henrietta Berkeley (Silvia). These questions are also at the heart of the larger infraction of familial relationship represented by the Duke of Monmouth (Cesario) and his rebellious attempt on the throne of England. At the center of both plots is the unstated but dominant fact of estate ownership and its complex relationship to female erotic desire.

Indeed, the estate itself is the object as well as the objectification of Philander's desire, and it represents Silvia's subjectivity and the subjectivity of the monarchy as well. As these valences of meaning accrue throughout Part 1 of *Love Letters*, the ethical underpinning provided by reference to the Song of Songs is gradually eroded by notions of possessiveness, progress, and power. As a result, the illusion of pastoral bliss is shattered by urban violence in *Love Letters*. The threatening streets of Jerusalem could not stem the Shulamite's passion nor stifle her voice nor prevent her return to the innocence of pastoral love. London does pose a threat to Silvia; her abilities to feel passion and to speak of it are not quelled, but they are corrupted. The return to pastoral innocence is out of the question. In a sense, though, that innocence was an illusion all along, for in England the country estate is bound up in the politics of London and vice versa. The settings are not opposite domains, but part of the

---

17   Donald R. Wehrs, "Eros, Ethics, Identity: Royalist Feminism and the Politics of Desire in Aphra Behn's *Love Letters*," *Studies in English Literature* 32 (1992): 466.

18   Ibid., p. 465.

19   Ibid., pp. 474, 471.

same place, a place that speaks at once to the venal and the transcendent desires that motivate human behavior in love and in the search for power.

The State of the Estate and the Estate of the State

Although this subtitle will no doubt strike many readers as a strained (and failed) effort at cleverness, what I mean to suggest is that on one level—and a very serious one—*Love Letters* is more concerned with the chiastic relationship between the country and the court than it is with the briefly mutual relationship between Silvia and Philander. Or to put it another way, the erotic plot of *Love Letters* is synecdochic rather than analogic. Philander's desire for Silvia is a desire for all of Bellfont, the novel's name for the Berkeley estate of Durdans. Of course, Philander enjoys a degree of "ownership" conferred by marriage. As Silvia comments, her brother-in-law is accorded "all the freedoms imaginable . . . to entertain and walk with me" on the grounds of her family's home (29). Strangely, however, such prerogatives are not often in evidence as Philander is more often skulking about, negotiating the distance between "*Dorillus*'s cottage" on the outskirts of the estate, through the meadow, grove, and garden into Silvia's room. If we did not know it from the evidence of his own letters, his very movements would alert us to the fact that he wants more of the estate than his marriage entitles him to have. He wants Silvia, of course, and perhaps more as well. The transgressive and excessive nature of his desire and his design turns the estate into a geography of secret enclosures; even what seem to be open spaces conceal as much as they reveal. Philander's movements in this environment are furtive because he pursues rights that his legitimate ownership has not conferred.

As a pastoral landscape, Bellfont has places, parts, purlieus, and parterres that are erotically charged, each space imbued with its special significance. The grove is particularly important. It is where the lovers acknowledge their mutual passion, where they meet clandestinely, where Philander fights a duel with his parentally sanctioned rival, Foscario. It marks, in other words, the growing intensity of the love affair and its movement from the protection of secrecy to the private confrontations that will lead to public exposure and scandal.

The grove also marks out or demarcates differences between the lovers. In a sense it is the locus of sexual difference where man and woman can express their essential natures. Significantly, the grove is the setting for the verbal dispute that initiates Silvia's seduction, a conversation that reveals differences we conventionally attribute to gender. To Philander, the grove is a sacred scene of privacy, a hallowed place of natural instincts uncontrolled by custom or law, a privileged space where the sexual can be raised to the plane of the spiritual. Here, Philander explains to Silvia, the "formalities" of honor are "laid aside" (15). Here, lovers can "love like the first race of men, nearest allied to God"; even—or especially—incestuous lovers can "[reap] the joys of Love without controul, and [count] it Religious coupling" (12). For Silvia the grove holds other, horticulturally supported, lessons of life and love:

> You grew up a Brother with me; the title was fixt in my heart, when I was too young to understand your subtle distinctions, and there it thriv'd and spread; and 'tis now too late

to transplant it, or alter its Native Property: Who can graft a flower on a contrary stalk? The Rose will bear no Tulips, nor the Hyacinth the Poppy; no more will the Brother the name of Lover. O spoil not the natural sweetness and innocence we now retain, by an endeavour fruitless and destructive; no, no *Philander*, dress your self in what Charms you will, be powerfull as Love can make you in your soft argument,—yet, oh you are my Brother still. (13)

For Silvia, at this juncture, fecundity is the point of love; she emphasizes the health and growth of nurturing and informed agriculture not the freedom and abandon of a wild and untended garden. Silvia, though the "innocent" one in this exchange, from the beginning understands that in the postlapsarian world, garden simplicity is the product of art as much as nature.

Yet her argument falters on this very matter. She has based her objection to Philander on the analogy of grafting, creating hybrids, altering the "Native Property" of the natural world. In fact, the horticultural development of landed property was dependent on the very techniques Silvia is determined (or says she is determined) to disallow. Chances are the trees at Bellfont have been transplanted from somewhere; most certainly they have been tended, cultivated, and maintained. Perhaps there are no hybrids in this grove as extreme and rare as Silvia describes, but to have no hybrids at all would be a highly unusual situation for a wealthy estate like Durdans (Bellfont). In her next letter, it is as though Silvia has recognized the speciousness of her argument. And it is as though the grove itself has corrected her—not by disputing the notion of species purity, but by asserting a natural force that overrides such considerations. As Silvia walks in the grove the morning following the attempted seduction, she finds herself more receptive to the power of Philander's argument than she had been the day before. She responds in a coupling with the earth that clearly prefigures the consummation of her love for Philander: "I threw my self down on that bank of grass where we last disputed the dear but fatal business of our souls: Where our prints (that invited me) still remain on the prest greens" (13–14). She sighs and kisses Philander's letter, throws herself on the ground in a fit of jealousy thinking of Mertilla, presses her "panting heart to the cold earth," and finally cries as she "traverse[s] swiftly the conscious Grove . . . the lovely silent shade favouring my complaints" (14). Whatever wrong Silvia and Philander are about to commit, it is not, she becomes convinced, a crime against nature. But more importantly, the grove stands in for Philander here. Silvia's love for Philander expresses itself as love for the grove; love for the grove and all it represents is bound up in her love for Philander as much as it is in his desire for her. With the grove as the point at which this chiasmus meets, it begs to be explained more fully as the point at which Whig and Tory desire potentially and potently fuse into a chiastic, ethical bond.

The grove is only part nature. Its cultivation and artificiality make it part too of civilization, and, in fact, in the narrative the grove is increasingly viewed as an extension of the house itself. For example, those who aid and abet the lovers are servants of the estate. At first, it is the household servants on whom the incestuous pair relies, but when Melinda and Silvia's page are dismissed from service "as supposed confidants of this dear secret" (91), the rustics—Dorillus, his daughter, his son, and various weeders—take over as the letter carriers, gate openers, and secret keepers. While this substitution may seem to chart a move from the house to the estate grounds, like the grove itself, the bucolic employees are liminal entities that draw our attention to the estate's own liminal status. What is the estate? Like Dorillus and company, its identity depends on its function.

The associations between the country estate and a pastoral Eden, while plentiful in the literature of the seventeenth and eighteenth centuries, are rarely deployed in the interest of advocating retreat and withdrawal from the scenes of power. More often, the estate is celebrated as a place in which the values of the nation can be clearly articulated, clearly illustrated in ordered life patterns and responsible maintenance, in tasteful spending and regenerative cultivation. In constructing themselves as hero and heroine of pastoral romance, Silvia and Philander eschew the buildings of the estate and attempt to redefine the estate grounds as the domain of private happiness. In doing so, they reinterpret the signs of the environment in which they live to fit with the pastoral paradigm. Perceptually, they recenter the Berkeley estate; the grounds and gardens, groves and meadows, woods and fields, comprise the setting of Part I of *Love Letters*. It is true that Philander is often situated "at *Dorillus*'s cottage" and that Silvia's apartment is the setting for the consummation of this affair. Indeed, the symbolic association of Silvia's room with her virginity is clearly established. Silvia sends Philander "a Key *Melinda* got made to the Door, which leads from the Garden to the back-Stairs to my Apartment, so carefully lock'd, and the original Key so closely guarded by my jealous Father" (55). Much is made of the bedroom itself as a sign of the physical union between Philander and Silvia. Two scenes are set in this room. The first emphasizes the precoital moment which is followed, not by immediate coitus, but by various impediments—first, Philander's impotence, and, then, delays occasioned by pressures from Cesario on the one hand and Silvia's family on the other. Yet, finally, the precoital image of Silvia "extended on a Bed of Roses" in a state of "wanton loose negligence" (58) is answered by a second bedroom scene in which Silvia recounts her behavior after "the *happy Night*" (87):

> often opening the conscious curtains, [I] survey the print where thou and I were last night laid, surveying it with a thousand tender sighs, and kiss and press thy dear forsaken side, imagin [sic] over all our solemn joys, every dear transport, all our ravishing repeated blisses, then almost fainting, languishing cry—*Philander* oh, my charming little God! then lay me down in the dear place you press'd, still warm and fragrant with the sweet remains that thou hast left behind thee on the Pillow. (88)

Compared to the trial transcripts of Lord Grey's appearance before the King's Bench on 23 November 1682, these scenes are not interior scenes at all.[20] In the transcripts, we are aware of the positioning of Henrietta Berkeley in closed rooms for interrogation, in coaches for escape, in private homes and inns and taverns for secrecy and concealment. That the room in Behn's novel, however, is an extension of the pastoral environs of the estate seems clear from the presence of roses in Silvia's chamber and from the echo in Silvia's postcoital behavior of opening the

---

20 Todd reprints extracts of the trial transcripts as Appendix 1 of her edition of *Love Letters*, pp. 443–61.

"conscious" curtains and embracing the print of Philander's body as she had earlier done on the grassy banks of the "conscious" grove.

The traditional pastoral association between the rural landscape and the themes of retreat and retirement might seem to be operative in Part 1 of *Love Letters* as Philander is torn between his ambitions and his attachment to the cause of Cesario (Monmouth) and his desire for Silvia. Early on, the contrasting demands of the dangers of urban politics and the sensuality and contemplativeness of rural pleasure seem the key feature of Philander's emotional conflict, reminding us, perhaps, of the dialogue between Meliboeus and Tityrus in Virgil's Eclogue 1. As Meliboeus puts it:

Beneath the shade which beechen boughs diffuse,
You, Tit'rus, entertain your sylvan Muse:
Round the wide world in banishment we roam,
Forc'd from our pleasing fields and native home;
While, stretch'd at ease, you sing your happy loves,
And Amaryllis fills the shady groves.[21]

As Meliboeus suggests, there are various reasons, ranging from ease to exile, for going into the country. Philander may find himself with good enough cause to retreat if Cesario's rebellion does not go according to plan, but meanwhile, he is drawn to the city by ambition and politics. Interestingly, though, he is urged by the same desires to remain away from London in the gardens of his father-in-law's estate. His conflict, then, is more perceived than real.

What Philander wants, what he desires, in Silvia, he desires also in Cesario. Many critics have pointed to the erotic homosociality (even homosexuality) of Philander's description of Cesario. In commenting on his wife's infidelity with the prince, Philander adopts the female point of view, but what he says of Mertilla applies with equal force to his own relationship with Cesario:

Cesario, whom the envying World in spight of prejudice must own, has unresistable Charms, that Godlike form, that sweetness in his face, that softness in his Eyes and delicate Mouth; and every Beauty besides that Women doat [sic] on and Men envy: That lovely composition of Man and Angel! with the addition of his eternal Youth and Illustrious Birth, was form'd by Heav'n and Nature for universal Conquest! and who can love the charming Hero at a cheaper rate than being undone. (17)

What Philander's language suggests here is something the narrative as a whole bears out: desire and envy are closely allied; the impulse toward the other (be that other lover, estate, or prince) is a heavenly, divine impulse; but the self, being human, not divine, is often undone in one way or the other by yielding to such impulses, by allowing the other's conquest, by—in a sense — saying "here I am" (assertion of presence and subjectivity) without the accompanying "send me" (acceptance of obligation in the face-to-face encounter with the other).

---

21 Dryden's translation. "The First Pastoral, or, Tityrus and Meliboeus," in *The Poetical Works of Dryden*, ed. George R. Noyes, Cambridge Edition of the Poets (New York, 1909), lines 1–6.

In another sense, however, the estates of England had said both to the monarchy after the Restoration of Charles II, and they said so in and with their groves. Any contemporary reader would have recognized Behn's emphasis on the grove as a royalist gesture, for one of the most severe ravages of the Civil War had been the destruction of forests and trees on estates. After the Restoration, landed families were encouraged to plant trees for the purpose of restoring Britain's woodlands— particularly the oak—which, properly managed, could ensure the country's naval competence in trade and in war for the next century. The issue was such a highly charged emotional one for Behn's contemporaries that John Evelyn's 1664 report to the Royal Society about "the Propagation of Timber in his Majesties Dominion" actually earned him the nickname "Sylva" after the title of his work.[22] Therein, Evelyn more than once assigns the blame for England's sylvan crisis to the "late prodigious Spoilers, whose furious devastation of so many goodly Woods and Forests have left an infamy on their Names and Memories not quickly to be forgotten!"[23]

The grove of the Berkeley estate, in addition to the fictional name Behn chose for the Berkeley's younger daughter, then, can be said to carry an ideological weight drawn from the circumstances of recent history. With the restoration of the Stuart monarchy, the forests too had enjoyed renewal and recovery (hence the traditional association of the oak with the Stuart family). A new revolution (the Monmouth rebellion) could mean disastrous consequences for the groves which serve as symbol of the relationship between the monarch and the health and security of England. But once more the invocation of the grove is ironic. The threat this time comes not from commoners who will lay waste the woods even as they discard the tradition of the monarchy, depose and perhaps destroy the legitimate successor to Charles II, whom Evelyn calls *"Nemorensis Rex,"* "God of the forest-trees, King of the grove."[24] Instead the threat is from noblemen, landowners who themselves want to be king.

Perhaps it is for this reason—that the threat comes from among the royalist ranks rather than from below—that in *Love Letters* we find the grove the site for sexual dalliance that is not merely transgressive, but incestuous as well. The Whig party, of course, drew its energy and drive from dissenters, the middle class, and from the "lower orders." But the contest for power was being waged between aristocrats. The Duke of Monmouth was the king's son. The Earl of Shaftesbury was a nobleman, as was Lord Grey, the model for Behn's Philander. Whatever the larger ramifications of the Whig/Tory tension during the Exclusion Crisis and after, the shorter view was simply who would be king. Ultimately, the Whigs would triumph over both court and landed wealth. Philander's treatment of the trees at Bellfont as he awaits Silvia's arrival for the consummation of their affair is telling. The carving of a mistress's name on the barks of trees is a pastoral convention, but reified through Philander it is also an act of appropriated ownership. What Philander records is not desire but possession "that all the world may wonder at my fortune . . . ; let it grow up to Ages that shall come, that they may know the story of our loves, and how a happy youth,

---

22 Guy de la Bédoyère, headnote to *Sylva* in *The Writings of John Evelyn* (Suffolk, UK, 1995), pp. 186, 174.

23 Evelyn, *Sylva*, p. 187.

24 Ibid., p. 183n.

they call'd *Philander*, was once so blest by Heaven as to possess the charming, the ador'd and lov'd by all, the glorious *Silvia*." He would not exchange the "happy coming night" even "to reign a monarch here" (71). Of course, he does not have to make such a trade, for possession of Silvia is impairment of the estate which is shoring up the monarchy that Philander hopes to destroy. Even as Philander carves his name on the trees at Bellfont, inscribing his own "monarchy," as it were, the Whig triumph which will elevate Parliamentary rule over monarchial power and aristocratic privilege is nigh unto assured.

The Grove and Incestuous Desire

The invocation of incest in Behn's *Love Letters* stands in contrast to the sister/spouse, brother/lover rhetoric of the Song of Songs. There, as we have seen, the language is an assertion of kinship, of reciprocity, of freedom of expression in public denied to lovers, but allowed to brother and sister. In Behn's *Love Letters*, almost the opposite is true. First of all, this is literal, not figurative, incest, according to the law of the time. By marrying her sister, Lord Grey became brother to Henrietta Berkeley, and thus, as Ellen Pollak has noted, "because the English concept of marriage in the seventeenth century was based on the legal and religious doctrine of the unity of husband and wife," the two are as near allied in the eyes of the church and the state as blood kin would be.[25] Secondly, as Pollak also maintains, the linking of incest with political rebellion, even regicide, adds urgency to the brother/sister relationship not present in the Song: "Behn incorporates the scandalous historical fact of the Berkeley-Grey affair into the political, thematic, and figural dimensions of her fiction by situating Philander's justifications for his adulterous and incestuous desire for Silvia squarely within the context of Restoration debates over the relationship and relative authority of nature and conventional morality."[26]

The mysterious combining of material essence that is supposed to be marriage is called into question by the pastoral libertinism of Behn's novel, as is the mysterious property of kingly succession.[27] For in the grove at Bellfont, as in all libertine pastoral environs, it is nature, not society, that makes the laws, and nature in the form of desire dictates both the coupling of Philander and Silvia and the coupling that produced Cesario (Monmouth) and thus legitimizes his claim to the throne. Such desire is

---

25   Pollak, *Incest and the English Novel, 1684–1814* (Baltimore, 2003), p. 61. Pollak draws on   the positions of Hugo Grotius (1625), Jeremy Taylor (1660), and Richard Cumberland (1672), all of whom argue that although marriages between brothers and sisters are "incestuous," they are forbidden by divine command and not by "the prime law of nature" (38). See also Pollak's discussion of the general dynamics of the "incest novel," pp. 1–26.

26   Ibid., p. 60.

27   This is indeed part of the problem with reading the *Love Letters* as propaganda. Although exploiting the case of the infamous Lord Grey and thereby serving to add to the ignominy being heaped upon him, Behn is also writing a narrative in which she allows full play to the dangerous ideologies supporting the lovers' affair and the Monmouth rebellion. See Francis F. Steen, "The Politics of Love: Propaganda and Structural Learning in Aphra Behn's *Love-Letters between a Nobleman and His Sister*," *Poetics Today* 23 (2002): 91–122.

driven by the longings of two bodies and does not result in the metaphysical union described by St. Paul in Ephesians as a "great mystery" by which "two be[come] one flesh" (Ephesians 5: 31–2). What happens in the garden at Bellfont is materialist desire, not holy wedlock. The materialist version of such mysterious forces insists on a difference (sexual) that underwrites the similarity and equality of desire, as Lucretius's own formulation would suggest:

> One fire, them [women] and their lovers doth enflame
> Their joyes are equall, their desires the same.
> Nor could all birds, beasts, heards [sic] and flocks encrease,
> Unlesse desires the females did possesse.[28]

Oneness of the sort described here, can be (and is in Behn's narrative) troped by the incest metaphor of lover as sister/spouse or brother/husband.[29] Opposite to the sacred reading of marriage as the creation of one person from two bodies, materialist or libertine ethics insists on the preservation of sexual subjectivity even, indeed especially, in the throes of other-directed desire.

Of course, the preservation of sexual subjectivity alone does not ensure ethical desire which also depends on the recognition of obligation. I will argue that double desire, Silvia's as strong as Philander's, infuses Part 1 of *Love Letters*, and I do so in contradistinction to Ellen Pollak's eloquent argument that Silvia's sexual appetite even this early is "an effect of power."[30] To deny Silvia actual physical longing for the man who has awakened her desire is to deny biological fact. Of course Silvia has desire, essential desire, for her brother-in-law. That is a material reality of her life, and evidence of her agency as a sexual subject.[31] But she is not only a sexual subject; she is also a sign, as Pollak justly observes, and what she signifies has, on one level, more to do with homosocial relations between men than with heterosexual longings, transgressive or otherwise. For, if, through double desire, sexual discreteness is preserved in the incestuous union of Silvia (Henrietta) and Philander (Grey), other material entities are denied being and substance by the same union. The sexual union between a man and a woman of wealth and status meant, in the late seventeenth century, the merging of estates, properties, fortunes, and families. Through his unlawful union with his sister-in-law, Lord Grey has rendered her unfit for such a merger; his violation of the Berkeleys' material identity is an act of theft by which he doubly damages the estate through unlawful possession of a part of the whole and through illegal behavior as a part of the whole.

---

28 *Lucy Hutchinson's Translation of Lucretius De Rerum Natura*, ed. Hugh de Quehen (London, 1996), p. 141. For Behn's interest in materialist philosophy (particularly Lucretius and Fontenelle) in the 1680s, see Todd, "'The hot brute,'" pp. 277–8, and her *The Secret Life of Aphra Behn* (New Brunswick, NJ, 1996), pp. 291–3 and 396–400.

29 While Pollak insists that Silvia's desire is constructed by Philander even in the early stages of their relationship, I believe the invocation of the Song of Songs and the pastoral imagery, settings, and themes suggest otherwise. *Incest and the English Novel*, pp. 63–4.

30 Ibid., 64.

31 In this view, I align myself with Judith Kegan Gardiner, cited above (n. 10).

Similarly, Monmouth is part of the king's identity, both as his son and as a noble subject. But to try to become king is to behave as Philander has done in an act of appropriation that calls the entire identity of the monarchy into question. On the level of both state and estate, then, there is a tension between the discreteness of the desiring subject and the participation of that subject in a larger identity. The negotiation between the demands of both is aptly figured in the idea of incest between brother and sister-in-law because such incest is a form of patricide as father/daughter incest is not. The challenge to the authority of the father, therefore, poses significant danger to the monarchial state (or the paternal estate). In a world populated with equals, all feel qualified, as well as entitled, to rule.

Regicide and patricide, then, underlie the incest motif in Behn's novel as they underlay the historical events which gave it rise. The point of the Rye House Plot, in which Philander's model, Lord Grey was involved, was to kill King Charles as well as his brother James, the heir to the throne. And as far back as the Popish Plot, in fact, Monmouth's behavior had been allegorized as that of the biblical Absalom who attempted to murder his father, David. Though Dryden, Behn, and others would reserve the stiffest blame for those surrounding and advising Monmouth rather than the king's son himself, they were fully aware that innocence in such a climate was impossible to maintain. Dryden would link Monmouth to Prometheus, one who had "a spark too much of heavenly fire."[32] Behn would take a more rigorous political stance allowed by the very different circumstances in which she wrote the final books of *Love Letters* (Charles having died, James having ascended, and Monmouth having been executed). Her change in attitude is reflected by a transformation in the garden of delight.

While a libertine irony invests the presentation of pastoral motifs in Part 1 of *Love Letters*, it does not predict or prepare us for the dark cynicism of Part 3's garden in which Silvia is symbolically returned to the paternal home. This gesture of repossession occurs at least partly because of Octavio's reverence for his uncle, his inability to stage rebellion. A committed royalist, Octavio is also a true lover, sharing none of Philander's caprice and restlessness. How does it happen, then, that this young man ends up murdering his uncle in a room in the country estate where "our Hero" was born? (299) Silvia blames herself, saying *"That sure she was born the Fate of all that Ador'd her, and no Man ever thriv'd that had a Design upon her, or a Pretension to her"* (306), and we might just agree. For if part of the strange fact that Octavio allows his besotted uncle to take Silvia to his home, to imprison her, to woo her, and to plan to marry her is due to a nephew's reverence for the uncle who reared him, another (perhaps more significant) part is attributable to Silvia herself. .

In Part 3, Silvia is no longer the desiring subject with the potential to realize both presence and obligation. She has not ceased to speak, but she has definitely stopped listening. Part 3 begins by informing us that Silvia has "absolutely resolv'd to give her self to that doting fond Lover, or rather to sacrifice her self to her Revenge" (257). With this news, we are aware that Philander's rejection continues to sting Silvia, eliciting aspects of her character that counterbalance her beauty, youth, and charm.

---

32   This is Dryden's description of Monmouth in *Absalom and Achitophel*, *Poetical Works of Dryden*, line 308.

"She was Imperious and Proud, even to Insolence; Vain and Conceited even to Folly; she knew her Vertues and her Graces too well, and her Vices too little; she was very Opinionated and Obstinate, hard to be convinced of the falsest Argument, but very positive in her fancied Judgment" (257). Among the "Vertues . . . that balanc'd her Vices," however, the chief is that she "lov'd *Philander* with a Passion, that nothing but his Ingratitude could have decay'd in her Heart" (258). Throughout this entire episode, Silvia seems self-contained, driven by the desire to "beget Desire," but incapable of returning it in kind (278).

The garden thus ceases to serve as a chiastic site in which lovers come together in one being while preserving their discreteness as individual and as sexual beings. The oblique incest that figures such a self/other exchange is tainted by possession, imprisonment, design. Octavio's uncle, Sebastian, struggles with the conflict between his devotion to family and his devotion to Silvia in a garden conversation with his nephew that is characterized more by silence than by speech: "both walked many silent Turns about the Garden" (289). Eventually they understand one another, however; once Sebastian determines that Octavio had never "*had the Possession of this fair Maid*" (289), he reveals his own love for Silvia. Octavio fights back with what is essentially the argument that while Sebastian may avoid true incest, he nonetheless opens himself to the reputation for such. Already there has been a lampoon, Octavio tells his uncle, "*for keeping a Beauty in your House, who they are pleased to say was my Mistress before*" (290). This information produces the direct opposite of the desired result, for Sebastian, enraged, vows to marry Silvia.

Sebastian "kept and guarded [Silvia] like a mighty Heiress" (291), but her room is just off the garden, and at night Octavio can come to her window to woo her and to plan their escape. Echoes of *Romeo and Juliet*'s pastoralism seem deliberate:

> she anon came to the Window, and putting up the Sash, leaned on her Arms and look'd into the Garden. Oh! Who but he himself that Lov'd so well as *Octavio*, can express the Transports he was in at the Sight? which more from the Sight within than that without, he saw was the lovely *Silvia*; whom calling softly by her Name, answered him as if she knew the welcome Voice, and cry'd, —*Whose there, Octavio*? She was soon Answer'd you may imagine. And they began the most indearing Conversation that ever Love could dictate. (293)

The self-conscious literariness of this scene speaks to a generational conflict, but the players are confused. Octavio is a royalist; Sebastian, on the side of the "states." Octavio's patricide later at the country estate on which he was born, his donning of a rustic's costume in order to get to the estate, the eliding of this episode into the story of Philander's affair with Octavio's sister (another case of oblique—and strangely doubled—incest), thoroughly mixes and confuses categories. But as categories of personal identity and identification become so jumbled as to be uninterpretable, the demarcation between outside and inside, garden and house becomes clearer. In Part 3, the conflation of room, bed, body, and nature that we see from Silvia's (and from Philander's) perspective in Part 1 never happens. Even the rustics who help Octavio gain access to Silvia are to be trusted only so far, their loyalty being to the owner of the estate not to lovers who belong to nature. In other words, in spite of the presence of a garden and reference to a country estate and allusions to pastoral scenes and motifs, this episode suggests a fuller investment of a pattern we noticed beginning to emerge in Part 1. In Part 3, it is quite clear that the realm of politics has thoroughly infested and infected the garden of delight. Primarily through the corruption of Silvia's sensibility, her inability, once betrayed, to re-achieve erotic desire for an other, the garden of delight has been transformed into a prison of personal power.

Behn's general perception seems to be that the pastoral ideal is often a convenient fiction used to entrap, ensnare, or exploit one of a couple, usually the woman, although Cesario in the end is presented as a pastoral victim to the machinations, black art, and ambitions of Hermione. Yet Behn also credits the ideal with the power to enrapture and transform. While Silvia's fate is regrettable, the trajectory of her growing cynicism cannot be read as an indictment of erotic pleasure. Calista's response is to move along a different path. Having experienced the beauty of pastoral love, the garden of delight, and having recognized the evil in the garden (Philander's inconstancy), she has recourse to a higher domain—a convent—in which retreat is permanent and return is a step closer to Eden and to God.

Chapter 3

Sexual Awakening and Political Power

In the amatory narrative, as formulated by Aphra Behn, the moment of awakening first love is typically followed by one or more discursive moments, discussions by characters or the narrator about subjects apparently unconnected with the panting, blushing, fainting, weeping ecstasy these narratives associate with mutual desire. Often, these interruptive, delaying meditations have to do with what we can describe as the political and philosophical implications of sexual attraction, for it seems to be the sense of these fictions that acute awareness of the bodily self is tied to acute awareness of self as political subject and agent. Behn, and, following her, Delarivier Manley are given to "freezing" the first moment of double desire—suspending action between the awakening of desire and its consummation—sometimes for dozens of pages wherein the plot or discursive commentary focuses on questions of state governance and power. The somewhat strange linkage they forge constitutes an important aspect of their understanding of both the nature of sexual desire and the structure of women's political identity.[1] In a sense, we could say, they see in the moment of sexual awakening the birth of a self-awareness necessary to participate in the actions of the world, the decisions of the body politic. So their fantasies of female desire are not simply fantasies of sexual appetite or emotional longing. They are also fantasies of power, influence, and political agency—in the family and in the home, certainly, but also in the nation and in the world.[2]

Behn and Manley approach the world from the same political vantage point—Toryism—about the same political phenomenon—the rise of the Whig state. Further, they adopt the same rhetorical stance, which I will call for convenience's sake at this point "satire," though that term must later be complicated and qualified considerably. Each also writes in the service of politicians and political parties at a particular moment of political crisis (the Exclusion Crisis for Behn, the ending of the War of the Spanish Succession for Manley). Finally, each of these women defines herself as both political agent and sexual subject. Each lived what we (and they) would call a libertine life; each espoused what we (and they) would recognize as conservative political beliefs in the sense that conservatism endorses the notion of an ideal past in lieu of pursuing a future of radical change. While these women lived at a time in which they could not hold political office, they did themselves enjoy and express

---

1   Ros Ballaster has discussed the seduction narrative in terms of its political significance, seduction and persuasion sharing the same rhetorical profile and obvious political power. See *Seductive Forms*, pp. 24–30.

2   After all, as Ballaster points out "[w]omen's only political instrumentality was to be achieved by playing the role of seductress." Ibid., p. 80.

political agency, and they gave political voice to their desiring female characters as well.

During the roughly fifty-year span between the Glorious Revolution in 1688 and the failure of Robert Walpole's ministry in 1742, the British republican state is born, and in some ways our authors can be seen as the midwives of this new nation which will retain its monarchy while operating as a parliamentary government. [3] Behn and Manley are concerned with the theoretical justification of the monarchy; yet each is also acutely (and astutely) interested in politics. These two focal points are really antithetical, as J.G.A. Pocock has meticulously explained in his study of the emergence of republicanism in Florentine thought. A true defense of monarchy would proceed from the argument of eternal truth, fixity of values, state alignment with permanent, ideal hierarchical structures. As Pocock points out, the ideal monarchy is underwritten by a belief that the next world is more important than this world; that God and the King are in essence one; and that the rest of existence is obviously of minor importance when compared with the monarch's and the deity's will and judgment. No actual monarchy will ever reach the ideal, of course, but belief in the system assumes belief in eternal and transcendent values. Monarchy cannot be convincingly justified in a world that accepts (or embraces) its contingencies, particularities, and transiencies without repining.[4] Yet this is precisely what Behn and Manley undertake to do. It is appropriate, therefore, that they link the particular, never recoverable, and—significantly—transcendent moment of sexual awakening with the dawn of political consciousness. It is equally appropriate that they position this political consciousness against the backdrop of the ideal monarchy. By doing so they draw attention to the nature of the republican state whose emergence they wrote to forestall.

For Behn, such a forestalling must have seemed possible. After all, her adult life spanned the years between the Restoration of the Stuart monarchy and the revolution which demonstrated that the civil conflict of the 1640s had left an indelible mark on the English kingship. Divine right could still be theoretically justified in a world in which the king "touched" victims of scrofula, a world in which broken vows brought fears of retributive justice from above.[5] For Manley, however, divine right had to

---

3   Robert Walpole, of course, remained in office until 1742, but from the mid 30s on, he faced a series of crises that eroded his authority and provided Tory Opposition with occasion for vituperation in the press and in Parliament itself. First came the Excise Crisis of 1733–34; then, the death of Walpole's friend and supporter Queen Caroline in 1737 stimulated the increasing antagonism of the Prince of Wales toward his remaining parent and the prime minister. In 1739, Walpole found himself forced against his will to lead England into war with Spain over the inspection of ships which cost Robert Jenkins's Ear (the "War of Jenkins Ear"), and in 1740—with the Spanish crisis not yet resolved—war broke out in another European theater over the succession to the Austrian throne. On Walpole's relationship to the writers of the time (and theirs to him and his policies), see Betrand A. Goldgar, *Walpole and the Wits: The Relation of Politics to Literature, 1722–1742* (Lincoln and London, 1976).

4   *The Machiavellian Moment: Florentine Political Thought and the Atlantic Republican Tradition* (Princeton and London, 1975), p. 4.

5   As J. Douglas Canfield has noted, the dominant trope of English literature written before 1689 is "the word as bond." *Word as Bond in English Literature from the Middle Ages*

be re-established. *The New Atalantis* examines the various perversions of desire that infect the political world, implicitly arguing that while the linkage between unchanging truth and state governance is quite natural—or should be—the tie has been severed. Though there was a time when Justice and Truth reigned on earth, they clearly have been driven from the contemporary scene. Undergirding Manley's satire is the assumption that with the right leaders, the right people in charge, Justice and Truth will once again prevail, but her focus is on those who are unfit for the positions they hold, those who have brought corruption and chaos into the world they govern.

Prophecy and Tent Pegs

The idea of divinely sanctioned kingship draws strength from the biblical example of David, but predating his leadership of Israel are those not denominated kings, but prophets, those not called rulers, but judges. Deborah is one such leader. This matriarchal figure is concupiscent, just, and powerful. She is introduced to us in all three of her aspects, and in the order I have employed, in the Book of Judges: "Deborah, wife of Lappidoth, was a prophetess; she led Israel at that time" (Judges 4: 4). She is a wife, a prophet, a leader. She has her own date palm tree ("the Palm of Deborah") located between Ramah and Bethel in Israel ("Ephraim") under which she sits: "and the Israelites would come to her for decisions" (Judges 4: 5).

Deborah's idea of prophecy is the same as that enacted by Moses and Joshua before her. She may make a habit of sitting under her tree dispensing wisdom and judgment, but when the need arises, she will get up and go in pursuit of justice. The narrative that centers on her is set in motion by her calling her army commander to her palm tree court. Here, she tells Barak that God has revealed a plan for deliverance of the Israelites who have been "oppressed . . . ruthlessly" by King Jabin of Canaan for the past twenty years: "'The Lord, the God of Israel, has commanded: Go, march up to Mount Tabor, and take with you ten thousand men of Naphtali and Zebulin. And I will draw Sisera, Jabin's army commander, with his chariots and his troops, toward you up to the Wadi Kishon; and I will deliver him into your hands'" (Judges 4: 3, 6–7). She implies, of course, that she would like her military commander to take this matter upon himself and go to Mount Tabor and get the job done. Barak's decision would seem to be an easy one as it is but his duty to follow the orders delivered by his leader who is herself following the directive of God. Something seems to have happened to manly resolve in Israel, however. Before the oppression under Jabin, the Israelites had such "champions" as Shamgar son of Anath, "who slew six hundred Philistines with an ox-goad" (Judges 3: 31); now, it turns out, the army commander is reluctant to lead forces ten thousand strong into battle when he has been prophetically guaranteed victory and when God himself has mapped out the military strategy. Barak does not answer "Here I am; send me." Instead, he says to Deborah, "'If you will go with me, I will go; if not, I will not go'" (Judges 4: 8).

---

to the Restoration (Philadelphia, 1989), pp. xiii–xiv.

Deborah is a kind leader who does not chide Barak for weakness. She agrees to his demand, but she tells Barak what the consequences will be: "'there will be no glory for you in the course you are taking, for then the Lord will deliver Sisera into the hands of a woman'" (Judges 4: 9). Barak makes no response; his need for her is so strong that forfeit of glory means nothing. Why does he need her? Perhaps he "needs the prophetess as a means of inquiring of the Lord."[6] Perhaps he needs her wisdom, her judgment to guide him. Perhaps he needs her physical presence (there is a tradition that Barak and Deborah are husband and wife).[7] Whatever the reason, it is acceptable to the Lord: "All of Sisera's soldiers fell by the sword; not a man was left" (Judges 4: 16). Sisera himself, however, escapes. What happens next is the fulfillment of Deborah's prophecy; Sisera is delivered into the hands of a woman, Jael, wife of Heber the Kenite.[8] When Sisera appears at her tent seeking water and shelter, Jael responds: "'Come in, my lord, come in here, do not be afraid'" (Judges 4: 18). She gives him milk and covers him with a blanket. No doubt exhausted from battle and, now, full and warm, Sisera falls into a deep sleep. At this point, Jael removes the pin from the opening of her tent and drives it "through his temple till it went down to the ground" (Judges 4: 21). To Jael, therefore, belongs the glory of Sisera's death.

When we first read Deborah's prophecy following Barak's request that she accompany him into battle, we assume she is the one who will receive glory for the coming victory. The song that follows the narrative does accord praise to Deborah as the mother of Israel who has delivered the land and its people from oppression: "Deliverance ceased, / Ceased in Israel, / Till you arose, O Deborah / Arose, O mother, in Israel" (Judges 5: 7). That Deborah is referred to as mother here is interesting, particularly in light of the end of the song. There, in consecutive verse vignettes, we are presented with the image of two women—one the heroic, stalwart Jael, and the other the anxious, suffering mother of Sisera. Jael is celebrated as the "most blessed of women," as the "wife of Heber the Kenite," and, again, as "most blessed of women in tents" (Judges 5: 24). The overt double reference to blessedness is matched by the covert double reference to marriage: i.e. Jael is a wife and is among the "women in tents," the one who provides for the stranger, as Sarah did for the angels of God. Jael's hospitality, however, is illusory, at least for enemies to Israel. Though she and her husband are not Israelites but Kenites, they bear friendship and loyalty to the people of Israel. When Sisera asks for water, therefore, Jael does not respond as Rebekah responded to the servant of Abraham. Jael fetches milk and says "drink," seeming perhaps to exceed the demands of the stranger, but, in fact, dulling his senses with a heavy soporific drink that allows her to overpower him.[9] The song

---

6   This view is expressed in the *Jewish Study Bible*, p. 518 n.4:8.

7   This rabbinic tradition is supported by the relationship between the names "Lappidoth" (torchlight) and "Barak" (lightning).

8   The Kenites were allies of the Israelites, but there was a friendship between the family of Heber and King Jabin of Hazor upon which Sisera was trading in order to elude his pursuers. Unfortunately for Sisera, Heber's wife felt no such friendship, though feigning amity allows her to fulfill Deborah's prophecy.

9   The narrative has it that Jael murders Sisera when he is "fast asleep" (Judges 4: 21), but the song implies an active struggle (*Jewish Study Bible*, p. 522 n.5:24–7).

recounts the events, emphasizing her substitution and her systematic execution of the guest:

He asked for water, she offered milk;
In a princely bowl she brought him curds.
Her left hand reached for the tent pin,
Her right for the workmen's hammer.
She struck Sisera, crushed his head,
Smashed and pierced his temple. (Judges 5: 25–6)

In the final image of this vignette, she towers over her guest: "At her feet he sank, lay still: / Where he sank, there he lay—destroyed" (Judges 5: 27).

The song then shifts focus, taking us to the home of Sisera's mother. She stands at the window, looking for her son, expecting him to return from battle any minute. She is becoming anxious, though, and she "whines" to her servants: "'Why is his chariot so long in coming? / Why so late the clatter of his wheels'" (Judges 5: 28). She is answered by the "wisest of her ladies," wise, perhaps, because she says what she knows her mistress wishes to hear. In fact, we are told that Sisera's mother, "too, replies to herself," so the words we hear are both what the servant says and the internal rationalizing of the nervous mother:

'They must be dividing the spoil they have found:
A damsel or two for each man,
Spoil of dyed cloths for Sisera,
Spoil of embroidered cloths,
A couple of embroidered cloths
Round every neck as spoil.' (Judges 5: 30)

The compulsive repetition in this verse suggests a desperate attempt to stave off knowledge. The mother's obsession with the rich cloth and her insistence on excess (two damsels, a couple of cloths, spoil draped around every neck) are poignant efforts to deny the increasingly obvious fact that pleasure and vitality are no longer possible for her son—or for herself, we feel.

The song ends with the lines "So may all Your enemies perish, O Lord! / But may His friends be as the sun rising in might!" (Judges 5: 31). One more sentence, not a part of the song, follows to conclude the story of Deborah, Barak, Sisera, and Jael: "And the land was tranquil forty years." Although both of these tag lines may seem to invite us to gloss over the complications of the events commemorated in the song, the song itself does not turn away from the hard truth that the procuring of tranquility is a messy, costly enterprise. Justice may be served by the actions recounted in Judges 4 and celebrated in Judges 5, but it is served at the expense of ethics and emotion. To call Deborah "mother" is to link her with the soon-to-be-grieving parent of Sisera, to call her "wife" is to acknowledge her relation to the righteous but treacherous Jael. She is a judge and a prophet, and in fulfilling those roles she serves the will of the Lord by restoring justice to a world gone wrong. The degree to which it has done so is marked in the suffering of the women who represent aspects of being—maternal, concupiscent—that have been warped by a climate of oppression, war, and corruption. In the complications her story brings forth, Deborah is the paradigm of the woman in a political world.

From the Cloister to the World and Back

While Jael certainly is represented as a heroine in Judges 4 and 5, we recognize in her behavior the perverse echo of Rebekah's responsiveness to Eliezer. In what kind of a world are women forced to murder through exploitation of hospitality and kindness? In a world where the Baraks refuse to answer the calls of their prophets and their God, the women must step forward, but at a cost.

The biblical text treads lightly on this ground. Barak is not held accountable for his weakness; Jael is celebrated for her strength. In some ways, the triumph for Israel is even greater than it otherwise would have been because Sisera's humiliation is graver. He does not die in battle, but in bed; he is killed not by a general or skilled warrior wielding weapons of might but by a woman driving a common tent pin through his head. Still, though narratively positioned in support of Deborah, Barak, and Israel, we hesitate to feel complete vindication. By shifting focus to Sisera's mother at the end of the song of victory, in fact, the text disallows our complete rejoicing. Triumph has come through the twisting of an ethical paradigm established in the beginning of Israel's history and recalled with every significant betrothal since—from Jacob and Rachel to Moses and Zipporah.

There are more Jaels than Deborahs in the fiction of Aphra Behn. These late-seventeenth-century Jaels, like the first, find themselves involved in a world rendered ethically complicated by human weakness. As in the paradigmatic biblical narrative, Behn's vision of human frailty is set against a stable system of divine strictures that offer clear, but too often unheeded, behavioral directives. While human suffering is a result of the violation of immutable law in Behn's world, it is also proof of ultimate justice.

In "History of the Nun," Behn offers her most thorough examination of the relationship between justice and the ethics of desire. Her eponymous protagonist, Isabella, fuses the characters of Deborah and Jael in a brief narrative set against a backdrop of worldwide religious conflict, the Candia War (also known as the fifth Venetian-Ottoman War and the War over Crete) which played itself out in the Mediterranean between 1645 and 1669. This narrative occurs during the final stages of that war in which the Christian forces yielded to the Turks—a matter that might seem to call into question, for a Christian readership, the idea of ultimate justice were it not for the fact that Behn is writing in the 1680s during renewed conflict that would eventually halt the expansion of the Ottoman Empire into Europe. Of course, a Protestant readership might have a very different reading of both the Candia conflict and the "Great Turkish War" than a Catholic-sympathizing readership would have. But Behn's audience was always the latter. Published in 1689, "History of the Nun," like *Love Letters Between a Nobleman and His Sister* earlier, argues the futility of attempts to elude the obligations attendant on a relationship with the divine. For Behn, this tale of domestic horror no doubt signified concern with the national crisis at hand. The deposing of the king would represent, to her and others of her ilk, a broken vow and a violation of sacred trust. Isabella's history stands warning that rectification will come and justice will be served, for "Of all the Sins, incident to Human Nature, there is none, of which Heaven has took so particular, visible, and frequent Notice, and Revenge, as on that of *Violated Vows*, which never go unpunished."[10]

Young though Isabella is, she seems to have almost the status of a Deborah for her community. She stations herself not under a date palm tree but at the grate of her cloister where "the whole World . . . of Strangers, came directed and recommended to the lovely *Isabella*" (219). These visitors do not seek her out for judgment or prophetic proclamations, but for some kind of vague inspiration. Isabella, like Deborah, signifies the connection between the human and the divine, and others are attracted by her combination of effortless charm and sincere piety: "however Diverting she was at the *Grate*, she was most exemplary Devout in the *Cloyster*" (219). Isabella's "Life was a Proverb, and a President [i.e. precedent], and when they would express a very Holy Woman indeed, they would say, *She was a very ISABELLA*" (220).

Unlike Deborah, Isabella is not a wife, and she never intends to be, but her resolution is articulated and her vows taken before she has experienced the physical and emotional passion of human love. Once that happens, Isabella's exemplary serenity is replaced by cunning willfulness. She becomes a Jael without Jael's justification. In other words, the ethical violations Jael commits in service to a just cause, Isabella commits in service to herself. Her desire awakened by Henault, the brother of her sister votary Katteriena, Isabella suffers the tortures of unrequited love until she overhears the siblings consulting about Henault's similar pains. From this point on, Isabella plays a double game, dissembling resolve and self command in order to pursue her passion. The text is explicit with regard to Isabella's ethical violation on this count: "There needed no more from a Maid of *Isabella*'s Integrity and Reputation, to convince any one of the Sincerity of what she said, since, in the whole course of her Life, she never could be charg'd with an Untruth, or an Equivocation, and *Katteriena* assur'd her, she believ'd her, and was infinitely glad she had vanquish'd a Passion, that would have prov'd destructive to her Repose" (228). Duped, Katteriena becomes the unwitting go-between in a courtship that leads to scandal and shame.

We might expect Aphra Behn to argue that Isabella's cause is just. The denial of natural human sexuality is a source of "abundance of Mischiefs and Miseries" in Behn's estimation, whether that denial come in the form of "Nunneries" or arranged marriages (213). But Isabella has taken the vow of celibacy against the advice of others; she has willfully asserted her own strength in assuming a life of chastity, and she just as willfully renounces that life despite the sacred vow she has taken. In exchange for her betrayal, she is awarded a life of hardship and barrenness. The report of Henault's death "fighting for the *Holy Cross*" in the Candia War renews the monastic instinct in Isabella. She secludes herself in mourning, and again becomes a model of "Piety, Charity, and all other excellent Qualities" which "gain'd her a

---

10 "History of the Nun," in *The Works of Aphra Behn*, ed. Janet Todd (7 vols, Columbus, 1995), vol. 3, p. 211. Further references to this text will be noted parenthetically.

wonderous Fame, and begat an Awe and Reverence in all that heard of her" (243, 244). She eschews love, though she has plenty who would love her, for "she was resolv'd to marry no more, however her Fortune might require it" (244).

Resolution notwithstanding, when Fortune does frown again on Isabella, her weakness becomes a kind of perversion once more. Villenoys, whom she had rejected years before in order to take the vows she spurned for Henault, arouses a new desire in Isabella. It is a complicated passion made up of memories of her husband (Villenoys had fought alongside Henault in the battle that took his life) and a taste for the exotic (Villenoys entertains her with battle stories and reports of "the Customs and Manner of the *Turks*" [245]). It is material need, this time not sexual, but monetary, however, that finally drives her to marriage again. When Isabella's aunt dies "and, with her, all the Hopes and Fortune of *Isabella*," the still young and beautiful woman says yes to Villenoys. Again, the narrator is blunt: "'twas for Interest she married again" (245). Comfortable in a secure marriage and a well-appointed home, Isabella has discovered the fact that desires once awakened, in fact, can be put to sleep again. Her love for Henault is not reactivated by his reappearance. Indeed, the opposite is the case. Afraid she will lose the life she has come to enjoy with Villenoys, she kills Henault. Then, afraid Villenoys will discover her crime and render her life miserable with reproaches and suspicions, she arranges his death as well. Unlike Jael who "never explains" but who "fulfills God's oracle . . . whatever she might have been thinking," Isabella deliberates and rationalizes her way to murder in pursuit of self-preservation.[11] Yet, interestingly, Isabella's story, like Jael's, does offer argument that immutable values and unchanging forces govern our world. Isabella's existence is underwritten by divine will, and God exacts a penalty for the broken vow that allowed Isabella to love and lose and love again. In the end, she accepts her death with dignity and relief that order has been reasserted. Ending her life with a "Speech of half an Hour long, so Eloquent, so admirable a Warning to the *Vow Breakers*," she faces execution with full conviction of the transcendent and permanent truths that assure justice in the world to come (257).

Isabella's history, then, is an argument for monarchial stability as opposed to political exigency. One effect of erotic love for woman is to be propelled into an existence defined by her husband or lover, to partake of his power or his weakness as part of his definition of self. But because eros is material and existence mutable such definition is impermanent, even at its best. Isabella is faultless in her devotion to Henault until his "death"; Henault is faithful to her, even beyond death, as it were. Nevertheless, things change; and as they change, power shifts. A woman, like a man, can find herself afraid of losing position or covetous of more material goods and greater status than she has by birth or situation. If she does so, she will define and protect the boundaries she seeks.

Behn celebrated the ideal of monarchial stability and divine directive, but she participated in a world of exigency and carnality. She was, after all, a spy, a double agent, and she was associated in her own time and for generations afterwards with harlotry (literal and metaphorical) as well as with prophecy. As such, she combines the characters of Jael and Deborah with a third, related, biblical paradigm—Rachav,

---

11   Tikva Frymer-Kensky, *Reading the Women of the Bible*, pp. 56–7.

the prostitute. Rachav gives succor to Pinchas and Calev when their lives are endangered on the spying mission they have undertaken for Joshua. Rachav helps the two escape their pursuers, making them promise before they go that they will remember her and reward her for her loyalty to them—a loyalty not born of kinship or political alliance, but of her conviction that "the Lord has given the country to you" (Joshua 2: 9). That she wishes to oblige these men is clear, but her motives are less so. Does she act out of fear ("dread of you has fallen upon us" [Joshua 2: 9]) or out of belief in their god ("the Lord your God is the only God in heaven above and on earth below" [Joshua 2: 11]) or out of an instinct for survival and a shrewd ability to gauge the likely outcome of the conflict at hand ("since I have shown loyalty to you, swear to me by the Lord that you in turn will show loyalty to my family" [Joshua 2: 12])? Rachav plies a trade that depends on the ability to raise and satisfy desire. While rabbinic tradition has it that, in her behavior toward the emissaries of Israel, Rachav has evidenced a change of character, it is not so clearly the case. She strikes a bargain with Pinchas and Calev that assures her future in the event of their success, and then she helps them succeed. Their desires and her desires are equally matched—which, arguably, has been the case all along. Why did they end up at the home of Rachav the prostitute, after all? Could it be that they were there for the obvious reasons?[12] Could it be that their willingness to help her was driven as much by desire as by gratitude? And, if such were the case, was justice any less served by the events that transpired?

Aphra Behn, the spy whose code name Astraea she retained as a literary and personal nom de plume for the rest of her life, would answer *no*. So would Delarivier Manley, but for slightly different reasons. As we have seen in her *History of a Nun*, Behn's *no* would come from the sense that justice is over and above human affairs and will work itself out according to a divinely ordered course of events, however we try to elude, trick, or prevent it. Manley's *no* would seem to stem from a sense that in pursuit of justice in an unjust world, agents and double agents, spies and judges, generals and wives, prophets and prostitutes, must all play a role.

Astraea Redux

When Dryden celebrated Charles's return to England as the restoration of Astraea or Justice, he invoked what Frances Yates has called a "phantom," the possibility of imperial revival. Associated with the values of, first, classical Rome and, later, the Holy Roman Empire, this phantom, in Yates's words, "exercised an almost undying influence," which she has traced through the reign of Elizabeth I.[13] The revivalist hopes are inevitably focused on the person of the monarch whose splendor and power will initiate a new Golden Age in which justice thrives and virtue reigns. After the disruptive events of the Civil War and the experiment with republicanism

---

12   As Frymer-Kensky puts it: "perhaps men who had been out in the wilderness all their lives headed for a bordello with soft beds and soft women" (35).

13   Dryden, "Astraea Redux: A Poem on the Happy Restoration and Return of his Sacred Majesty Charles the Second" in *The Poetical Works of Dryden*, pp. 7–11. Frances Yates, *Astraea: The Imperial Theme in the Sixteenth Century* (1975; rpt. London, 1993), p. 2.

that characterized the period we now call the Interregnum, it was to be expected that the phantom would reappear, along with all the imperialist, universalist trappings that characterized its previous incarnations. Perhaps it was to be expected too that the savior/monarch, being male, would be accompanied by a female emanation of Justice. Elizabeth had embodied Astraea, but Charles simply employed her as a spy and patronized her as a playwright and penalized her as a propagandist gone too far. And, as befits an Emperor of his habits, Charles had an Astraea especially concerned with sexual justice.

When Astraea left the earth due to her disgust with corrupt human behavior, she went to reside in the constellation of Virgo. This aspect of her identity was central to Queen Elizabeth's invocation of the phantom of imperial rule. For the Restoration, however, such associations were replaced with a naturalized, "innocent," and free sexuality influenced by Epicurean philosophy. In her poem "The Golden Age," Aphra Behn celebrates a sexual desire. "[n]ot kept in fear of Gods, no fond Religious cause,/Nor in Obedience to the duller Laws." She bemoans the "Politick Curbs" created "to keep man in" and asks with umbrage:

> Who by a fond mistake Created that a Sin;
> Which freeborn we, by right of Nature claim our own.
> Who but the Learned and dull moral Fool
> Could gravely have forseen, man ought to live by Rule?[14]

She castigates "Honour," in particular, for the damage the concept has done to women by robbing them of their enjoyment of sexual pleasure ("Honour! that rob'st us of our Gust" [l. 119]) and by teaching them to view their sexuality as a means to power rather than as a therapeutic conjoining in the act of love:

> Honour! who first taught lovely Eyes the art,
>   To wound, and not to cure the heart:
> With Love to invite, but to forbid with Awe,
> And to themselves prescribe a Cruel Law. (lines 122–5)

What does it mean, this transforming of Astraea from Virgin to votary of female sexual pleasure? What do we make of the cultural significance of the "awakening" signified by Aphra Behn's appropriation of this name? When did it happen and why? How and why does the virgin Justice become the goddess of female desire?

The transformation in England seems to have had something to do with the political use made of Honore D'Urfe's pastoral romance *L'Astree*. In the romance itself, Astraea is a lover, but she falls victim to the pains of jealousy. Feeling justified in anger, Astraea spends most of the narrative separated from the faithful Celadon, in a state of suspension related to but different from the prolonged moment between the awakening of desire and its consummation. This romance chronicles many states of desire, but the overarching theme is the separation of true lovers through a misunderstanding. The driving emotion is the longing for reunion with reparation.

---

14   "The Golden Age: A Paraphrase on a Translation out of French," in *Poetry*, vol. 1 of *The Works of Aphra Behn*, ed. Janet Todd (7 vols, Columbus, 1992), vol. 1, lines 109–10; 112–6. Further references will be cited parenthetically.

The first English translation of this romance was produced in 1651, and the same year saw publication of Leonard Willan's *Astraea, or, True Love's Myrrour*, a verse drama based on d'Urfé's pastoral romance. Willan's dedicatory preface was addressed to Mary, Duchess of Richmond and Lennox, the daughter of Charles I. Here, Willan elaborates the analogy between Astraea and the deposed royal family. He begins by emphasizing the *"Hymenal* Amitie" shared between goddess and princess, and then he reflects on their similar fates:

> *Astraea* is figured to descend from noble *Progeny*, who to avoid the Military Fury of debording [overflowing] Multitudes (which passing frequently through *Gaule*, descended like an irresistable Torrent on the *Roman* Empire) were constrained to betake them to the humble Sanctuary of a *Pastoral* condition: This Circumstance will meet no trivial *Analogie* in the Eminence of your Extraction, and Consequence of your present Rural Retreat: So that (with permission) may evidently be concluded, that in reference to your Natural perfections, Civil Transactions, or Accidental Occurrence, *Astraea* may (in equity) presume to be either your *Type*, *Parallel*, or *Character*.[15]

This "type, parallel or character," then, becomes a way of reading, of understanding, recent political events, the separation of England and the Stuart monarchy figured as the separation of lovers as well as the banishment of Justice. Significantly, it was as a spy for Charles that Behn first assumed the name that would be her signature; her lover and fellow double agent, William Scott, was known as Celadon.[16]

Aphra Behn died the year following publication of the third part of *Love Letters*. Twenty years later, she was, in a sense, summoned back to help her Tory descendant Delarivier Manley address another political crisis through the exploration of erotic desire.[17] Manley's Tory satire, *The New Atalantis*, begins with the return of Astraea to the earth, not in triumphal restoration, but on a reconnaissance mission, as it were: "Astrea (who had long since abandoned this world, and flown to her native residence above) by a new formed design, and a revolution of thought, was willing to revisit the earth, to see if humankind were still as defective, as when she in a disgust forsook it."[18] Met by her mother Virtue, dressed in rags, Astrea hears from her of a world not simply defective but systematically corrupt. Mock Justice prevails in her absence, but more significantly, from Virtue's point of view, Love is perverted by Interest who officiates at the marriage ceremonies of this netherworld: "he presides over the feast, he joins their hands, and brings them to the sacred ceremony of the bed with so much indifferency, that were not consummation a necessary article, the unloving pair could with the utmost indifferency repair to their several chambers" (5–6). The "offspring of such an union" is not "that sparkling genius, the product of a noble free-born love" (6). Consequently, the "times are . . . defective of heroes, and if

---

15 Leonard Willan, *Astraea, or, True Love's Myrrour, A Pastoral* (London, 1651), p. v.

16 See Janet Todd, *The Secret Life of Aphra Behn*, p. 51.

17 As Ros Ballaster puts it, "*The New Atalantis* . . . reincarnates the figure of Aphra Behn's fictional and poetic persona, Astrea, in order to authorize her own position of female satirist" (*Seductive Forms*, p. 114).

18 *The New Atalantis*, ed. Rosalind Ballaster (London, 1991), p. 4. Further references will be cited parenthetically in the text.

some excel others, 'tis only like trees planted in the same soil. Chance gives them the height over their companions, or more properly speaking a dexterous management of vice" (6). And who should be the most dextrous of them all but the new anti-heroes, John Churchill, the Duke of Marlborough, and his wife, Sarah? There are plenty of others, but these two emerge early and often as the standard by which other corrupt lovers are judged.

This anti-hero and heroine represent the first interesting divergence from the Tory satire of Aphra Behn. The Cesario of *Love Letters'* Part 3 anticipates Manley's various renditions of John Churchill, for at that point in the narrative Cesario embodies the fundamental contrast inherent in the character of a military leader whose prowess in battle and whose authority over men is countered by his domestic emasculation. Henrietta Wentworth and Sarah Churchill were both represented by Tory satirists as domineering women whose principle aim was to marry in order to harness masculine power in service of their own ambition. In Behn's works, this negative trajectory of desire (awakening -> delay and struggle -> consummation -> appropriation of power) is contrasted to a positive narrative pattern (awakening -> consummation -> restoration of justice -> imperial revival). In Manley's political vision, revival of empire is a bit more complicated. Awakening is followed by delay, as in Behn, but in the Marlborough episodes that delay is the result of calculation. A hasty, prudent marriage intervenes between arousal and consummation; the chiasmus of double desire becomes another figure altogether, one with a third term—a syllogism perhaps. That third term is marriage, and the logic it advances rests on the manipulation of desire. While the Duke of Monmouth was the product of "free-born love," Marlborough is the creature of a calculated concupiscence.

By the early eighteenth century, Tory and Whig alike were influenced by the theory of contract governance set forth most thoroughly by Locke in his *Two Treatises of Government*. While Bolingbroke's *Idea of a Patriot King* offered an alternative vision of monarchial power that preserved the cultural notion of central, elevated, heroic authority, it was Locke's view that spoke to the times in its combination of Hobbesian pragmatism and something along the order of deistic idealism. So, although during the early eighteenth century party politics redefined itself according to new parameters, the discussion shifted in intent and focus. No longer overtly focused on the issue of succession to the English throne (though covertly, as I will explain below, continued anxieties about succession exerted political pressure), Tories and Whigs vied openly for control of government. Generally the distinction between the two parties remained that of nobility versus commoners, conservative versus progressive, old money versus new. But both parties laid claim to an imperial vision centered not on the monarch so much as on the leaders of society who represented the people's side of contractual theory. The difference between the parties with regard to this vision crystallized during the debate over the ending of the War of the Spanish Succession.

Both Tory and Whig were concerned with marshaling imperial rhetoric in the service of national definition. The Whig strategy can be generally described as a strategy of transference wherein heroic qualities that in imperial discourse had served to define the prince or emperor are celebrated in the citizens (statesmen or military heroes) who advance the national cause. During the War of the Spanish

Succession, Godolphin and Marlborough were elevated to the cultural space that in preceding centuries had been reserved for royalty. Though the quit-claim ceremony prescribed by Queen Anne at the deeding of Blenheim and the creation of the hereditary dukedom bear some cultural resemblance to the ceremony attendant on the appointment of London's Lord Mayor, the grandeur, expense, and regality of Blenheim Palace elevates the military hero to the symbolic level of monarch and the iconographic level of God.

Imperial revival, from the Whig point of view is, as we say of Whig ideology in general, progressive in one way—that is, it separates the ideas of birth and worth. But in the "shorter view" it is, if not conservative, preservative, wishing to assure the settlement of 1689 remain unchallenged by a revivification of the Astraea Redux myth. For the War of the Spanish Succession's heroes and the imperial revival they represent were fashioned in direct opposition to this potential narrative. As Catherine Gallagher and others have pointed out, in English minds, the arguments justifying the war were not universalist or imperialist in the old sense of the term but particular and nationalist in aim and objective. The point of the war was to keep James II from asserting his claim to the throne, to ensure the Hanoverian solution to the succession.[19]

The Tories, of course, could not openly oppose the Hanoverian settlement, despite the reigning monarch's distaste for the idea. And, though certainly some notable Tories engaged in covert Jacobite schemes and some works playfully built on the standard version of the Astraea Redux theme, the official Tory strategy pursued a different logic, which was like the Whig argument, based on a theory of contract government. The Tories, however, tended to employ a marital metaphor or the metaphor of family to pursue both the negative and the positive sides of their argument for political power.[20] The idealized, heroic virtues are commingled in Tory rhetoric with observations about love, marriage, and family.

In accord with this new view, Manley activates another version of the Astraea Redux myth centered, as the 1701 Act of Succession would seem to dictate, on the figure of Elizabeth, Princess of Palatine and Queen of Bohemia, to whom the Hanoverians owe their right to the throne. Astraea presents the rewritten myth which underpins not only *The New Atalantis*, but the Tory platform in general:

> There was an emperor, who gave life to a daughter, born a masterpiece of nature for beauty, virtue and sorrows. She was married to a neighbouring Prince, who had more ambition than success: puffed up with the vain hopes and pride of his new father's empire, he thought nothing too great for him to attempt; he put on the royal diadem and called himself king of a people, who were oppressed and held in slavery by a nation more mighty than themselves. The consequence of it was, his being forsaken, first by his imperial father-in-law, then by all his inferior allies; he lost not only his new-assumed sovereignty, but his own hereditary principality. The queen his wife, a miracle of suffering goodness, wandered with her wretched children from territory to territory and at length refuged in the court where she was born. (6–7)

---

19 See Gallagher, *Nobody's Story: The Vanishing Acts of Women Writers in the Marketplace, 1670–1820* (Berkeley, 1994), pp. 120–2.

20 See Müllenbrock, *The Culture of Contention*, pp. 40–1.

The emperor is James I; the daughter Elizabeth, Queen of Bohemia, whose husband Frederick ("elected" King of Bohemia) embarked on costly wars that resulted in his fall and exile. While he is clearly a version of the populist threat (King Monmouth and, more pertinent, here "King" Marlborough), she is a new kind of heroine, admired for her suffering patience, as unlike the Tory renditions of Sarah Churchill as one can get.

The exiled, mournful queen is a model of wronged Justice, righteous anger. In the "pulling apart" of king and country, she stands for the justifiable anger of thwarted love. Unlike Sylvia, whose jealous rages at Philander's philandering prefigure a perversion of love, this wronged queen demonstrates that such negative passions have a proper function in the sexual/political world, fueling the movement toward reconciliation and reunion. Though in vain, the queen's "cries, her tears and beauty, [essayed to] excite her countrymen to arm in her husband's defence, and to re-seat him in his native rights" (7). Unsuccessful in her own lifetime, because of the viciousness of the country that "should have armed in the defence of virtue, with which they had no acquaintance," the queen nonetheless interested Astraea in her cause. The goddess pleads the case to Jupiter who promises that "the good queen should receive a double portion of bliss hereafter in the happy regions, when her years of wandering were accomplished," but that restoration would not occur "till a Prince descended from the beautifullest of her daughters, should obtain the sovereignty over 'em" (7). This prince, of course, is the future king of England whom Astraea hopes to sponsor and educate in the heroic virtues that will "merit [him] the empire over mankind" (8).[21] *The New Atalantis*, however, is not about the education of the prince, but the "education" of Justice in the vices of the world, "the better to teach my young Prince how to avoid them, and accomplish him" (8).

The modifications to the narrative of restored Justice underwriting the satire Manley fashions in response to the specific political situation of 1709 are significant, first, as they serve to mediate between the time of the narrative's action (set in 1702) and the narrative's intent, i.e. to influence the shape of the future, the course of the war or, to be more Tory in perspective, the course of the peace which would bring the war to a close. They are also significant in terms of the evolving definition of female desire as it plays itself out over the span of the eighteenth century. Perhaps the most interesting modification to the traditional narrative has to do with the recasting of characters from the monarchial past. Whereas in the Restoration period, the signal instance of injustice was the execution of the King and the imposition of Puritan rule in place of legitimate, divine right leadership, in the early eighteenth-century version of the myth, injustice involves domestic chains of obligation that avoid the issue of divine right entirely. Elizabeth, queen of Bohemia, has been wronged by "her husband's ambition, and her father's supineness" (7); her sufferings and anguish are personal, not constitutional. But there are national implications. The overreaching of Frederick of Palatine, on the one hand, and the failure of James I to respond to

---

21 See Ballaster's note explaining that as in 1702 "George Lewis [the future George I] would have been forty-two years old, it seems likely that the young prince referred to is his son, George Augustus, the future George II" (*New Atalantis*, p. 270 n.17). The action of *The New Atalantis* takes place in 1702 but the political situation addressed is that of 1709.

this overreaching, on the other hand, have combined to render homeless one who should have been protected and honored as the mother of England's royal progeny, as a claimant to the throne herself in the event of her brothers' premature deaths. This queen thus becomes symbolic of the effect of the contest for power that had characterized English politics since the 1640s.

Championed by the mythical female adviser, Astraea, the wronged queen serves also as analogue to the sitting monarch in 1709, Queen Anne, who too is victim, *The New Atalantis* implies, of a political climate characterized by a combination of the unlawful accruing of power (ambition) and a decadent, sybaritic wallowing (supineness). Like *Love Letters'* Philander (early on) and Cesario (until the end), the entire nation is driven by the alternating, antithetical impulses to amass political power and to luxuriate in sensual delights. Counterbalanced by no one good thing, this energy drives through the court, the city, the country, infecting every level of English existence, but particularly the lives, indeed the very nature, of women.

The anxiety produced in English culture by the ascension of Anne to the throne is everywhere evident in early eighteenth-century English satire. For some reason, perhaps having to do with the personal presence of the woman herself (nearly constantly pregnant during the course of her reign), certainly having something to do with her reliance on female advisers (clear to the court and court observers long before her actual ascension), anxieties about female power seemed to emanate from her court in a way they never did from the court of her female predecessor, Elizabeth I. Elizabeth successfully "masculinized" the monarchial side of her being and desexualized the female side, a rhetorical and cultural strategy that probably would not have struck the eighteenth century as convincing even if the monarch had attempted it. But she did not. Anne's world was a woman's world in many ways; her court was the setting for power contests between ministers whose relationship to her was less important than their ability to influence those women surrounding her and the men to whom they had intimate access. Astraea the Virgin—the myth that Elizabeth tapped to shore up her monarchial power—needed to be educated in the sexual manners of the times to be able to function in the concupiscent world presided over by Queen Anne.

As noted above, the temporal setting of *The New Atalantis* is 1702, the year of William III's death and Anne's ascension. The first glimpse we see of the new Queen (the "Empress" of Atalantis) is through the reportage of the gossipmonger Intelligence who tells Justice and Virtue of the manner in which the king's death is received: "I have already been at the new Empress's court, and left her to condole with her she favourite, over some flasks of sparkling champagne" (13). This sentence bears its contradictions with a light touch, but a sharp precision. Intelligence's former presence at court contrasts with her present absence; the idea of condolence is posited against the flasks of sparkling champagne. The phrase "she favorite" adds an aura of seediness; the celebratory drinking party underscores the sense of transgressive pleasure contained in the two word description of Sarah Churchill. These women are acting like men, and there is implicit criticism in the way their behavior is described.[22]

---

22   Cf. William Congreve's *The Way of the World* in which Mirabell stipulates to Millamant that she "on no account . . . encroach upon the men's prerogative and presume to

There is something in the scene worth reporting—its "unnaturalness," perhaps—and Intelligence is in a rush to spread the news. She has another secret to tell, too: that Justice and Virtue are abroad and that she herself has been commissioned to attend them and that Truth will (for once) accompany her.

The "Truth" about Anne's monarchy as revealed in *The New Atalantis* is that the queen has little to do with the exercise of power, governed as she is by her favorite, Sarah Churchill, and the real "emperor" of the country, John Churchill, the Duke of Marlborough.[23] In two extended meditations on the political climate surrounding Anne's court, Manley (in the voice of Intelligence) exonerates the Queen by focusing criticism on the ambition and manipulativeness of the Marlboroughs. In the first episode (really concerned with the rise of Marlborough through the reigns of Charles, James, and William), the reflections on Sarah's manipulation of Anne are brief, but telling. As Manley represents it, Sarah intervenes when Anne ("the Princess") experiences her own sexual awakening by "Count Lofty" who "please[d] the Princess, whilst yet she was a maid." We are told little more about this romance— just that the princess "tenderly received" Count Lofty's addresses and that he wrote a poem to her declaring his love (24). There is no indication that Lofty himself is a true lover, for Intelligence has it that he is motivated by his "ambition" not his desire. But the princess's response seems to fit the paradigm of the young virgin awakened to her sexual nature for the first time. While it is true that "Jeanitin's" intervention and the consequent breaking off of the affair have no tragic consequences, still the poignancy of loss inflects the language with which Intelligence reports the Princess's marriage to "the Prince of Inverness": "The young Princess had admirable good inclinations, but without consulting them, they had married her, according to royal custom, to the Prince of Inverness, before she had ever seen him. . . . The Princess has since been an example of conjugal happiness, they have loved and deserved each other; nor could there be any objection against her, but in so entirely resigning her self up to the Countess's management"(24).

Again, in the later episode, Princess Olympia is portrayed as "born to bless her people," but "mistaken in her choice" of favorites (201; 205) for far too long. Having replaced "Madam de Caria" (Sarah Churchill) with the virtuous "Hilaria" (the Tory Abigail Masham) whose "soul [was] fitted for grandeur" and whose "wit, . . . [and] judgement . . . [were] of the finest frame" (205), Olympia is pursuing the path of regal justice as Astraea defines it: "I will have my Prince indeed distinguished [sic] and employ those of the most virtue and capacity, but on any terms I forbid him to oppress his nation with the pride and avarice of favourites" (211). This observation is followed by a poem celebrating God's constancy through the course of a hurricane

---

drink healths, or toast fellows." Act 4, scene1, lines 297–9.

23 A point underscored by Frances Harris's study of the Duchess of Marlborough: "In the final reckoning, Sarah's chief significance in Augustan politics lay in the influence she exercised through her male relations and associates, rather than in her more famous role as 'Mrs. Freeman' to Queen Anne's 'Mrs. Morley.' Yet it took her many years to accept the limitations of her position as a woman in this respect, to acknowledge bitterly that 'the things that are worth naming will ever be done from the influence of men.'" *A Passion for Government: The Life of Sarah, Duchess of Marlborough* (Oxford, 1991), p. 3.

which is in turn followed by a depiction of constant love, by now a metaphor for stability of state. *The New Atalantis* ends where Manley's next satire, *Memoirs of Europe* begins, with a celebration of the virtues of Lord Peterborough, Tory hero and constant lover, a husband faithful even after the death of his wife.

Manley's satiric project is to reveal the dire need for political (as opposed to monarchial) leadership, the longing for a "great good man . . . [to] stand up and fearlessly regulate these disorders" (12) that she describes in episode after episode of *The New Atalantis* in particular. And in pursuit of this project, she, like Behn, employs amatory, erotic devices to explore the desire for political stability. In *The New Atalantis*, however, sexual awakening does not provoke desire for an other that represents ultimate satisfaction, and the narratology does not pursue the rhythm found in Behn's narratives of sexual/political desire: i.e., the drawing out of narrative fulfillment and the delaying of consummation. Instead, *The New Atalantis* is full of brief, heated sexual moments, liaisons described and defunct in a matter of paragraphs. In effect, the sexual metaphor accompanying observations of political power emphasizes the insatiability of female desire. The implied accumulation of experience and lovers and money and power trades on an existing negative stereotype about awakened female sexual appetite—its voraciousness and its unquenchability. Barbara Villiers ("the Duchess"), mistress to King Charles ("Sigismund") and John Churchill ("Fortunatus"), is the first and best example of avid, urgent, and ravenous desire; in Fortunatus's estimation "she could not be long in a bedchamber, with a handsome young gentleman, without consequences" (23). This kind of appetite finds analogue in the appetite for wealth that the Churchills demonstrate which is shown to be just a version of the same kind of insatiability. The Duke's "unbounded, unwearied desire of wealth" bodes two possible consequences, in the opinion of Intelligence: "Will he one day set it all at stake upon a royal cast, or an imperial squander? Or descend to his grave, choked with greediness of gain, and a most prodigious, accumulated mass of wealth?" (17)

The absence of satisfaction, the frantic search for pleasure and power, is one characteristic of this world. The omnipresence of the female sexual body is another. As Mrs. Nightwork reveals, this body is often politically dangerous, demanding private attention when public duties call. The ludicrous stories with which she regales the inquisitive triumverate—Intelligence, Virtue, and Astraea—include tales of surreptitious births, masked deliveries, children smuggled away before they become incriminating evidence, "incognito within incognito," as Mrs. Nightwork puts it, all testifying to masculine potency and female vulnerability (140). But these stories also suggest self-regulation of the female body in the interest of power and position. Barbara Villiers, Mrs. Nightwork reports, defied knowledge and common sense to keep up the appearance of reputation during a difficult pregnancy, by attending the Queen on horseback at the risk of her life. She could have avoided doing so by "taking off the mask and owning her self indisposed," but she chose instead "to conceal a thing that all the court already knew" (139). Significantly, Sarah Churchill experiences a similar fate and makes a similar choice. Mrs. Nightwork describes her in the character of "a certain, now great, lady [who] fell in labour when she was at court in waiting and was forced to appear the next day at dinner in the quality of maid, though she had just given the world sufficient proof that she could no longer justly be called one" (140).

Such bodily control, such a de-emphasizing of biological imperatives, implies female dominion, perhaps suggesting anxiety about the cost of the cultural dominance witnessed in the present court and in the manners and luxuries of a capitalist age. Such an argument has been convincingly made in several recent studies, but the point bears repeating. In Charles's time, of course, anxieties about "feminization" emanated from the sexual license practiced by the king and the influence or distraction represented by his various sexual partners.[24] In Anne's time, the fear seems to be of a masculinization of women rather than a feminization of men, and two aspects of this masculinization seem particularly threatening: the definition of male as object of desire and the appropriation of masculine counsel and reason. As objects of desire, characters like Fortunatus and his replacement in Villiers's affections, Germanicus, receive a detailed, voyeuristic portraiture usually associated with the female form:

> Upon the bed were strewed, with a lavish profuseness, plenty of orange and lemon flowers. And to complete the scene, the young Germanicus in a dress and posture not very decent to describe. It was he that was newly risen from the bath, and in a loose gown of carnation taffety, stained with Indian figures. His beautiful long flowing hair, for then 'twas the custom to wear their own tied back with a ribbon of the same colour; he had thrown himself upon the bed, pretending to sleep, with nothing on but his shirt and nightgown, which he had so indecently disposed, that slumbering as he appeared, his whole person stood confessed to the eyes of the amorous Duchess[.] (20–1)

Of course, Germanicus is feigning sleep, his posture a posturing to arouse the Duchess's desires. But the significant thing is not the difference between the fact and appearance of aggression, but the assumption that the Duchess will be aroused by the sight of a passive youthful beauty that is also assumed to be titillating to the readership (male and female alike). While her seduction of Germanicus reinscribes culturally defined gender roles (he embraces her; she shuts her eyes and allows herself to be "taken"; she feigns confusion at the discovery that her lover is not the Count but another handsome young man), female will and agency appropriate the culturally endorsed masculine prerogative to define, direct, and pursue desire in this scene of seduction. Other seduction scenes in *The New Atalantis* rehearse the familiar story of masculine aggression and female victimization and recount instances of power preying on vulnerability to the end of suffering and retribution or despair. Few, if any, episodes argue the mutuality of desire. Sex is about self-gratification of one kind or another in this world. Newly popularized facts about female sexuality, particularly the nature of female clitoral orgasm, seem to be combining with a feminocentric

---

24   On October 27, 1662, for example, Samuel Pepys records in his diary that he has heard gossip that "the Queene doth know how the King orders things, and how he carries himself to my Lady Castlemayne and others, as well as anybody; but though she hath spirit enough, yet seeing that she doth no good by taking notice of it, for the present she forbears it in policy; of which I am very glad. But I pray God keep us in peace; for this with other things, doth give great discontent to all people." *The Diary of Samuel Pepys*, ed. Robert Latham and Willliam Matthews (11vols, London, 1995), vol. 3, p. 235.

court to produce cultural anxieties—if not about masculinity per se—at least about women's need to define themselves and their desires through men.

The cabal described in Volume 2 of *The New Atalantis* brings together these various musings and anxieties in the description of the world in which sexual difference is purportedly not an issue. The struggle for dominance is avoided by the exclusion of men from the world of the cabal. Intelligence denies the rumors of lesbianism, but her references to the possibility raise in the readers' minds the titillating transgressiveness of sexual satisfaction without the societal and biological restrictions attendant on heterosexual love: loss of reputation, subservience in marriage, the pain of childbirth. Still, even in this scene of same-sex gratification, it is clear that the exclusion of men does not imply the exclusion of masculinity. Although the cabal "momently [sic] exclude the men" (155), they discuss with cabal members who are unmarried "how to behave themselves to such who they think fit they should marry, no such weighty affair being to be accomplished without the mutual consent of the society." "[A]t the same time," we are told, the cabal laments "the custom of the world, that has made it convenient (nay, almost indispensable) for all ladies once to marry" (155–6). Accommodation to the practices of "the world" is one way sexual difference is retained; but another more significant is in the depiction of the most overtly lesbian relationship described in this section. The "Marchioness of Sandomire" dresses as a man and "with her female favourite, Ianthe, wander[s] through the gallant quarter of Atalantis in search of adventure" (157).

The satiric point, of course, is to suggest the depravity of Whig sexual appetite, and the "beastliness" of Whig female desire combines with its predatoriness and its material ambition to underscore the criticism of the Marlboroughs in particular as opportunists who prey on society for the aggrandizement of their family at the expense of the rest of the nation. Such solipsism is figured in the negative stereotype of the lustful, insatiable woman whose attraction to her own sex is simply an extension of her own self-absorption. At the same time, the lingering memories of the elemental binarism between man and woman provide a sense of profound melancholy that seems to derive from the longing for difference, the remembrance of desire no longer experienced. Thus it is that Lord Peterborough, Tory and faithful, loving husband, becomes the antidote to the ills of the world as defined by Whig power.

Manley closes *The New Atalantis* with a portrait of Peterborough as he prepares to attend the "inauguration" of the empress (267). This portrait is in essence a fantasy of restoration—but a restoration of Justice as a concept, not the restoration of a particular line of royalty. Peterborough (the Count of Valentia) represents ancient values, "antique glory, when renown fired the breast of mortals and the universal love of mankind was their only regard: when to be a leader was understood as of one exposing himself with a willing bravery for the benefit of his followers, the spoil of the field equally divided, the hero reserving nothing to himself but the reputation of conquest" (268). The opposite, in other words, of Marlborough.

Peterborough serves as foil to Marlborough, not only in his public life but in his private life as well. For if the Tory configuration of the marriage of Sarah and John Churchill served to criticize the Whig government, the idealization of the Peterborough marriage offered a Tory alternative founded on mutual and unending desire. At the beginning of Manley's next satire, *Memoirs of Europe*, the Peterborough marriage is eulogized (Lady Peterborough just having died) and the nature of Tory desire posited as providing the foundation for social stability as well as personal satisfaction. As Horatio (Lord Peterborough) tells Merovius, "there is no Possession how *full* soever, where *Desire* may not abide! If it be only *employed* in wishing a *Continuation* of what we *enjoy*, 'tis enough to render it inseparable from Love."[25]   But Horatio/ Peterborough's love persists beyond the possibility of such continuation. Does that not mean his love is, in fact, divorced from desire? Merovius thinks so. "if *Love* be a *Desire*, it would when in Possession, be *no more Love*, since we cannot *desire* what we *enjoy!*"[26] But, as it turns out, we can. "[B]ecause we cannot possess without (in some manner) uniting ourself to it, it necessarily follows, that *Love* is a *Motion* of the *Appetite*, by which the *Mind unites itself to that* which appears to it *amiable* and *Good*."[27] In other words, love is an appetite that goes beyond appetite. Opposed to the fantasy of control and willfulness that characterizes the world of Atalantis, *Memoirs* posits this vision of desire that is clearly based in physical response to an other, but that also persists after sexual satisfaction. The ideal love, *Memoirs* suggests, is a love that begins in the body and ends in the mind. If we think of desire and love this way, we see, as Peterborough saw, that arousal of desire can lead to a steady commitment, a continuing appetite, that outlasts death itself.

By Manley's account, Justice is a human concept, dependent on training, wisdom, education, proper maternal guidance, and care. Justice is also a divine abstraction. Part of the implication of the narrative framing of *The New Atalantis* is that proper leaders are not born but made. In this sense Astraea Redux, despite Manley's use of abstractions throughout her satiric landscape, is a practical matter, not a divine narrative pattern. This argument meets Whig claims to power head-on, positing quality against quality in a contest for the kind of civic leader defined by society as desirable and good. On the other hand, the idealized portrait of Peterborough as that civic leader reinscribes the Astraea myth, mapping it onto a domestic scene. Like the Queen of Bohemia, Peterborough experiences a dispossession that speaks more to personal than national sorrow. In his continued devotion to the woman he loved, he, like Elizabeth, Princess Palatine, serves as a national symbol of suffering and patience, sure to be rewarded in the next life, but also a source of inspiration and guidance in this life. Both are symbols of Virtue, and Peterborough in particular gives force to the central argument of Manley's satire: corruptions in the state begin and end with corruptions in relationships between men and women. When desire for power and material gain replaces desire for the person of another, the creation of double desire, i.e. mutual and reciprocal love, becomes impossible. The overarching narrative that bespeaks eternal satisfaction through desire that continues beyond possession is replaced by brief narratives of desire-possession-abandonment, narratives that comprise the bulk of Manley's satiric project. In narratology as well as in theme, then, *The New Atalantis* documents the melancholy postcoital moment in which sorrow and regret accompany the fear of dispossession.

---

25   *Memoirs of Europe, Towards the Close of the Eighth Century* (London, 1710), p. 30.
26   Ibid., p. 31.
27   Ibid., p. 31.

At the center of Manley's dystopic vision is the notion that unsatisfied and unsatisfiable female desire is a driving political force—one that has shaped and defined the Whig oligarchy that Manley so detests. So is Manley, arguably the most forceful woman writer of her generation, suggesting that female power is a symptom of political corruption? In one sense the answer is *yes*. Chief among the heinous architects of the world Manley would reform is Sarah Churchill. It is clear, as other critics have pointed out, that Manley both despises and admires Churchill. Her admiration is centered on the power Churchill accrued—both for herself and for her husband. Her criticism seems leveled at the price paid for such power. In another sense, however, the answer to the question "is female power a symptom of political corruption?" is *no*. At the heart of Manley's criticism of Churchill is the fear—or perhaps the recognition—that sexual fulfillment and political power are exclusive categories. Both objects of female (as well as male) desire, *The New Atalantis* presents them as incompatible alternatives in the world as constructed by Marlborough. Female power, in this sense, is not a symptom of political corruption so much as it is a symbol of the displacement required by the world presided over by Marlborough. Incapable himself of fashioning political change, he relies on his wife to accomplish the necessary transformation from a feudalistic society to a capitalist one. And she does so, Manley suggests, at the expense of her sexuality, at the expense of her natural desire.

Of course, there is another thing to be said about *The New Atalantis*. For all its satiric stance against the warping of natural desire, Manley's narrative preserves as well a sense of the avidity (if not voraciousness) of female sexual appetite. While the world she depicts teems with transgressors and manipulators and victimizers, it is also a world in which women can and do both deploy and enjoy sex. These women exist in a political world of shifting borders and changing realities. Tikva Frymer-Kensky has said the same thing about Jael and Rachav:

> Both are women marginalized within their own society, Rahab as a prostitute and Yael as a Kenite in Canaan. As a result, neither has a stake in the power structure of Canaan. They are living their normal lives, each in her own house, when political events encroach upon them as the Israelite men come to Rahab's house and Sisera to Yael's tent. Each has a 'moment of truth' when her destiny is thrust upon her and she has to demonstrate her loyalties.[28]

In demonstrating the loyalties celebrated by the texts that record their actions, Jael and Rachav, like the women of the *New Atalantis*, exercise a clear sexual agency. Rabbinic and midrashic tradition includes enthusiastic praise of both women for their loveliness, their desirability, and their own carnal knowingness. Rachav and Jael are two of the four beauties of the Bible (the other two being Michal and Abigail); and stories abound that emphasize the pleasure of physical love with them. One tradition explains that Jael weakens Sisera through sexual intercourse ("interpreting the seven verbs of the fall of Sisera as seven ejaculations of Sisera"); the Babylonian Talmud

---

28 Frymer-Kensky, p. 57.

records a rabbinic dictum that "one need only recite the name 'Rahab, Rahab' to come to climax").[29]

Other strands of commentary deny such interpretation, representing Jael as chaste and Rachav as reformed; still other strands penalize the women for possible shortcomings—ulterior motives or confused ethical priorities. It should come as no surprise that realities, exigencies, prejudices, and dreams are reflected in the biblical interpretative tradition. In a perfect world, of course, there would be no need for interpretation. But in a perfect world, one would not need to stab a sleeping enemy with a tent pin, and one would not need to become a prostitute to feed oneself and one's family. Certainly, in a perfect world, the restitution of justice would not depend on treachery and betrayal of the sort that, from the Canaanite view, characterizes the behavior of Jael and Rachav. In a perfect world, all acts of love, all gestures of nurture and care would proceed from responsiveness to the other and would lead to the knowledge of God. The longing for such a world infuses the biblical texts, of course. It also informs the Stuart-centered narratives of Aphra Behn. Even more poignantly, this longing drives the Tory satire of Delarivier Manley wherein the fading, but discernible, ideal of free, mutual, fulfilling love is tied to both the moment of sexual awakening and the dream of civic governance possessed of truth and dedicated to justice.

---

29   Ibid., p. 346.

Chapter 4

Hieroglyphics of Desire

As Astraea and Virtue approach the capital in the early pages of Delarivier Manley's *The New Atalantis*, they catch their initial glimpse of the character who is to be their guide through the muck and mire of modern desire. Virtue is the first to remark Intelligence's presence: "See, my dear Astrea, . . . how busy Intelligence appears, like a courtier new in office! She bustles up and down and has a world of business upon her hands; she is first lady of the bedchamber to the Princess Fame, her garments are all hieroglyphics" (13). Full of good, bad, and "medium" news, Intelligence is "rarely concerned with" the truth. But when she is arrested, "in the name of Jupiter" and ordered to serve Virtue and Justice, all that changes: "You are to inform us of all we shall demand," Virtue tells her; and moreover, "Truth is summoned to attend you on this occasion" (13). Intelligence is captured and corralled, as it were, against her wayward will, her hieroglyphic secret knowledge made legible by the presence of Truth.

While Egyptian writing was developed not to conceal but to reveal, the seventeenth and eighteenth centuries commonly accepted hieroglyphics as a secret, mystical code. At least that was William Warburton's view in 1741 when he tackled the subject in the second volume of his *Divine Legation of Moses* in order to "trace up *Hieroglyphic* Writing to its Original; which an universal Mistake concerning its primeval *use*, hath rendered extremely difficult."[1] This mistake, he explains, "is that which makes the *Hieroglyphics* to be invented by the *Egyptian* Priests, in order to hide and secrete their Wisdom from the Knowledge of the Vulgar" (2: 66). Originally, hieroglyphic writing was very simply designed "for recording Men's Actions and Conceptions" (75); it was quite late in the development of the written language that it became a vehicle for the expression of political secrets and religious mysteries (2: 96, 128–32). Of course the early nineteenth-century decoding of the Rosetta stone would substantiate Warburton's claims. In the eighteenth century, however, Warburton notwithstanding, the patina of magic and mystery remained attached to the notion of hieroglyphics. After all, hieroglyphs tend to be featured, as Liselotte Dieckmann explains, in the working out of "the basic problems of all Platonic thinkers" which she defines as follows: "the relationship between matter and spirit, appearance and reality, outward form and true meaning, tangibility and idea."[2] Fascination with such problems is more characteristic of the Renaissance than the long eighteenth century, but we do witness in the later period the occasional

---

1   *The Divine Legation of Moses Demonstrated* (1741) (4 vols, New York, 1978), vol. 2, p. 66. Further references will be cited parenthetically in the text.

2   Liselotte Dieckmann, *Hieroglyphics: The History of a Literary Symbol* (St. Louis, 1970), p. 2.

invocation of hieroglyphics especially when, as in the passage quoted from *The New Atalantis* above, there is some interest in negotiating the relationship between "the world of appearances and the world of ideas, form, or essences."[3] More generally, the notion of language as both sensory and extra-sensory, as providing material access to the world beyond matter, informs the practice of eighteenth-century writers interested in representing the mysterious intersection of body and spirit. It is not surprising, therefore, that fable, allegory, and emblematic language persist as means of expressing and exploring the enigmatic nature of sexual desire.[4]

Warburton treats gesture as a kind of hieroglyphic communication. The ancients, he argues, considered action to be language as a matter of course (2: 81).[5] After all, what is action but "apt and significant signs" that forward "mutual Converse"? (2: 83) In support of his view, he cites many instances from the book of Kings, in particular, that suggest the mode of conversing by motion in a "perpetual Representation of *material Images*":

> As where the Prophet *pushed* with Horns of Iron, to denote the entire Overthrow of the *Syrians*; where *Jeremiah*, by God's Direction, *hides* the Linen Girdle in a Hole of the Rock near *Euphrates*; where *he breaks* a Potter's Vessel in Sight of the People; *puts on* Bonds and Yokes, and *casts* a Book into *Euphrates* where *Ezekiel*, by the same Appointment, *delineates* the Siege of *Jerusalem* on a Tile; *weighs* the Hair of his Beard in Balances; *carries* out his Household-stuff, and *joins together* the two Sticks for *Judah* and *Israel*.

"By these actions," Warburton concludes, "the Prophets instructed the People in the Will of God, and conversed with them in Signs" (2: 83). Though the actions themselves could seem "unbecoming . . . the Dignity of the Prophetic Office," to such commentators as the Jewish philosopher Maimonides and later Christian writers who resolved the difficulty by interpreting the actions as visions, not behavior, Warburton insists that the language of action was just what it seemed to be, the expression of meaning through a physical act. God speaks to the prophet in visions, but the prophet speaks to the people in actions.

The eighteenth-century novel, too, privileges action as a particularly potent form of communication or expression. We can call to mind familiar gestures from the canonical works of eighteenth-century fiction: Trim's dropped hat in *Tristram Shandy*, Pamela's displaying of herself in country garb in Richardson's first novel, Parson Adams's flinging of his copy of Aeschylus into the fire in *Joseph Andrews*, Roxana's eastern dance in Defoe's novel; Evelina's refusal to dance in Burney's first

---

3   Ibid., p. 2. Dieckmann observes that in the eighteenth century "hieroglyphics" "lost its immediacy and [was] used [when used at all] in a well-accepted seventeenth-century sense which no longer need[ed] any discussion" (129).

4   Warburton explains that apologue, fable, proverb, simile, and metaphor are all aspects of hieroglyphic language in that they all serve to express abstract thought through specific images. Ibid., pp. 87–93.

5   Francis Bacon likewise discusses gesture and hieroglyphics as sensible language: "gestures . . . are as transitory hieroglyphics, and are to hieroglyphics as words spoken are to words written, in that they abide not; but they have evermore . . . an affinity with the things signified" (Quoted by Dieckmann, p. 102).

narrative. The works under consideration in this study also feature prominent actions that reveal information—particularly information relating to desire.

Warburton traces all kinds of figurative language back to the hieroglyph of picture or of action; apologue, proverb, fable, simile, allegory, and metaphor alike are just "symbol[s] of something else understood" (2: 92)—not mysteries or secrets, but ways of clarification for a people whose "Language was yet too narrow, and ... Minds . . . too undisciplin'd. . . to support only abstract Reasoning and . . . direct Address" (2: 87). Later on, though, hieroglyphics were marshaled in the service of political secrets expressed in coded epistolary correspondence (2: 128–32) and in the service of religious mysticism through symbols worn as amulets or charms (2: 153–54). So, in summation, Warburton identifies four categories of Egyptian hieroglyphic writing—the first two (basic hieroglyphics and symbolic hieroglyphics) designed to reveal; the second two (epistolary or civil and hierogrammatic or religious) designed to conceal.

As intriguing as what Warburton says about hieroglyphics is why he embarks on such an extended meditation about a subject so seemingly disconnected from his main purpose (i.e. to prove that the doctrine of life after death—in his words "the Doctrine of a Future State of Reward and Punishment"—is not part of the Mosaic dispensation).[6] Warburton is making two separate but related points in this address to a rational readership, whose deistic tendency is to deny the divine dispensation of any faith as well as to erase distinctions between faiths: first, that the Jewish doctrine is as divinely sanctioned as the Christian religion and, second, that the Christian religion adds to the older belief the assurance of reward or punishment after death.[7] Further, as Jonathan Lamb has explained, Warburton looks to the absence of such a doctrine in early Jewish thought as evidence of the need for a state religion. In *The Divine Legation*, Warburton "undertook to prove by a system of universal illustration that the foundation of the Jewish nation under Moses was unique in that it did not depend on the prospect of a future state of rewards and punishments to enforce people's obedience to the law."[8] The reason the "nascent state" of Israel does not need such a doctrine is that Moses had a "hidden contract" with God, a "private assurance" of an "extraordinary providence" that inextricably tied the people's happiness to their obedience.[9] The efficacy of this arrangement

---

6   Ibid., title page, p. [i].

7   As David Sorkin has noted, "Warburton wanted to defend the divine origin of Judaism and its inseverable link to Christianity because some deists had attacked Christianity by disparaging its Jewish foundations, and some believers, in turn, had acquiesced to that severance in order to defend Christianity." He goes on to describe Warburton's chief "project" as the effort to "establish the true nature of Judaism and Christianity by delineating their respective relationship to natural religion." "William Warburton: The Middle Way of 'Heroic Moderation,'" *Nederlands Archief voor Kerkgescchiedenis* 82.2 (2002): 274; 275 and passim.

8   "The Job Controversy, Sterne, and the Question of Allegory," *Eighteenth-Century Studies* 24 (1990): 3. See also Melvyn New, "Sterne, Warburton, and the Burden of Exuberant Wit," *Eighteenth-Century Studies* 15 (1982): 255–6 on the paradoxical nature of Warburton's position—and the encyclopedic learning and exuberant wit with which he defended it.

9   Ibid., p. 3.

is superseded in Warburton's formulation by Christianity. Yet, it is essential to his argument that Moses' laws be understood as a divine, though limited, advance from the paganism of the Egyptians.[10] It seems necessary to Warburton to elaborate the nature of Moses' mind and learning before tackling his main project. The point of the discussion of hieroglyphics is to establish the iconic nature of the Egyptian culture in which Moses and the Israelites were steeped and which they both reject and crave. The iconoclastic Israelites (with Moses as leader) persistently and inconsistently struggle against the tendency to revert to idol and image worship. The rejection of hieroglyphics as a language is simply part of the rejection of an Egyptian learning that nevertheless continues to have a great appeal.[11]

Hieroglyphics, in a sense then, serve as metonymic signs of the larger issue of assimilation. How Egyptian were the Israelites? How Egyptian was Moses? How did this enslaved people retain a sense of identity upon which to build a nation? How much of that identity is entwined with the other who served as host and oppressor for so long? In Exodus 23: 9, God commands the Israelites that they never forget the experience of bondage in Egypt; it is to be central to the Israelite identity both for its own sake and for what it teaches about their relationship to those who may regard them as the defining other: "You shall not oppress a stranger, for you know the feelings of the stranger, having yourselves been strangers in the land of Egypt." Further complicating the matter is that the word for stranger (*ger*), used here three times is also the word used in rabbinic commentary for "convert."[12] At what point does the stranger *ger* become the convert *ger*? At what point is the Israelite an Egyptian, the Gentile a Jew? Or, in terms of the focus of this study, terms familiar to feminists concerned with any written text or cultural act, is it possible to speak in your own voice or act with autonomy and self-determination when you are writing and talking in someone else's language, when you are living in oppression in someone else's land, according to someone else's laws?

Concealing and Revealing

The answer, according to a midrash concerning Queen Esther, is yes. "Cut off from intercourse with Jews," by virtue of her marriage to King Ahasuerus, Esther, the midrash informs us, "was in danger of forgetting when the Sabbath came."[13] Her

---

10	As Sorkin puts it, according to Warburton, "Judaism was 'good' only in the relative sense that in its time it prepared the way for Christianity" by "freeing" the Jews "from the idolatries and other pagan practices to which they had grown accustomed in Egypt and, then, subjecting them to a special administration to prevent recidivism." Ibid., p. 279.

11	Warburton argues that "[a]ll Hieroglyphic Writing was absolutely forbidden by the second Commandment, and with a View worthy the Divine Wisdom; Hieroglyphics being,. . . the great Source of the most abominable Idolatries and superstitions. . . . [T]o cut off therefore all Occasion of Danger from Symbolic Images, Moses, as I suppose, altered the Form of the *Egyptian* Letters, and reduced them into something like those simple Shapes in which we now find them" (2: 140).

12	On *ger*, see Friedman, *Commentary on the Torah*, Gen. 15: 13n.

13	I Targum 2. 9.

Sabbath is a chief aspect of her identity; to lose track is to lose the sense of who she is, who her people are. Her solution to this dilemma is to develop a code that will serve to remind her. She has seven attendants upon whom she relies to help her remember—not by directing that they do so, but by renaming them and assigning their duties in such a way that the maids themselves become a secret code by which Esther can remember her people, her God, and her own identity:

> The first one she called *Hulta*, 'Workaday,' and she was in attendance upon Esther on Sundays. On Mondays, she was served by *Rok'ita*, to remind her of *Rek'ia*, 'Firmament,' which was created on the second day of the world. Tuesday's maid she called *Genunita*, 'Garden,' the third day of creation having seen plants produced in the world. On Wednesday, she reminded herself by *Nehorita*'s name, 'the Luminous,' that it was the day on which God had made the luminaries, to shed their light in the sky; on Thursday by *Ruhshita*, 'Movement,' for on the fifth day the first animated beings were created; on Friday, the day on which the beasts came into being, by *Hurfita*, 'Little Ewelamb'; and on the Sabbath her bidding was done by *Rego'ita*, 'Rest.' Thus she was sure to remember the Sabbath day week after week.[14]

The midrash's emphasis on a secret code is appropriate for a text that is about so many levels of communication. Decrees, edicts, annals, writings, and scrolls abound in the book of Esther, as does the language of gesture. It is her refusal of King Ahasuerus's command to put on "a royal diadem" and appear at her husband's banquet "to display her beauty to the peoples and the officials" that bans Queen Vashti from the King's presence forever—a punishment "written into the laws," no less, "of Persia and Media, so that it cannot be abrogated" (Esther 1: 11, 19). Queen Vashti's gesture (or non-gesture, as the case may be) is more than a private whim; it is "read" by the entire court as a threat to masculine prerogative in general: "For the queen's behavior will make all wives despise their husbands, as they reflect that King Ahasuerus himself ordered Queen Vashti to be brought before him, but she would not come" (Esther 1: 17). In fact, the sage Memucan tells the king that women are already on the verge of "citing" Vashti's behavior as precedent to officials of the king. "[T] here will be no end of scorn and provocation!" he predicts (Esther 1: 18).

Although King Ahasuerus does emerge in the narrative as one of the less astute potentates of biblical history, his court is highly literate and, to his credit, he himself seems to like intelligent women. When he comes to choose a replacement for Vashti he prefers, once again, a woman of wit, education, and strength of character. Yet his attraction to female intelligence seems more a matter of instinct than design. His conscious efforts are expended on beauty. Esther is naturally "shapely and beautiful" (Esther 2: 7), but she, along with the other favored virgins, receives a full year of allure-enhancing treatments at the king's expense. Oils, perfumes, cosmetics—and "rations"!—are systematically applied ("six months with oil of myrrh and six months with perfumes and women's cosmetics") to render these women as pleasing

---

14 Ibid. We are told in the book of Esther itself that the king, upon first seeing the beautiful girl, "hastened to furnish her with . . . the seven maids who were her due from the king's palace" (Esther 2: 9). It is on this detail that the midrash is built.

to this king as they can possibly be (Esther 2: 9; 12). And Esther does please. She pleases most of all—and the king indicates as much by placing the royal diadem on her head, hosting a court banquet in her honor, and remitting taxes for all the provinces (Esther 2: 17–18). By these royal gestures, Esther herself, the officials of the king's government, and the people of the kingdom are informed that she has replaced Vashti as Queen.

On the advice of her cousin and surrogate father, Mordecai, Esther "does not reveal her people or her kindred" (Esther 2:10). The sign of her secret identity is ever present, however, in the person of Mordecai himself. Mordecai "would walk about in front of the court of the harem" while Esther was going through her period of approval and beautification; after she receives the diadem, he moves his center of operations to the palace gates where, we are told, he "sits" (Esther 2: 11; 19; 21). We are not told exactly what Mordecai does besides sit; perhaps he sells some sort of goods there, offers some sort of service to the courtiers who come and go. What we are told is that he becomes a spy, at least for a day. He overhears two of the court eunuchs plotting to kill Ahasuerus. Mordecai tells Esther; Esther, in turn, reports it to the king "in Mordecai's name" (Esther 2: 22). Once the matter is investigated and found to be true, the criminals are executed by impalement and the whole incident, at the direction of Ahasuerus, is written up "in the book of annals" (Esther 2: 23).

From this point on, the narrative proceeds as a complex orchestration of various levels of communication. Mordecai refuses to bow to Haman, the king's chief courtier. Haman begins to form a genocidal plan to "do away with all the Jews" (Esther 3: 6) and has lots cast before him until he finds an auspicious day to make his secret plot official. The king is persuaded that the unassimilated Jews ("whose laws are different from those of any other people" [Esther 3: 8]) are trouble; he allows Haman to draw up edicts and decrees to be distributed "to every province in its own script and to every people in its own language" (Esther 3: 12), sealed with the king's signet ring. These documents, to be displayed publicly in each province, announce that on the thirteenth day of the twelfth month in every province of the kingdom the people are "to destroy, massacre, and exterminate all the Jews, young and old, children and women . . . and to plunder their possessions" (Esther 3: 13).

The city of Shushan is "dumbfounded" (Esther 3: 15), but Mordecai finds a way to communicate and to act. He tears his clothes and puts on sackcloth and ashes, clear signs to Esther that her cousin/tutor/guardian is in mourning. But for what? She sends a eunuch to inquire, and she is both told the story and also given the written documents to peruse. In addition, Mordecai sends instructions by way of the eunuch. It is up to Esther to save her people.

The culturally bilingual Esther understands that her task is complicated, and she proceeds by indirection—seducing the king and flattering Haman.[15] Luck also plays a role—the king passes a sleepless night listening to a reading of his "book of records"

---

15   As Tamar Frankiel points out, the biblical text understands that "sexual power is part of a woman's inherent power—differing in degree, quality, and extent for each woman." Unlike the willful, pleasure-seeking, self-centered Vashti, Esther uses her sexual power "to the good of the Jews of Persia." *The Voice of Sarah: Feminine Spirituality and Traditional Judaism* (New York, 1990), p. 31.

(Esther 6: 1), the annals that contain the story of Mordecai the Jew's uncovering of the assassination plot. Suddenly struck that Mordecai should have been rewarded for his loyalty, the king seeks advice from the first courtier he sees as to the appropriate gestures of honor. Haman, who has come to demand Mordecai's instant death, ends up advising the king to give the Jew a diadem, royal attire, and a parade! In a final irony, Haman is impaled on the stake he had erected for Mordecai's death—and not really because of his behavior toward Mordecai. The king, after all, had given Haman carte blanche. He knew full well about the edict and plans for massacre and mayhem. What he had not remembered was Mordecai's earlier service; what he had not known and what Esther reveals at the final banquet she hosts for Haman and the king is that Esther herself is a Jew. The "evil Haman" is her "adversary and enemy" (Esther 7: 6), adversary and enemy to all Jews, adversary and enemy to the king himself! Esther's proclamation causes the king to leave the room in agitation; Haman, convinced his destruction is imminent, pleads with Esther. The king, returning to the room, sees Haman prostrate on the sofa, and in a singularly obtuse act of misreading decides that the courtier merits instant death for the effrontery of attempting "'to ravish the queen in my own palace!'" (Esther 7: 8).

The book of Esther ends with three acts of writing. Mordecai writes the record of the events and charges Jews in all the provinces of King Ahasuerus's kingdom to observe yearly a feast day in honor of this grief turned to joy. Queen Esther also writes a dispatch "confirming with full authority the aforementioned one of Mordecai the Jew" (Esther 9: 29). Her letter "was recorded in a scroll" (Esther 9: 32). Finally, the events, their sequence and consequence, are entered in the annals of the king.

Esther's triumph is a triumph of communication and interpretation. She skillfully manipulates signs; she responds clearly to clear acts of communication. She doggedly investigates when signs point to enigmatic meanings; she remains silent as others misinterpret specific signs in meaningful ways. Esther's triumph is also a triumph of co-existence without full assimilation. She and Mordecai function in the kingdom of King Ahasuerus as reminders of the other—of the Jewish other, certainly, but in a broader sense, of all the others who exist in the king's multi-lingual empire. Haman had striven to unite the kingdom in hatred of one people. The dumbfoundedness of the people on hearing the genocidal edict suggests that they understood the ultimate effect of such unitedness. To silence one other is to silence all.

Yet the demands of nation are such that it requires great effort to preserve otherness within identity. On one level, in fact, it would seem almost impossible. The story of Esther is really the story of the alliance between Ahasuerus and Mordecai. Esther can preserve her own sense of self, as well, because she is one in a harem of various wives, her identity confirmed and sustained by a variety of relationships— with her maids, her eunuchs, the courtiers, and her cousin. Her desire is focused on this preservation of self, extended to her people. Her love is not directed toward lover as other, but toward her people and her God.

Concerned about a different Sabbath, but the same principle, Robinson Crusoe marks lines on a post, making "every seventh notch . . . as long again as the rest" so that he would not "forget the Sabbath days from the working days."[16] The reckoning

---

16 *Robinson Crusoe*, ed. John Richetti (New York 2004), p. 52. See also p. 83.

of time by signs that speak hieroglyphically to the demands of a transcendent and timeless other is a recognition of the paradox of ethical obligation, i.e. the sensing of presence where presence is not phenomenological but, in Levinasian terms, "beyond being." The signs are phenomena, of course, but what they signify is not phenomenon but enigma. As one commentator on Levinas has put it: "The Other does not appear within the world but is an interruption or disturbance of it. In other words, the Other does not appear, but phenomenology gives access to the Other's nonappearance."[17]

In his 1965 essay "Enigma and Phenomenon," Levinas asserts that "all speaking is an enigma."[18] This observation is certainly true on occasions when speakers wish to protect themselves from overt rejection by one who does not choose to enter into relation at the subject's demand. For example, "[o]ne diplomat makes an exorbitant proposition to another diplomat, but this proposition is put in terms such that, if one likes, nothing has been said." Or, perhaps, "[a] lover makes an advance, but the provocative or seductive gesture has, if one likes, not interrupted the decency of the conversation and attitudes; it withdraws as lightly as it had slipped in." Or, again, "[a] God was revealed on a mountain or in a burning bush, or was attested to in Scriptures." We can dismiss these words, these gestures, these illusions, Levinas says:

> It is up to us, or, more exactly, it is up to *me* to retain or to repel this God without boldness, exiled because allied with the conquered, hunted down and hence absolute, thus disarticulating the very moment in which he is presented and proclaimed, unrepresentable. This way the Other has of seeking my recognition while preserving his *incognito*, disdaining recourse to a wink-of-the-eye of understanding or complicity, this way of manifesting himself without manifesting himself, we call enigma—going back to the etymology of this Greek term, and contrasting it with the indiscreet and victorious appearing of *phenomenon*.[19]

Anyone who speaks, even one who speaks within and to the dominant culture in commonplaces that seek to deny disruption, will open the possibility of new signification, renewal, enigma to those "listening at the doorway of language" (74). Desire may be awakened by words that say more than the speaker intended to say, thoughts that seem beyond the thoughts meant to be conveyed. "Human sexuality" itself is enigma, a response to phenomena that goes beyond the phenomenological. After all, Levinas concludes, "[a] face can appear as a face . . . only if it enigmatically comes from the Infinite" (77). So sexual desire is nothing more nor less than "the expectation of an unknown, but known, face" which speaks as much to our longing for God as it does to our longing for human connection and physical pleasure (73).

---

17   Headnote to "Enigma and Phenomenon" in *Basic Philosophical Writings*, p. 65.

18   Ibid., p. 73.

19   Ibid., p. 70. As Levinas's editors point out, the Greek word *ainigma* means a riddle or an obscure word— which I would associate with a hieroglyph (p. 179 n.12).

Keys and Correspondences

It is one thing to talk about the enigma of human desire in a Levinasian register, quite another to read about its phenomenological manifestations in the squalid world of early eighteenth-century politics. The voracious lusts chronicled in *The New Atalantis* seem to spring from neither God-longing nor longing for human connection. Most seem divorced from pleasure as well. Sexual desire in this world seems to have become the handmaiden of power, the tool of oppression, the instrument of manipulation. Yet, I maintain, these hieroglyphics of desire document a doubleness similar to that we witness in Queen Esther's use of sign and symbol in the palace of King Ahasuerus—and for the same reason. Manley writes as a stranger in a strange land both to preserve a sense of self and to participate in the defining and directing of nation. Like Mordecai and Esther before her, Manley is both of and apart from the world in which she lives. She combines the two biblical figures, in a sense, becoming a double agent, as it were—both spy and queen—whose access to knowledge comes from being fully participatory in the corruption she would combat. She observes and listens; she interprets and writes. She manipulates the signs and symbols of a corrupt society in pursuit of a just world.

While we might be inclined to regard early eighteenth-century print culture as a far remove from the court and kingdom of Ahasuerus, in fact, the two cultures share a sense of the importance of writing to the establishing of national identity and to the articulation of individual identity within a nation. Manley's hieroglyphics, her coded satires, are designed to expose the secrets of political and sexual intrigue, but enigmatically. In the partisan world of early eighteenth-century politics, language became overtly slippery.[20] Libel laws, economic uncertainties, and shifts in political power contributed to a culture in which enigma was lingua franca. Nevertheless, as Catherine Gallagher has argued, the pointedly clever names and sharply exaggerated personae in Manley's satiric narratives were signs meant to reveal, not obscure, identities.[21] If the masked identities of the characters were not sufficiently transparent or at least decodable for the "language community"—i.e., the British reading public—keys quickly appeared to help initiate the uninformed and to whet the appetite for further identification by the avidly curious who knew or thought they could guess the identities of the prominent personages involved. Manley's design was to write the history of the court; her *New Atalantis*, in particular, serves as the annals of the kingdom established and presided over by the Duke and Duchess of Marlborough.

As the paradigmatic story of Queen Esther illustrates, a sharp paradox underlines a culture of writing. Words are put on paper in an effort to capture and secure meaning, but such efforts always fail. Experience reveals that, with regard to governance of any kind, written documents can actually increase the potential for instability and unpredictability. Haman had a surefire plan, after all, until Ahasuerus decided to read. The more texts there are, the less control any single person has over the way

---

20 For the legal and literary ramifications of this "slipperiness," see C. R. Kropf, "Libel and Satire in the Eighteenth Century," *Eighteenth-Century Studies*, 8 (1974): 153–68.

21 Gallagher, *Nobody's Story*, p. 125.

others interpret the world. Anything written can be rewritten; in fact, each act of reading is, in a sense, an act of rewriting. That the eighteenth century was particularly preoccupied with the stability and precision of language in general is too clear a truism to need much elaboration. Swift's *Tale of a Tub*, Sterne's *Tristram Shandy*, and Pope's *Dunciad* come to mind as works almost solely devoted to the perplexities and dubieties surrounding meaning in a world of proliferating printed matter written by bad writers whose careless use of language, according to the satirists, signified moral as well as linguistic failings. More generally, suspicion regarding figurative language and mystical symbolism infuse the thinking of political theorists and practicing clergymen alike. "Plain sense," "clear expression," balance, and harmony are the stylistic ideals of the period, endorsed by everyone from Thomas Sprat to Samuel Johnson.

The reason for such widespread anxiety about language—both spoken and written, but particularly written, particularly printed—is not far to seek. The eighteenth century is a period in which both religious and political power are becoming less and less centralized. More people are invested with a sense of authority for determining meaning while at the same time meaning is increasingly located in the realm of abstract signs. Of course, the English language had never been a pictorial language, so that kind of abstraction is nothing new. But print technology distances language a step further from authority by introducing the concept of reproducibility (hence impersonality and corruptibility) into the notion of "text" or "work." Are words on flimsy printed pages anything but ephemeral, destructible, valueless notions? Are they supported by any kind of stable authority? These questions were predominant in the minds of many during the eighteenth century, not only in reference to prayer books and deeds of conveyance, but also with regard to the financial infrastructure of England. The emergent economic system founded on the printed sign of paper currency had not yet earned the confidence of the public. Indeed, it would reveal itself to be unstable and wildly fluctuating on several notable occasions during the early decades of the eighteenth century.

The proliferation of paper and words on that paper, its material destructability, its transient power and its fragile claim to permanence were acutely felt during the early part of the eighteenth century, and the fickleness of the printed word was often linked to the wayward instability of female desire. According to Catherine Gallagher, women had a special place in the "emergent civil humanist model" of masculine excellence which "accepted that the worthy man would have private interests and commercial dealings as well as a private life in which he cultivated himself merely for the sake of personal cultivation."[22] The stereotypical identification of feminine desire with waywardness and instability made the feminine an appropriate referent for the uncertainty of the new economic reality, but the conventional association of the feminine with private life also elevated woman's position as a cultivator of the private man made possible by the new economy. The containment of (female) desire—as Gallagher points out—became doubly (and contradictorily) significant— its location as well as its regulation was important to the civil humanist model of social interaction.

---

22   Ibid., p. 107.

In a sense, Manley's entire career as a writer can be explained as an exploitation of the cultural need to contain female desire. To that end, her "language," her system of signs and symbols, is both adopted from and adapted to a culture of misogyny.[23] On their surface, Manley's scurrilous vignettes and scandalous narratives accuse her female targets of lascivious insatiability, devious and deviant behavior, and a hunger for power that overwhelms every other emotion, including their sexual appetites. This language of scandal participates in a cultural language of misogynistic satire.[24] Manley's satirical stance is indebted to negative stereotypes of female behavior because, as Gallagher explains, "[w]hat was desired of . . . [the woman political writer] was desire itself, the introduction of the passions into a proto-political civil discourse, where their regulation might also be displayed."[25] "[S]atire on a woman in a woman's voice," Gallagher explains, "was particularly relished," and so it should be no surprise to find the termagant, the amazon, the hysteric, the irrational, the demonic, the fickle, and the insatiable among the patterns drawn upon to create aspects of Sarah Churchill, the Duchess of Cleveland, and other women associated with the court.[26] This language of stereotype is complicated in Manley's work, however, by the fact that she employs it both in blame and in praise. For, just as surely as it underwrites the criticism she would bring to bear on Whig feminization of culture, it also underpins the significance she would claim for herself as spokesperson for the Tory view.

Although such doubleness is evident in *The New Atalantis*, it is *The Adventures of Rivella* that most completely examines the paradoxical nature of this world of keys and correspondences along the lines suggested by the ethical paradigm derived from Queen Esther's story. After all, in *The New Atalantis* Justice and Virtue are decidedly *ger*, exiled and distanced from the corrupt proceedings they come to witness as visitors—or, we might even say, as bewildered, unhappy tourists. They observe and represent from the vantage point of the stranger who is *not* attracted by the land in which he or she has come to dwell. In *The Adventures of Rivella*, Manley adopts a different strategy, creating a completely self-referential world of words, gestures, and paper. The hieroglyphs "Rivella," "Calista," "Cleander," "Oswald," "Lord Crafty," "Tim Double," and so on, when identified, lead merely to other constructs of language. Who is Rivella? Delarivier Manley. Who is that? Her books. Her letters. Scandal. Gossip. Lies. The trail of references leads from one set of papers to another; narratives, stories, legends, books—her words against other words against other words—all in the end amounting to the same thing: the driving force, as Manley herself puts it, of "self-love"—or, as Queen Esther or Robinson

---

23   Gallagher notes Manley's participation in the Juvenalian tradition of misogynistic satire. Ibid., p. 118.

24   Felicity Nussbaum has documented the standard perceptions as they inform Tory satire written by men. *"The Brink of All We Hate": English Satires on Women, 1660–1750* (Lexington, 1984), pp. 1–7 and passim. Gallagher has extended Nussbaum's argument to explain aspects of the partisan writings of both Susannah Centlivre and Delarivier Manley, *Nobody's Story*, pp. 106–14.

25   Gallagher, *Nobody's Story*, p. 113.

26   Ibid., pp. 114–15.

Crusoe might have put it, of the need to maintain a sense of self and separateness while living in, and as a part of, an alien land.

The autobiographical account exploits many categories of contradiction—praise and blame, men and women, virtue and vice, beauty and repulsiveness. And, as Lovemore's opening remark to D'Aumont suggests, the contradictory impulses are not restricted to the character and life of Rivella. The act of narration itself is propelled by the counter forces of the teller's impulse and the listener's demand: "There are so many things praise, and yet blame-worthy, in Rivella's conduct, that as her friend, I know not well how with a good grace, to repeat, or as yours, to conceal, because you seem to expect from me an impartial history."[27] D'Aumont's desire to love Rivella motivates the telling of her history, but, Lovemore realizes, the fulfillment of that desire involves a complex negotiation of revelation and concealment. At the outset, then, he acknowledges the difficulty of telling the story D'Aumont wants to hear, for to keep desire alive the contradictions must be exposed but never resolved. To reveal and conceal at the same time is the essence of Manley's narrative art and of the art of her self-creation (through the voice of Lovemore). As her narrative suggests, it is the essence of desire itself.

Manley's exploration of desire involves the continual invocation of interpretive possibilities. In the very first paragraph, in her own voice (quoted by Lovemore), Rivella introduces two ways of reading her own conduct in terms of gender categories: "I have often heard her say, if she had been a man, she had been without fault. ... [W]hat is not a crime in men is scandalous and unpardonable in woman" (47). Later, Lovemore invokes this attitude more negatively: "I pitied her conduct, which I saw must infallibly center in her ruin . . . The casuists told her a woman of her wit had the privilege of the other sex, since all things were pardonable to a lady *who could so well give laws to others, yet was not obliged to keep them her self*" (69). But, by this point he too has begun trading in contradictions. His judgmental remark follows quickly upon the revelation that he has asked Rivella to live with him "because it could no longer do her an injury in the opinion of the world which was sufficiently prejudiced against her already" (67). Rivella's retort on that occasion—"she must first be in love with a man before she thought fit to reside with him" (67)—accords with her response to Lovemore's continued criticism of her conduct: "[s]he looked upon all I said with an evil eye; believing there was still jealousy at the bottom" (69). Fixed categories of praise and blame based on essential definitions of sexual character and social propriety simply fail to provide the basis for judging Rivella here and elsewhere. She claims to be innocent and appears to be guilty; Lovemore would protect her true "innocency" by exploiting her apparent guilt: the casuists would allow for a redefinition of appropriate female conduct based on Rivella's unusual wit that allows her to transcend boundaries others must observe.

As Rivella's conduct is open to contradictory interpretation, so is her physical appearance the site of dispute. Again, Manley emphasizes the fracture between what seems to be and what really is, this time invoking the categories of public and private: "Few, who have only beheld her in publick, could be brought to like

---

27   *The Adventures of Rivella*, ed. Katherine Zelinsky (Peterborough, 1999), p. 47. Further references will be cited parenthetically.

her; whereas none that became acquainted with her, could refrain from loving her," Lovemore says (47). It is the private domain in which Rivella is said to triumph, and it is there that her physical being is defined as alluring, fascinating, attractive in spite of features that would mark her as anything but beautiful (she is fat; her skin is marred by small-pox).[28] Her eyes, hair, lips, teeth, and feet are her best physical features, but in the end her appeal has to be explained as more than the sum of her parts. Lovemore concludes that all beauty is thus:

> love in the general is well natured and civil, willing to compound for some defects, since he knows that 'tis very difficult and rare to find true symmetry and all perfections in one person. Red hair, out-mouth, thin and livid lips, black broken teeth, course ugly hands, long thumbs, ill formed dirty nails, flat, or very large breasts, splay feet; which together makes a frightful composition, yet divided amongst several, prove no allay to the strongest passions. (48)

This grotesque anatomy serves to offset the fact that Rivella has little claim to personal beauty, and the result of Lovemore's long and contraindicatory description is that D'Aumont remains "resolved to be in love with Rivella": "I can easily forgive want of beauty in her face, to the charms you tell me are in her person" (49). The narrative proceeds to her history, D'Aumont hoping to discover "no hideous vices in her mind, to deform the fair idea ... of fine hands and arms, a beautiful neck and breast, pretty feet, and . . . limbs that make up the symmetry of the whole" (49).

The remainder of the narrative recounts Rivella's love affairs, her bigamous marriage, her involvement with men and women of fashion, her scandalous reputation, her complicity in legal chicanery, her emergence as a self-described misanthropic author. In the end, D'Aumont is fully as charmed as he was in the beginning, his eagerness to meet Rivella in person unabated and his enthusiastic approbation unabashed: "let us not lose a moment before we are acquainted with the only person of her sex that knows how to *live*, and of whom we may say, in relation to love, since she has so peculiar a genius for, and has made such noble discoveries in that passion, that it would have been a *fault in her not to have been faulty*" (114).

The narratives of Sir Peter Vainlove (Lord Skipwith) and the Meanwell/Crafty (Albemarle) lawsuit confirm the notion that identities created to conceal truth actually reveal truth—but the truth revealed has more to do with the person interpreting the "hieroglyphic" identity than the "hieroglyph" itself. Sir Peter Vainlove is a portrait of Sir Thomas Skipwith, theater producer and, reputedly, Manley's lover. Skipwith (like Vainlove) was a noted rake, and Manley's narrative undermines what she presents to be his carefully cultivated reputation for sexual prowess. She exposes the means by which he creates "his own vain false reputation" (71)—the exchange of letters, words which substitute for deeds he can no longer perform. Through the agency of her narrator, Lovemore, Manley admits to desire for Vainlove. But, the narrative

---

28 Katherine Zelinsky, conversely, reads the sentence on p. 47 referring to the smallpox as an assertion that the disease had left Rivella unscarred. We disagree in our understanding of the referent to "it" in the comment that Rivella's face "has scarce any pretence to it." Zelinsky, apparently, takes "it" to mean "smallpox"; I take "it" to mean the "beauty" Rivella had as a child. See *The Adventures of Rivella*, pp. 47 and 47n.2.

maintains, the two never became lovers due to Vainlove's broken constitution, not his prior obligations:

> he found she [Rivella] was a woman of fire, more than perhaps he could answer, [and] he was resolved to destroy any hopes she might have of a nearer correspondence than would conveniently suit with his present circumstances, by telling her his heart was already prepossessed. This served him to a double purpose, *first*, to let her know that he was reciprocally admired: and *secondly*, that no great things were to be expected from a person who was engaged, or rather devoted to another. (70–1)

This passage serves Manley to a double (cross) purpose as well: first, to exonerate herself from the charges of having given Skipwith a venereal disease (how could she have done so if he was unable to make love to her?) and, secondly, to maintain her authority in matters of passion and desire—an authority on which her scandalous narratives depend.[29] These opposing aims serve, like Vainlove's opposing aims, to fuel the desires of others by at once promising and denying the pleasures of fulfillment. Readers expecting to hear a vindication are treated instead to a denial of fact that proves more titillating in its description of frustrated passion than an account of consummated but morbid desire could ever be.

In the lengthy narrative based on the convoluted Albemarle lawsuit, Manley extends her observations on the relationship among concealing, revealing, and the force of desire. According to Katherine Zelinsky, the overt purpose of the judicial narrative is to relegate (through the agency of Lovemore) woman to the private sphere by demonstrating the inappropriateness of her involvement in legal and political matters: "in his detailed account of Rivella's involvement in the most public and protracted trial of the century . . . Lovemore is most resolute in his judgments about women's proper sphere, for he finally recontains her within the private (feminine) realm of romance, within the only cultural space where, as a veritable *feme covert*, she has any legitimacy and authority as a speaking subject" (28). While it is true that at the end of the narrative, Rivella (according to Lovemore) agrees "that politicks is not the business of a woman" (112), it is rather difficult to take this view seriously as it caps off an account in which prevarication is shown to be the common denominator of all human utterance. Further, while the thrust of the Albemarle trial was economic, the text suggests that it, like all forms of human behavior, including politics at the highest level, is influenced at every turn by the complications attendant on erotic passion—Manley's acknowledged area of expertise. In fact, the roots of the Albemarle case lie in one of the most politically significant events of the last age, the novel asserts, the political machinations that resulted in the Popish Plot of 1678, the origin of which was none other than a lover's quarrel between Lord Crafty and Hilaria.

The world Manley describes is, as Gallagher has pointed out, a material world focused on possession, investment, symbolic monetary value, and shifting, unpredictable economic stabilities. In this world, the object of desire takes on much

---

29 See Carol L. Barash, "Gender, Authority and the 'Life' of an Eighteenth-Century Woman Writer: Delarivière Manley's *Adventures of Rivella*," *Women's Studies International Forum* 10:2 (1987): 165–9.

greater significance than the subject of desire. If women begin to lose their agency as desiring subjects as we seem to agree they do in the modern world, the reason is a complex association of female sexual character with this kind of economic circumstance. Manley is, like Esther, a dexterous and confident speaker of many languages, reader of many codes. She is playful as she transgresses all kinds of boundaries, donning the male character to speak her own tale, adopting, adapting, rejecting, and rehabilitating misogynistic female stereotypes to her own ends. She makes a virtue of desire and desiring even as she capitulates in the end to the cultural demand that she be more object than subject. But in her world, the object is so clearly constructed that we are still aware of the way it speaks to subjective desire. Women as well as men are depicted as formulating and then pursuing passions. As cultural norms shift, however, such acknowledgment will become more and more difficult. The desiring and desired woman in Manley's world can understand and speak the language of others while maintaining a sense of self. If, in the early eighteenth century, such a woman is a hieroglyph that both conceals and reveals, she will become by mid-century a cryptic cipher upon whom meaning is projected. We will explore this theme at length in the next chapter's discussion of women in the sentimental novel, but it is interestingly anticipated by Eliza Haywood and her biblical paradigm, Zipporah, both of whom still speak, in voices we have no difficulty hearing, but in languages we no longer fully understand.

Allegory and the Regulation of Desire

Unlike her predecessors, Behn and Manley, Eliza Haywood did not engage in self-constructions in which she deliberately blurred the distinction between public and private modes of desire by infusing her work with the implications of her own sexual nature.[30] She did not create herself as a desiring subject nor did she present herself as an object of desire. In fact, what self-revelation she allowed was contradictory, and as David Oakleaf has put it, "there is evidence that she wanted her private life to remain private."[31] What we know for certain of Haywood's life is what she published, in which plays she acted, in which public quarrels she participated, which writers honored her and which satirized her in print. In other words, what we know of Haywood is comprised of public utterance, and it has to do with her public life.

The most famous hieroglyphic image associated with Haywood, in fact, is not one of her own creating, but that fashioned by Alexander Pope for the *Dunciad* wherein she is exhibited as the prize in the urinating contest between booksellers Thomas Osborne and Edmund Curll.[32] The passage is so familiar, and so despised

---

30 The following discussion is indebted to my conversations with Julie Barfield as well as to her unpublished work on the fiction of Eliza Haywood and its invocation of the material world.

31 David Oakleaf, "Introduction" to Eliza Haywood, *Love in Excess, or The Fatal Inquiry*, Broadview Literary Texts (Peterborough, 1994), p. 5. Further references to the novel will be cited parenthetically.

32 My anonymous reader informs me that "pissing contest" works better than "urinating contest," here and later, and I agree but find myself a bit too (paradoxically) prudish on the

(or so admired), that to quote it here might seem unnecessary heresy. Yet, for its importance and its strategy in the construction of Eliza Haywood, it is worth considering the lines again:

> See in the circle next, Eliza plac'd
> Two babes of love close clinging to her waste;
> Fair as before her works she stands confess'd,
> In flow'rs and pearls by bounteous Kirkall dress'd.
> The Goddess then: 'Who best can send on high
> The salient spout, far-streaming to the sky;
> His be yon Juno of majestic size,
> With cow-like-udders, and with ox-like eyes.
> This China-Jordan let the chief o'ercome
> Replenish, not ingloriously, at home.' [33]

Subtextual notes continue Pope's attack on Haywood, as he twice justifies his animus using two separate rhetorical strategies: first, the sincerity of moral outrage; next, the inflationary language of satiric disdain. The first note claims that the game— i.e., the urinating contest—is described for the purpose of exposing "in the most contemptuous manner, the profligate licentiousness of those shameless scriblers . . . who in libellous Memoirs and Novels, reveal the faults or misfortunes of both sexes, to the ruin or disturbance of public fame or private happiness" (2.149n). The poet is particularly offended, the note says, that the main perpetrators of such scandal are of "that Sex, which ought least to be capable of such malice or impudence," and he has therefore, justifiably, "drawn as vile a picture as could be represented in the colours of Epic poesy." This note is followed by an elaboration: "*Eliza Haywood*; this woman was authoress of those most scandalous books called the *Court of Carimania*, and the *New Utopia*." Thus in the first commentary on this portrait, Pope identifies Haywood by name and by class: he excoriates her for what and who she is and what and whom she represents.

A gloss on line 157 again attacks both women as a class and Haywood as a member of that class: the placing together of alternative prizes, Haywood and a chamberpot (jordan) is parallel to a scene in the *Iliad* 23 in which a lady and a kettle arc sct up as prizes. "There," Pope points out, "the preference in value is given to the *Kettle*, at which Mad. *Dacier* is justly displeased." Rectifying the Homeric error of judgment, Pope says, he treats "Mrs. *H* . . . with distinction, and acknowledge[s] her] to be the more valuable of the two" (2.157n). So the insult to Haywood is actually dictated by female critical judgment! Pope is all too happy to acquiesce to the point of view that Haywood is the more appropriate material reward for victory,

---

matter to make the revision. It is just not what I would say, and as this is a book about women's voices, I have to be true to my own. Readers who prefer the more colloquial expression, however, are invited to substitute it in the mind's eye and ear.

33   Pope, *The Dunciad Variorum*, book 2, lines 149–58, in *The Poems of Alexander Pope*, one-volume edition of the Twickenham text, ed. John Butt (New Haven, 1963), pp. 384–5. I quote from the *Variorum* in order to cite the glosses. In *The Dunciad in Four Books* published in 1743, the lines on Haywood occur slightly later in Book 2 (ll. 157–66), but remain the same. See *Poems*, p. 741.

and he points out that such acquiescence entails the agreement that kettle, jordan, and woman are of the same order of being: they receive the fluids of the male body; they contain the products and by-products of masculine appetite.

To reduce Haywood to such an object is to insist on an embodiment the author herself sought to escape. Her works, her words, were all of her self that she authorized for public consumption, and unlike her predecessors she chose not to draw attention—in her fiction anyway—to her own physical being, her desires, the state and condition of her body, the physical manifestations of the erotic passions she enjoyed in her life. Perhaps her presence on the stage belies the claim that her body was never a part of her public self-construction; but many of the roles she undertook point emphatically away from the physical self to the words on the page. One thinks, for example, of the characters she played in Henry Fielding's *Euridyce Hiss'd* and *Historical Register for 1737*—the Muse and Mrs. Novel respectively. In Haywood's fiction, words, names in particular, point to a moral reality that extends beyond the body of the text. Names seem, in fact, to disembody the characters, elevating them to the status of ideas in the way that allegory typically does. But unlike typical allegorical narratives, Haywood's fictions deal with a moral landscape in which all values are subject to redefinition. Her purpose, like the purpose of Behn and Manley before her, is to examine the effects of erotic passion on the lives of the characters she creates. And through nomenclature she elevates this examination to the status of a moral discourse responsive to the demands of lives complicated by increasing focus on the needs of the self as an economic as well as an erotic entity.

Haywood's first novel, *Love in Excess*, was published in 1719, the same year as Daniel Defoe's *Robinson Crusoe*, and it is no accident, I would argue, that the two enjoyed equally phenomenal success. Although the two works seem to be focused on entirely opposite aspects of the human experience—Crusoe's physical and moral challenge to survive and thrive in isolation as opposed to the effect on community of the pleasures and dangers of erotic love—in fact, the two narratives are strikingly similar in their moral thrust. In a sense, we can sum up the composite "message" of the two works thus: homo eroticus and homo economicus are one and the same being in the world of 1719, both driven by excessive desire, both in need of regulation and self- control in order to profit from that desire, both directed by the texts that contain them to consume rather than to be consumed.

Love in Excess begins with the end of the War of the Spanish Succession. Although the setting of the narrative is France, and the brothers who are the focal points of narrative interest are soldiers of the defeated army, the language in which the narrative is written is, of course, English and the readership would recognize a cause for national celebration in the triumph of Britain and her allies over the French and theirs. The displacement serves not to idealize the defeated, but to turn attention from military matters to matters of the heart, the domain of the French, but also now—in the time of the peace that follows the Treaty of Utrecht—the domain of the English as well. This shift from war to love, tied particularly to this conflict, becomes something of a cultural cliche in eighteenth-century England, as witnessed by Laurence Sterne's similar invocation of the pattern in *Tristram Shandy*; it is following the Peace of Utrecht, after all, that Uncle Toby can devote his attention to the Widow Wadman.

The significance of the movement of energy from war to love is specific to this conflict in England's history. The establishment of trade routes and other economic privileges that was part of the package of the settlement ensured England's dominance of trade and other capitalistic activity. While the exercise of military might and physical valor would be important components of the colonial enterprise, other skills were needed to turn the military triumph into a real source of global strength. In particular, desires of all kinds would have to be managed, disciplined, and directed. It is significant that examination of the wayward sexual desire attributed to both genders in the works of Behn and Manley yields in the fiction of Haywood and Defoe to concern about the focusing of desire and the necessary displacement of male sexual energy.

That such is the case in *Robinson Crusoe* is too evident to need elaboration here. That such is the case in *Love in Excess* is not so clear. After all, the entire novel seems to be *about* masculine erotic desire and the search for the appropriate "object" of that desire. But it is just that formulation that represents a shift in the depiction of passion, a shift that seems connected to the general positioning of men and women in a new kind of economy, one driven by the need to possess objects of worth and beauty. Although there are some scenes of reciprocity in *Love in Excess*, those scenes are outnumbered by tableaux that feature a woman as beloved object and a man as desiring voyeur. Part 1's "story within" concerning Brillian's love for Ansellina provides examples of both reciprocal desire featuring two subjects and masculine desire that objectifies the beloved in a frozen image.[34] The two declare their love for one another in an exchange of verses written, significantly, on the pedestal of a statue of Diana, the goddess of the hunt. Brillian writes of his unrequited passion: "*Hopeless, and silent, I must still adore / Her heart's more hard than stone whom I'd implore*." And Ansellina responds with a challenge: "*You wrong your love, while you conceal your pain, / Stones will dissolve with constant drops of rain*" (77). Her verse alludes, interestingly, to the final image in the fourth book of Lucretius's *De Rerum Natura* in which the poet explains that husband and wife will know contentment, not through passionate love, but through years of companionship, through "custome" in Lucy Hutchinson's translation: "So on hard rocks, still-dropping water weares / The solid stone, by its continued teares."[35]

This image of mutual affection born of long and close acquaintance is in direct contrast, however, to the kind of love experienced by Brillian whose adoration reaches its height as he beholds Ansellina "at her toilet" (81). He realizes that his romantic imagination—the very quality Lucretius warns against—is contributing at least in part to his admiration of his love. Nonetheless, he celebrates that moment as he recalls it for his brother D'elmont: "either it was my fancy, or else she really did look more amiable in that undress than ever I had seen her, tho' adorned with the utmost illustrations" (81). Further, he explains that his response—"those little delicacies, those trembling aking transports, which every sight of the beloved object

---

34 "Story within" is J. Paul Hunter's term. See *Before Novels: The Cultural Contexts of Eighteenth-Century Fiction* (New York, 1990), p. 47.

35 *Lucy Hutchinson's Translation of Lucretius*, book 4, lines 1320–21.

occasions"—are the very means by which one "distinguishes a real passion from a counterfeit" (82–3).

This kind of passion bears little resemblance to D'elmont's experience of love up to this point in the tale. He has felt passion for Amena, but, that having failed, he does not balk at marrying her rival, Alovisa. Indeed, we are told, "[a]mbition was certainly the reigning passion in his soul, and Alovisa's quality and vast possessions, promising a full gratification of that, he ne'er so much as wished to know, a farther happiness in marriage" (83). As it turns out, however, he will seek further happiness when his passion for Melliora is stimulated by moments of tableaux such as the one in which he watches her read Fontenelle's *Discourse Concerning the Plurality of Worlds*. In the work of Aphra Behn, this book of "natural history" would no doubt serve to counter D'elmont's romantic fantasy. Here, however, it is introduced only to be repudiated: "I am confident, had this author ever seen Melliora, his sentiments had been otherwise than now they seem to be, and he would have been able to write of nothing else but love and her" (109). He responds more positively to her later choice of reading matter, Ovid's *Epistles* (117), which he declares a sign that she has "come over to our party" (118). Deny that conclusion though she does, Melliora engages in a conversation with D'elmont regarding the demands of love versus those of friendship, a discussion that in effect conflates and inflates the two terms to idealized categories supported by literary examples and culminating in a final tableaux in which a sleeping Melliora reveals her desire for D'elmont as that young man watches her sleep. Finding his desire reciprocated, D'elmont presses for physical consummation, but Melliora, awake, resists, and the two are interrupted by the mischievous, also smitten, Melantha. Unfulfilled, but heightened desire, serves to propel both D'elmont's and the reader's interest through the remaining pages of the narrative (roughly half of the story remains to be told at this point). Haywood has settled on a formula of delayed gratification in pursuit of what's "better." And, as her name asserts, Melliora *is* better. In a sense, then, the driving force of D'elmont's passion remains ambition, not for contentment, but for whatever is "better" than what he currently has.

The names of D'elmont's first three mistresses seem to embody Haywood's thesis. Alovisa, a form of "Eloisa," invokes the medieval heroine, most familiar to Haywood's readers from John Hughes's 1714 *Letters of Abelard and Heloise* and Alexander Pope's 1717 poem "Eloisa to Abelard." The latter in particular emphasized Eloisa's desire and Alovisa, like Eloisa, is a passionate woman driven and ultimately destroyed by love. Unlike Eloisa, however, though she is a desiring subject, she is not the object of her lover's desire. Amena, her first rival, is pleasant, as her name suggests. And it is this benign sweetness that is the first threat to Alovisa's passion for D'elmont. Given the choice between Alovisa's aggressive desire and Amena's passive receptiveness, D'elmont prefers the latter, but in fact he feels no keen drive toward possession of either woman. Eventually, he marries Alovisa whose fortune appeals to his ambition. But that marriage is destroyed when D'elmont finally falls in love. Melliora offers something better. It is not asserted in the text that she actually will bring more fortune or prestige to D'elmont. Indeed, that does not seem to be the appeal. She is just, from his point of view, "better," and aiming for "better" is what this narrative, like its 1719 bookstall companion, *Robinson Crusoe*, is about.

Like *Robinson Crusoe, Love in Excess*, seeks to redeem the urge for advancement. Haywood does so by linking ambition and love, admitting that both can have disastrous consequences, but asserting, quite directly, that the obsessive drive toward possession of a beloved object is a trait of the noblest individuals: "*Covetousness, envy, pride, revenge*, are the effects of an earthy, base, and sordid nature, *ambition* and *love*, of an exalted one" (206). Here Haywood divorces ambition and love from nature, linking them instead with the divine, a sentiment that her use of image, sign, symbol, and word underscores. For, palpitating hearts, blushing countenances, heaving bosoms, distracted hair-pulling, notwithstanding, love is largely a matter of the disembodied imagination in this text; the hieroglyph that speaks to the mystery of love has been replaced, for D'elmont, by the cipher upon which the lover can project his or her fantasies of desire.

No scene so clearly illustrates the change that has occurred in "libertine" thought as that between D'elmont and Ciamara in the third volume. Ciamara is driven by fundamental physical passion, a kind of love, the narrator tells us "which aims chiefly at enjoyment, [and] in enjoyment ends" (250). This kind of love is denigrated in favor of that provoked by "interiour beauties" and the "divinity" of soul. It is this kind of love alone that will remain unsatiated by possession; through this kind of love between men and women "*sense* elevates itself to *reason*, the different powers unite and become pure alike" (250). Ciamara's opulent home is decorated with ceiling paintings and tapestries that depict famous mythological lovers: Venus and Adonis; Jupiter and Leda; Diana and Endimion; Cupid and Psyche (229). But these myths speak to loves among the gods, and humans who aim that high are sure to be disappointed. Ciamara's name commemorates the pain of unfulfilled love; Marah is the Hebrew word for "bitter," an adjective Naomi applies to herself after her husband and sons die: "Turn back my daughters, for I am too old to be married. Even if I thought there was hope for me, even if I were married tonight and I also bore sons, should you wait for them to grow up? . . . Oh no, my daughters! My lot is far more bitter than yours, for the hand of the Lord has struck out against me" (Ruth 1: 12–13). Hopelessness attends those who attach their dreams to high romantic myths. A new kind of myth features fulfillment in "a cottage," as D'elmont puts it (229), a love to which anyone can aspire just as D'elmont himself aspires to union with Melliora. Further it is, as Melliora's name suggests, a "better" love than "love in excess."

The story of D'elmont's pursuit of Melliora is punctuated with stories of others' pursuit of him, from Alovisa to Melantha to an unnamed woman who tantalizes him by dropping a valuable Angus Dei which he retrieves and returns only to be treated with the view of another image, a glimpse of her momentarily unveiled beautiful face. He is protected in this instance by "the image of Melliora, yet unenjoyed, all ravishingly kind and tender" (189) as he will be when Ciamara attempts to seduce him and when, at the end of the narrative, the sad, devoted, and doomed Violetta declares her love. If D'elmont's history suggests that love is within the reach of the ordinary mortal man, the experience of these women reveals that it often hovers just outside a woman's grasp. The kind of love that is in excess in this narrative is female desire. D'elmont chooses the object of his affection, but female lovers inspired by tableaux and romantic dreams find themselves ravaged by passions they cannot control and objects of affection they cannot command. The images and signs that male lovers employ to fuel their desire for the object of their passion are symbols of defeat for the desiring woman. D'elmont quotes verse to Melantha, but the lines do not serve seduction as did the poetic exchange between Brillian and Ansellina. Instead, they are cautionary lines, teaching her to be an object, warning her against her own desires: "All naturally fly, what does pursue / 'Tis fit men should be coy, when women woe [woo]" (138). And as Alovisa experiences the death of her husband's desire, she figures it as a movement from living being to image—the opposite of D'elmont's favorite means of invoking Melliora and the narrative drive of the text toward the consummation of that passion. For Alovisa, "the heroe, and the lover are extinct, and all that's left, of the once gay D'elmont, is a dull, senceless picture"(141)—a cipher that spells her annihilation as it disallows the animating projection of her desire. Convinced of D'elmont's passion for another woman, Alovisa takes revenge against his image: "She tore down the Count's picture which hung in the room, and stamped on it" (147), but ultimately it is she herself who is destroyed as she immolates herself on her husband's sword, a forced penetration that symbolically punishes her for the willfulness of her behavior, the aggressiveness with which she pursued and possessed D'elmont.

Love in Excess is but one among Haywood's fictions to employ allegorical tactics to map narrative structure and identify narrative theme. In *The Injur'd Husband*, for example, Beauclair's love for Montamour and friendship with her brother Vraimont represent the happy union of Beauty, Light (Enlightenment), Truth, and Great Love. Betsy Thoughtless, entrusted to her guardian, Mr. Goodman and her mentor Lady Trusty, nevertheless marries the unworthy Mr. Munden (mundane, worldly) with whom she is miserable, partly because of her belated recognition of her feelings for Mr. Trueworth. Names in Haywood's most famous novel are transparent, though the characteristics of Goodness or Worthiness are not transferable by marriage. Mrs. Mellasin does not become good by virtue of her union with Mr. Goodman; and though arguably Betsy's marriage to Munden does make her less thoughtless, it does not make her worldly or ordinary after his example. Betsy's marriage to Trueworth does not in itself change her, though it does nominally recognize the change she has already undergone. The names suggest a trajectory of development, an idealized plot of romance and love: the thoughtless, but good, young coquet should respond to true worth; she should guard against the vanity that could distract her and detract from her value. This theme of *Betsy Thoughtless* is so clear and pursued in such a straightforward manner that it may be partly responsible for the fact that the early reviewers found the novel dull and insipid: "how can we greatly interest ourselves in the fortune of one, whose character and conduct are neither truly amiable nor infamous, and which we can neither admire, nor love, nor pity, nor be diverted with?"[36]

The allegory of *Betsy Thoughtless*, like that of *Love in Excess*, highlights the conjunction of love and value. And, like *Love in Excess*, *Betsy Thoughtless* pursues in

---

36 "A Review of Miss Betsy Thoughtless," *Monthly Review* 5 (October 1752): 393–4. Reprinted as Appendix B in Eliza Haywood, *The History of Miss Betsy Thoughtless*, ed. Christine Blouch, Broadview Literary Texts (Peterborough, 1998), p. 638.

allegory a trajectory of improvement, inculcating, as it were, a valuing of aspiration and quest for "the better." The use of sign, symbol, and image in this narrative, moreover, argues tacitly for cultural agreement as to the nature of this "better," and in that fact represents a departure from the thesis of the earlier work in this regard. While D'elmont just sought something "better," Betsy Thoughtless must learn to identify what is truly worthy as well as learning to be truly worthy of desire. The novel suggests strongly that there is cultural consensus—not only in the legitimizing of desire for the better but also in the definition of the nature of "true worth" which includes sexual propriety, acceptance of sexual differences that mark that propriety (i.e. emphasis on modesty in women and valor in men), fiscal responsibility and stewardship in both sexes, and chastity prior to marriage, fidelity afterward for women and men alike, though masculine indiscretions are to be overlooked if they do occur.[37] Emotional excess, indeed excess of any kind, is to be avoided, the ideal being, as Lady Trusty explains, "a proper medium" in all things (495).

The presence of signs, symbols, and images that open themselves to allegorical interpretation point toward cultural consensus. In *Betsy Thoughtless* the very word "hieroglyphic" is used to draw our attention to shared cultural values represented by easily readable cultural codes. It occurs in a scene in which Trueworth's intended bride unwraps some cloth that is to be made into a dress. It is white damask which her brother, Sir Bazil, interprets as "an omen of marriage" (363). Harriot protests that he has converted a simple piece of cloth "into a hieroglyphic"—or, as Warburton would put it, into a "symbol of something else understood." [38] The white damask cloth is a sign of intention. No one misses the significance of the cloth; no one disputes its symbolic value. It is a cultural symbol that reveals its meaning clearly. If a mystery does persist, it is the mystery of marriage itself. What does marriage mean for Harriot, for any woman? Presumably, Sir Bazil uses the word "omen" as a synonym for "sign" or "symbol," but, in fact, the marriage foretold by the cloth indeed will turn out to be an ill-fated one. While Harriot becomes a bride, she does not live to be a wife. She dies three months after the wedding. Did the hieroglyph portend this dire event? Or is there a sense in which all wedding dresses are "omens of marriage" implying the death of the woman's self as she becomes first a bride, then a wife? Can a bride retain a sense of self, of strangeness, or must she be fully assimilated into the identity of her husband?

That the answer in *Betsy Thoughtless* is both no and yes is suggested by a "hieroglyph" associated with Betsy herself and deployed in reference to both her love for Trueworth and her disdain for Munden, her husband. The squirrel that Trueworth gives to Betsy is a sign of his love. Her valuing of the pet increases as she comes to value Trueworth more. On the other hand, Munden's violent, impulsive murder of the animal is an expression, not of his anger toward his rival Trueworth, but of his brutality and dangerous hostility toward his wife. Betsy has no trouble interpreting his behavior as a sign of his character and her condition: "'Monster!'— cried she,—'unworthy the name of man;—you needed not have been guilty of this

---

37 *The History of Miss Betsy Thoughtless*, ed. Christine Blouch, p. 495. Further references will be cited parenthetically.

38 *Divine Legation of Moses*, vol. 2, p. 92.

low piece of cruelty, to make me see to what a wretch I am sacrificed'" (508). The squirrel, like the white damask cloth, is a symbol, a substitution for "woman" which defines and proscribes her. In accepting the definition, the woman, in essence, erases herself. In *Betsy Thoughtless*, such erasure is not in itself presented as undesirable from the woman's point of view. In fact, Betsy increasingly longs to be absorbed into the identity of the man she loves. Yet marriage in and of itself is not enough to effect such union of sensibility and identity. Betsy may feel herself "sacrificed" in her marriage to "a wretch," but the fact that she can say as much indicates that, in her mind, she continues to occupy the subject position in the story of her life. The squirrel may be a hieroglyph of Betsy's love, but the pet's violent death is not an omen of Betsy's fate. Unlike Harriot, Betsy survives her marriage, and she does so because of her increasing awareness of the nature of her own desire .

Betsy represents the most complex signifier of the narrative. Her various mispositionings in contexts that suggest things about her character and behavior that are not in fact true are invoked for the didactic purpose of emphasizing the importance of clear signs to the value of the individual, particularly the individual marriageable woman. Defined as a coquet in the best of these dubious settings, a prostitute in the worst, Betsy is never morally compromised in the reader's judgment inasmuch as we are privy to all the circumstances that surround her decisions and behaviors. But the misreading of Betsy's character does cost her Trueworth's affection and attention; it does result in physical harm to those (men) who feel honor-bound to protect her; and it is responsible for the ill-fated marriage to which she finds herself consigned by default as Munden seems the best suitor after Trueworth's defection. In the beginning, Betsy is herself without desire, though she enjoys being the object of the desire of others. As the novel progresses, Betsy's passive enjoyment becomes an active pursuit an active pursuit of passivity, that is. Her own desire begins to formulate itself as a longing to be valued by a man of true worth.

Through the negative examples of Flora Mellasin and Miss Froward in terms of sexual appetite and the negative example of Mrs. Mellasin in terms of other kinds of material desire, the role of woman as actively desiring subject is cast in a highly negative light. In fact, Trueworth describes Flora's behavior as an effort "to enforce desire" in a male lover (381) rather than as a pursuit of her own sexual appetites, language that essentially denies her subjectivity by focusing on the masculine response. And, in essence, that is the disciplinary effect of the entire novel. Much female action stimulated by desire is punished in this text, either by plot complications that illustrate the negative consequences of such behavior or by the moralizings of an authoritative narrator who draws attention to the difficulties and dangers attendant on the occupation of the subject position. The didactic thrust of the novel is to recommend care of one's reputation, control of the signs that allow others to project value and therefore to long to possess.

The female characters in *Betsy Thoughtless* are ciphers, at best and at worst. At best, they reflect the desire of a truly good man for propriety, beauty, stability, and faithfulness. At worst, they hide perhaps horrible secrets of their own wayward, willful desire as Lady Mellasin illustrates. Goodman's mistake in reading such a character has material and moral consequences for him, as it would for any good man. Women's aggressive, acquisitive behavior is linked inevitably in this novel to transgression; even Betsy's purchasing of Trueworth's picture (an act stimulated by her growing recognition of the value of what she has lost) is tainted by illegitimacy, as the portrait is intended for his bride, Harriot. Through possession and contemplation of his image, Betsy does not so much nurture secret desires as she blunts the pain of a longing for something she is sure she has lost. Her fetishizing of Trueworth's image—her idol-worship, as it were—is indeed a sign of her waywardness. She is like the Israelites, deprived of the presence of Moses and God, who turn to the golden calf. But, as some rabbinic commentators read the building of the calf as a misguided expression of the need to worship rather than a sign of the perverse longing for an idol,[39] so we can see Betsy's possession of Trueworth's portrait as an expression of her need for worthy love and her regret at having recognized that need too late. She does not, after all, pursue her passion. She simply acknowledges it. Such acknowledgment without action seems the path of redemption in the world depicted in this novel. Betsy is rewarded in the end with true worth both in what she values and in the value she has accrued.

Eliza Haywood's own life refuses, but does not refute, the "lesson" of *Betsy Thoughtless*. Haywood left herself a cipher open to the worst constructions. She did not, as did Behn and Manley, make any effort to explain or justify her unconventional life; she did not renounce her early fiction or defend herself against charges of licentiousness. Her later fiction, long seen as a repudiation of her early work, has been read so by critics wishing to project a narrative of redemption onto the life and career of the writer who left us so little evidence of the way she "constructed" herself. In fact, she wrote to a market; she wrote to please; and what she seems to have understood about the nature of the market she addressed was the need of readers and lovers alike to project their own desires onto an object. Her later fiction did not capitalize on secrets and mysteries; it offered moral plots with clear didactic messages onto which a reading public could project their fantasies of control.[40] The blank that was her life, however, allowed a different kind of projection—one revealing a hostility and violence toward female desire that will become increasingly evident as the century progresses.

Bridegroom of Blood

Hostility speaks to cultural tension—seismic shifts, as it were—which allegory can be invoked to mask or to attempt to clarify, as we have seen in the fiction of Eliza Haywood. Such tension can call to mind the ethical relation, but in the end it eludes ethics. Demands of nation, in particular, may simply deny us the luxury of hearing another's voice, may prevent us from speaking clearly in our own.

---

39   See Plaut, p. 650, and Nehama Leibowitz, *New Studies in Shemot*, trans. Aryeh Newman (2 vols, Jerusalem, 1996), vol. 2, pp. 549–51.

40   Significantly, Warburton pursues a similar strategy in *Divine Legation*. Staking out a position of moderation between those who would level all religions to the same ground and those who would divorce the Christian religion from its Jewish foundation, Warburton insists on allegorical readings of those texts (like the book of Job, for example) that would challenge his overarching thesis if read as historical accounts of individuals. See Lamb, pp. 3–5.

Imagine a man estranged from his people, and exiled. This man marries a woman in the land he inhabits. He is so grateful to her and her father for giving him succor and shelter and purpose that he names his first son in honor of their treatment of him. He is not striving to remember his former identity. He is content to be the welcome stranger. Suddenly, though, this man receives a message he cannot ignore. He is to return to his people who are themselves in a strange land. He is to lead them from that land to another in order to form a nation. He sets out with his wife and his son to accomplish this task.

This leader of course, is Moses; his wife is Zipporah; his son, Gershom. The three are at the center of what Robert Alter has called "the most enigmatic episode in all of Exodus."[41] It is, as he says, a "haunting and bewildering story"[42] Moses, in compliance with the demand of God, is returning to Egypt with his small family— his Midianite wife and their sons:

> At a night encampment on the way, the Lord encountered him and sought to kill him. So Zipporah took a flint and cut off her son's foreskin, and touched his legs with it, saying 'You are truly a bridegroom of blood to me!' And when He let him alone, she added, 'A bridegroom of blood because of the circumcision.' (Exodus 4: 24–6)

There are many perplexities in this brief passage. It is not clear from the pronouns themselves whether it is Moses or the child that "the Lord" seeks to kill; indeed, as Richard Elliott Friedman has pointed out, it is not clear that the Lord seeks to kill anyone as a more literal translation of the Hebrew in Exodus 4: 24 would read thus: "And he was on the way, at a lodging place, and YHWH met him, and he asked to kill him."[43] Friedman, indeed, posits that Moses may be seeking his own death in this obscure and bewildering episode.[44] It is not clear whose legs Zipporah touches with the severed foreskin; it is not clear whom "He" leaves alone at the end. Or, perhaps it is Moses that ceases to importune God—and "he let Him alone," rather than the reverse.[45] There are further confusions regarding interpretation. Why has the child remained uncircumcised to this point? What does the touching of the legs (or feet in some translations) mean? Why does Zipporah call Moses a "bridegroom of blood"? Why does she repeat the phrase, adding what seems to be a redundant explanation? Are the final words even her words? Alter follows the JPS translation by rendering the passage thus: "Then did she say, 'A bridegroom of blood by the circumcising.'" Tikva Frymer-Kensky, however, sees the ending reference to circumcision as an editorial explanation on the part of the narrator, rather than Zipporah's actual words:

---

41 *The Five Books of Moses: A Translation with Commentary* (New York, 2004), p. 330 n. 24.

42 Ibid.

43 This is Friedman's translation.

44 Friedman points out that Elijah and Jonah ask God for death, and Jeremiah bluntly asserts that death is preferable to assuming the prophetic task. *Commentary on the Torah*, pp. 184–5.

45 Again, Friedman's view. The imprecision of the pronoun references makes this reading perfectly plausible, even compelling.

"Then she said 'A bridegroom of blood' about the circumcision."[46] Needless to say, the Hebrew text does not include quotation marks at all. To add another bit of confusion, Zipporah speaks an unusual dialect. What she says ("bridegroom of blood") is reported in an "unique Hebrew phrase '*hatan damim*' for which no parallel has been found in ancient Near Eastern literature."[47] Friedman sees her act as "a passionate response to her husband's wish to die: You have a wife! You have a son, who should live to marry and be part of the covenant!" Finally, there is even some uncertainty about whom Zipporah addresses. Is she talking to her husband? Or is she talking to God?[48] Or both? Or one in the first instance, the other in the second?

How to explain? Commentary turns to Arabic for one explanation to elucidate "bridegroom of blood": "the word . . . *chatan* is related to the Arabic *chatana*, a circumciser, suggesting that there was a connection between marriage and circumcision. H. Junker has shown that in the Arabic realm circumcision was a prerequisite for marriage (hence the etymological bond). The rite resembled the bringing of first fruits and represented an offering of blood which cleansed and atoned."[49] W. Gunther Plaut, however, summarizes the standard interpretation: "The majority of commentators have held, however, that Moses' omission to have his child circumcised was the reason for the attack and that God, through a messenger, was the one who threatened to punish him. Moses, so it is argued, had lived under Midianite law—hence the child was called *her* son—and circumcision of young children may not have been the custom in that land."[50] Of course, it is more than custom for the children of Israel, and as Moses sets forth to found a nation that will occupy the land promised to Abraham, Isaac, and Jacob, he must adopt the distinctive patterns of life and behavior that define his people. Zipporah's enigmatic cry is probably a cry of frustration at the illness that has descended on her husband during a time of already difficult change; her repetition and explanation of the phrase "bridegroom of blood" can be heard as spoken in a softer register, as a sign of increased intimacy once the danger of illness is past. The illness that threatened the family has strengthened their bond, their closeness.[51] The circumcision, a covenantal sign, indicates that the bond is of spiritual and national, not simply domestic, import. Zipporah and Moses had been living as Midianites; they now define themselves by a clear and certain sign as Israelites in covenant with the God of Abraham.[52]

Zipporah, like Esther, is a skillful reader of situation and a proficient communicator—especially in the language of gesture. Like Esther, she has her own private language, signified by the "unique" expression she utters twice during her

---

46   Frymer-Kensky, p. 29.

47   *Etz Hayim: Torah and Commentary* (New York, 2001), Exodus 4: 25 n.

48   Frymer-Kensky, pp. 30–31.

49   Quoted in Plaut, pp. 415–16.

50   *The Torah: A Modern Commentary*, p. 415.

51   I am indebted to Rabbi Scott Saulson for this reading. E-mail exchange 18 February 2006.

52   As Plaut points out, many Eastern civilizations practiced circumcision (416 n.3). Yet, for all the cloudiness of this episode, its clear intent is to firmly establish Moses himself (through his own or his child's literal or symbolic circumcision) as a member of the tribe of Abraham.

husband's illness and recovery. Like Esther, Zipporah also asserts her identity through those with whom she lives. The child is "her son"; Moses is the "bridegroom," both denominated in relation to her. And, like Esther again, Zipporah does retain her own identity. In Zipporah's case, however, such self-preservation may not be entirely her own choosing. After the crisis in the wilderness, she and her children apparently return to Midian at Moses' desire. They reappear at the Israelite encampment at Sinai, after the Exodus from Egypt, brought by Zipporah's father, Jethro, perhaps in an effort to reunite the family. There is a new son, Eliezer, whose conception presumably predated the Exodus, but whose birth occurs afterwards as his name attests. Literally, the name means "(My) God is help," but the biblical text explains more fully why the name was chosen, glossing "Eliezer" thus: "The God of my father was my help, and He delivered me from the sword of Pharaoh" (Exodus 18: 4). We might expect a joyful meeting, as perhaps Jethro intends, after such separation and such difficulties, but, if so, we are disappointed. Moses simply inquires of his father-in-law as to the health and wellbeing of his wife and sons. He speaks with Jethro about the organization of a judiciary council, heeds Jethro's advice, and bids him farewell. Jethro, his daughter, and his grandsons return to their own land. If we read Zipporah's gesture of ceremonial circumcision as an acceptance of the identity and customs of her husband, a taking on of covenantal responsibilities for her own and her family's sake as well as for his, her return to Midian is heartrending. Having accepted the identity of her husband and her husband's people, she is now to be severed from him and them. She returns to her father's home with her sons whose bodies and whose names serve as perpetual reminders that she is now a stranger in her own land.

When Sensibility supplants Libertinism as the prevailing ethos of British culture, eighteenth-century women writers too find themselves in a world they do not recognize, speaking in voices not their own. Like Zipporah, like Eliza Haywood, they become aliens in the country they call "home."

Chapter 5

His Sister's Song

In 1990, I taught a course entitled "Women and Literature" to a group of college sophomores, juniors, and seniors, most of whom were not English majors. I taught the course as a survey of eighteenth-century women novelists. We began with Jane Austen's *Persuasion* and worked backwards from Frances Burney's *Evelina*, to Sarah Scott's *Millenium Hall*, to Sarah Fielding's *David Simple* to Aphra Behn's *Love Letters Between a Nobleman and His Sister*. In spite of what I still regard as the aphoristic truth of Brigid Brophy's remark that "the most fascinating subjects in the universe are sex and the eighteenth century," the choice of material for this particular class was probably a mistake.[1] The students' needs and interests would have been better served by a more contemporary and a more contemporarily feminist syllabus. Still, there was one moment that has stuck with me for over fifteen years. It happened late in the term, during the two-week period in which we discussed Behn's *Love Letters*. A student who was also taking a course in the Victorian novel came up to me after class and asked me this question: "What happened?" As she elaborated on that theme, it became clear that her perplexity could be better stated thus: "Since Aphra Behn had, in Virginia Woolf's words, earned women the right to speak their minds, why did they stop doing so during the nineteenth century?[2] Why did the fiction of that time, even fiction written by women, depict so many suffering angelic women or demonized transgressive women?" To me, today, the question seems to encompass this book's prevailing concern: "What had happened to female desire, subjectivity, and agency?"

At the time, I explained the shift as an unhappy result of the rise of sentimentalism. And despite the refinements and sophistications introduced over the past fifteen or so years into our formulations and estimations of sentimentalism and sensibility, I stand by that explanation. Sometimes the easy answer, it seems to me, is the right answer. That sentimentalism silenced women writers on the subject of female desire is, I maintain, irrefutable. Yet the more complicated phenomenon has to do with the echo of women's voices preserved in the works of mid-century male writers who sing, as it were, their sisters' songs.

The Song at the Sea

After the Israelites cross the Sea of Reeds to freedom, Moses sings a song of victory known as the Song at the Sea (*Shirat ha-Yam*) or more simply as Song (*Shirah*).

---

1   Review of *Fanny Hill*, *New Statesman* (15 November 1963), p. 710.
2   Woolf's comment is in *A Room of One's Own* (San Diego, 1929), p. 66.

As one standard commentary notes, the Song "does not celebrate the splitting of the sea. It celebrates the Israelites' commitment to faith in God after experiencing the splitting of the sea."[3] It documents belief that God intervenes in human affairs on behalf of his people. The poem is powerful and unusual. The original Hebrew is strikingly descriptive and the poetic effects stunningly distinctive. As W. Gunther Plaut has said, "no translation can fully render its special flavor, its rare poetic forms, its alliterations and assonances . . . The internal rhythm of the strophes is also hard to reproduce in translation: they alternate between couplets, triplets, and quatrains and end in a single line . . . which comes as a sudden and glorious climax, the final bars in a great poetic symphony "[4] Liturgically, the poem is emphasized by a special trope and also by the requirement that worshipers stand during its public recitation—an honor accorded only one other passage from the Torah, the Ten Commandments.

The Song dramatically affirms the special care of God and the Israelites' faith and gratitude. It also links Moses' leadership to poetic prophecy—a connection that will also distinguish David, king of Israel and, by tradition, author of the Psalms. Moses' authorship of the Song at Sea has never been firmly established, of course, but tradition holds the Song in such high regard, and its linguistic markers are so unusual, that without the certainty of specific authorship, scholars nevertheless tend to favor the explanation that the poem (despite some references that seem in various ways anachronistic) is of ancient origin and that it is "most likely in substance his own, speaking in accents of his own age and out of the overwhelming marvel of the salvation he and his people had witnessed."[5]

The Song is lengthy—eighteen verses. It is introduced with the statement that "Moses and the Israelites sang this song to the Lord," all singing as though in one voice: "I will sing to the Lord, for He has triumphed gloriously; / Horse and driver he has hurled into the sea" (Exodus 15: 17). The song ends with the triumphant assertion that "The Lord will reign for ever and ever!" (Exodus 15: 18) Between beginning and end, the song makes reference to the dramatic events of the parting of the sea and the drowning of Pharaoh's army; it looks forward to the establishing of sanctuary and nation. It lovingly and memorably expresses amazement and gratitude for God's unique power and his special dispensation: "Who is like You, O Lord, among the celestials; / Who is like You, majestic in holiness, / Awesome in splendor, working wonders!" (Exodus 15: 11). It is a song that unites singer, people, God, past, present, future. It is followed by a prose summary of the events just witnessed: "For the horses of Pharaoh, with his chariots and horsemen, went into the sea; and the Lord turned back on them the waters of the sea; but the Israelites marched on dry ground in the midst of the sea" (Exodus 15: 19). From prelude, through poem, to summary, chapter 15 of Exodus seems so complete a moment that we cannot help but

---

3   *Etz Hayim*, Exodus 14: 31–15:1 n.

4   *The Torah: A Modern Commentary*, p. 491.

5   Ibid. Plaut also summarizes the scholarly challenges to this position in the discussion on this page. This rabbinic commentary represents a liberal approach to tradition. The standard Orthodox view, of course, is that Moses is the inspired author of all of Torah. Therefore, for traditional commentators, the authorship of the Song and the period at which it was written are not subjects of debate.

wonder about the final two verses. Everything is done, celebrated, and summed up, yet there is a singer who is not finished: "Miriam the prophetess, Aaron's sister, took a timbrel in her hand, and all the women went out after her in dance with timbrels. And Miriam chanted for them, 'Sing to the Lord, for He has triumphed gloriously; / Horse and driver He has hurled into the sea'" (Exodus 15: 20–1).

There are many mysteries in these brief verses. Why is Miriam called "Aaron's sister" and not "Moses' sister"? Why is she called a prophetess? Why is she named for the first time here? In Exodus 2, when she plays a key role in saving her brother's life from the Pharaoh's edict that all the Israelite infant boys should be put to death, she is called "his sister" and "the girl." Now, she has a name. Do we assume she is the same sister? What does it mean that the women have timbrels? Certainly, there is a tradition of dance and song in ancient Israel's worship practices. But why do only the women dance here? And were they so certain of their successful escape from Egypt that they took timbrels with them in preparation for the celebration to follow? Why does Miriam sing only the first two lines of the song that Moses sang? Is she echoing him? Or does her song, which includes none of the seemingly anachronistic details in the longer song, actually predate his? Is Moses' song an elaboration of Miriam's song? Is Moses singing his sister's song?

Most of these questions are addressed by commentary to, ultimately, the same end. There seems to be something missing here—information we have simply lost. As Tikva Frymer-Kensky has put it: "The Pentateuch . . . preserves traces of what appear to have been far more extensive traditions about the prophet Miriam, one of the three leaders of Israel."[6] Similarly, Plaut acknowledges "[t]he tradition that preserved Miriam's song may have had a separate source in which Aaron and Miriam were closely linked with each other, a bond at which Numbers 12 hints, where Aaron and Miriam conspire against Moses."[7] Of course, it is in Numbers 12 that the Mosaic tradition wins out. Miriam and Aaron are annoyed with Moses on two counts. First, there is this Cushite wife of his. "'He married a Cushite woman!'" they exclaim in disapproval (Numbers 12: 1). What the point of their disapproval is remains unclear, though the feminine singular form of the verb "spoke against" (va-t'dabber) points clearly enough to Miriam's being the instigator of the protest. Rashi thinks Miriam is voicing concern for Moses' wife whom she feels Moses neglects in favor of his role as leader of the people.[8] Others feel the statement points to disapproval of the wife herself—perhaps as a dark-skinned foreigner ("Cushite" being a common reference to Nubians or Ethiopians). In any event, Miriam's querulousness does not end with complaints concerning her sister-in-law. Indeed, she and Aaron move quickly to what would seem to be the true source of their discontent: "'Has the Lord spoken only through Moses? Has He not spoken through us as well?'" (Numbers 12: 2). Moses is humble, but God is not, and, in Moses' presence, the Lord chastises the siblings severely, telling them clearly the difference between his address to them and

---

6   *Reading the Women of the Bible*, p. 327.

7   Plaut, 490 n.20.

8   It should be noted, too, that there is disagreement as to whether this Cushite refers to a wife Moses has taken in addition to his Midianite wife Zipporah or to Zipporah herself, Cushan being a Midianite tribe. See, for example, *Etz Hayim*, Numbers 12: 1 n.

his conversations with Moses. With an ordinary prophet, "I speak . . . in a dream"; with Moses, "I speak mouth to mouth, plainly and not in riddles" (Numbers 12: 6, 8). Having said as much, the Lord leaves, blasting Miriam with a leprosy that turns her skin white as snow. [9] Aaron is horrified when he turns to his sister and sees her covered with scales. He pleads with Moses, and Moses, in turn, pleads with God: "O God, pray heal her!" God agrees reluctantly: "If her father spat in her face, would she not bear her shame for seven days? Let her be shut out of camp for seven days, and then let her be readmitted" (Numbers 12: 14). At Moses' direction, we assume, the people wait patiently for her period of shame to end. Miriam's healing and her readmission to community having been realized, all march forward to a new encampment in Paran.

In this episode, Miriam is not permanently dishonored, but she is chastened and relegated to a lesser prophetic sphere than her brother Moses with such divinely attributed violence that we might legitimately suspect one tradition is ousting another with undue force. Within the dominant narrative, Miriam retains a place, but only at the will of Moses. It is significant that Moses himself does not take umbrage at anything Miriam does or says, however. He is quiet throughout the entire episode, except for the moment he turns to God and pleads for his sister's life. She may be silenced, but Moses honors her. Perhaps he is remembering the Song at the Sea or perhaps he is thinking back to a moment before that—the moment his sister spoke to Pharaoh's daughter and said "shall I go and get you a Hebrew nurse to suckle the child for you?" (Exodus 2:7). God speaks to Moses mouth to mouth without riddles. The Torah, on the other hand, records no direct conversation between Miriam and Moses at all. Nevertheless, whether Miriam's Song was an echo of Moses' Song or vice versa, it is clear that there would have been no song at all had Miriam been silent. Whatever Moses says and does, he is, in a very real sense, always singing Miriam's song.

Conversing With Richardson in the Voice of a Woman

The same can be said of the eighteenth-century's most important creator of narrative centered on women's experiences—Samuel Richardson. His complex relationship with the women of his time is informed by a dynamic similar to that which we see in the Mosaic narrative. He honors women, and he advocates for women. But tradition deemed him the more important prophet, and both his status and the roles he explored for women in his fictional worlds served to drown out the voices of the actual women of his time.

Samuel Richardson was undeniably supportive of his female friends' literary ambitions. Witness his advice to Sarah Fielding that "Mr. Dodsley advertise the cry [sic], on the filling of the town" and his attendant moan of regret: "I cannot bear that a piece which has so much merit and novelty of design in it, should slide

---

9   Friedman sees this as "a provocative case of punishment to suit the crime and a powerful biblical statement regarding racism. It is as if God says to Miriam: 'You don't like a woman with dark pigmentation? Then you don't have to have *any* pigmentation!'" (Numbers 12: 10 n)

into oblivion."[10] He was characteristically sympathetic with regard to society's diminishing of female talent and achievement. When Margaret Collier complains that she has been supposed the author of Henry Fielding's *Voyage to Lisbon* because it falls so short of that writer's usual performance, Richardson commiserates. Of course, he also blames women themselves for this state of affairs: "the capable ones . . . hide their talents in a napkin, and are afraid . . . of shewing themselves capable of the perfections they are mistresses of."[11] He castigates such "*degraders* of their own sex" and wonders that their concern for masculine approval would drive them to conceal their strengths: "Unworthy of such blessings, let such men not dare to look up to merits so superior to their own; and let them enter into contract with women, whose sense is as diminutive as their own souls. What loss would a woman of high attainments and of genius have, in a man of character so low, as to be afraid of the perfections of the woman who would give him the honor of calling her his!"[12]

As I will discuss more fully later, Richardson's fiction indicates that his own attitude toward female superiority was more complicated than his remarks to Collier suggest. And perhaps her imbibing of that complexity through Richardson's novels accounts for some of Collier's perplexity. The moral universe Richardson creates in his fiction would value such female strength, but, as she points out in her letter of response, the manners and morals of real men have not been as yet transformed by Richardsonian ideals. Even "men of real good sense, great parts, and many fine qualities . . . are . . . afraid of rivalship of understanding in their wives":

> Where shall we find husbands for our dear uncommon geniuses of girls?—Are not they under a kind of necessity (if they ever intend to marry) to continue their napkins in plaits before marriage nor ever dare to unfold them, even after marriage, to the generality of men, except they could meet with a noble-minded Sir Charles Grandison, or such as have grace enough to endeavour to tread in his steps.[13]

Here Collier articulates the dilemma for women of sense and ability, but her admiration for Richardson, I would suggest, makes it problematic for her to insist on the acuteness and accuracy of her own perception in the face of his moral—indeed ethical—ideals. So she seeks, seemingly, an occasion to demonstrate the existence of the kind of reciprocity Richardson advocates and she finds it in the "good old folks" with whom she boards in her retreat on the Isle of Wight.

These are uneducated people, and Collier's appreciation for their kindness is accompanied by a sense of her own social superiority; the posture she characteristically strikes with regard to this couple and her situation on the Isle of Wight in general is one of benevolent condescension. She adopts a tone of gracious acquiescence to

---

10 Samuel Richardson to Sarah Fielding, January 17, 1757, in *The Correspondence of Samuel Richardson, Author of Pamela, Clarissa, and Sir Charles Grandison*, ed. Anna Letitia Barbauld (6 vols, London, 1804), vol. 2, pp. 108–9.

11 Samuel Richardson to Margaret Collier, December 24, 1755, Ibid., vol. 2, pp. 81–2. He continues to complain about female "napkin'd talents" in his January 5, 1756, letter to Collier, vol. 2, pp. 92, 92–4.

12 Ibid., vol. 2, pp. 82–3.

13 Margaret Collier to Samuel Richardson, February 11, 1756, Ibid., vol. 2, pp. 97–8.

unhappy circumstances, including the circumstance of having as her most constant companions "minds . . . innocent and ignorant of the world."[14] Collier reads *Clarissa* and *Sir Charles Grandison* to them and is entertained by their observations and interest in the narratives. The couple, she tells Richardson, "believe both Clarissa and Sir Charles to be real stories." "[A]nd I don't care to undeceive them," she declares, just before describing them as individuals who, in their humble way, illustrate Richardson's ideal: "They love each other, and the husband rejoices in the balance of sense being on her side, which it is, in some degree, and glories in her being able to read and write, which he can scarcely do."[15]

Collier's vague discomfort with the notion of female intellectual superiority may speak as much to cultural mythologies as it does to social realities, for suspiciousness about women's reasoning is fundamental to a culture built around originary narratives that emphasize the destructive power of woman's unfettered curiosity.[16] The myth of Pandora and, most potently, the story of Eve's seduction and seductiveness lurk just beneath the surface of any eighteenth-century representation of woman's reasoning and provide a linkage in the minds of typical readers and writers of the period between female learning and female licentiousness.[17] The separation of these two ideas was no small task for Richardson to undertake, but undertake it he did, in his first work of narrative fiction, the story of an educated and morally superior servant girl.

Devices and Desires

In some sense, the separation of female learning and female lasciviousness seems the prevailing preoccupation of Richardson's novelistic career. Success would not come immediately, for readers were quick to perceive in Pamela too much wit to accord with proclaimed innocence. In fact, the two most famous anti-*Pamela*s target the heroine's self-awareness and perceptual acuity rather than her social overreaching. A character so precociously intelligent and observant, both Henry Fielding and Eliza Haywood assert, cannot be as innocent as Richardson maintains—not in life, anyway. Her story is a romantic fiction, the truth of which is exposed similarly by Fielding and Haywood. Fielding's Shamela and Haywood's Syrena are in confederacy with their mothers (and in Fielding's case, a lover too) to exploit male sexual desire for female profit. Innocence is the disguise by which they dupe their prey.

Shamela is deservedly known as the best of the anti-*Pamela*s, and as pure parody, it is unparalleled. Fielding's invocation and "explanation" of scenes from the novel itself, his narrative's brevity in contrast to the original's prolixity, the edgy exuberance of the names he substitutes—Shamela, Squire Booby, Parson Tickletext—economically expose the chief vulnerabilities of Richardson's text—its weighty seriousness and unconscious moral dubiety. Haywood agrees with Fielding,

---

14   Margaret Collier to Samuel Richardson, December 31, 1755, Ibid., vol. 2 pp. 99–100.

15   Ibid., vol. 2, p. 89.

16   For a discussion of the tradition of satire against women's learning, see Felicity A. Nussbaum, *The Brink of All We Hate*, pp. 148–58.

17   Ibid., pp. 15, 27, 124, 135.

particularly on the latter count. But her anti-*Pamela* is not a parody so much as it is an antidote "which has really its Foundation in Truth and Nature" as *Pamela*, the implication is, does not. So Haywood's Syrena Tricksy was "train'd up to deceive and betray all those whom her Beauty should allure."[18] "Innocence . . . never forsook her Countenance" (1), and she "excell'd the most experienc'd Actresses on the Stage, in a lively assuming all the different Passions that find Entrance in a Female Mind" (2). She is the opposite of Richardson's Pamela, a character of "Feign'd Innocence" and "Mock-Modesty" (two alternate subtitles, title page and 1) whose skill at deception calls Pamela's own virtue into question.

In Richardson's *Pamela*, the heroine's reading and writing argue for her innocence. Her unselfconscious, open epistolary style commands the reader's trust. Her chosen reading is characterized by simplicity and piety. Her "reading" of events is similarly innocent. Reluctant to draw conclusions from the evidence she sees, Pamela remains guiltless of the kind of intellectual control that asserts authority. This point is particularly intriguing, for even as Richardson's central character fails to "make sense" of the events of her narrative, readers (male and female alike) are provided textual evidence that encourages—indeed demands—judgment of character and circumstance. The reader who remains as innocent as Pamela misses much of the pleasure provided by the text.

In fact, the very genesis of *Pamela* draws attention to the contradiction at the heart of a tale about an unselfconscious young woman who writes her own story. Richardson's *Familiar Letters* was not designed to instruct readers in articulating the sincere outpourings of their hearts. Instead, it was meant to teach decorous and appropriate self-construction to be shared with others of like moral sensibility. Such self-construction, of course, would reinforce the morality, the matrix of middle-class virtue, that Richardson was helping to establish as normative. Richardson's belief in the conjoining of sincerity and rhetorical skill is far from naive; nevertheless, it is a belief open to the ridicule of skeptics who were quick to point out that "feign'd innocence" or "mock modesty" effectively presented are indistinguishable from true innocence and true modesty. Pamela *must* be self-conscious in order to write so eloquently, but her posture of passivity denies the control she exercises.

Not surprisingly, Hubert Gravelot and Francis Hayman's authorized illustrations for the octavo edition of *Pamela* conspire with Richardson to reinforce the notion of Pamela's passivity. Only two of the twenty-nine plates show Pamela's letters, and in both Mr. B holds the epistle. In the first illustration, Pamela looks demurely downward as Mr. B holds a letter she has written; in the second (for volume 3), she does not look so shy. She looks at Mr. B, but again he is the dominant actor in the scene, holding a letter with one hand and reaching out to touch her with the other in a gesture of possessive affection. Joseph Highmore's unauthorized, but admiring, paintings, nine in all, depict only one scene in which a letter appears (see frontispiece). The caption to the eighteenth-century engraving of this painting buttresses the image's reverential treatment of the heroine with a justification of her behavior: "Pamela is represented in this first Piece, writing in her late Lady's dressing

---

18   *Anti-Pamela: Or, Feign'd Innocence Detected, in a Series of Syrena's Adventures* (London, 1741), p. 3. Further references will be cited parenthetically in the text.

room, her History being known only by her Letters."[19] The defensiveness of the final clause speaks to a reluctance to acknowledge the obvious. In an epistolary novel dominated by the letters of one character, the main action is writing, but the images officially associated with the narrative are depictions of the scenes she describes, not the act of describing itself. Philip Mercier's two representations of Pamela suggest why. In one, he shows Pamela rising from her bed, revealing a bare left breast and right thigh, an inkpot, candle, and letter on the nightstand.[20] The second illustration is of Pamela putting on a stocking in a similarly seductive posture; in this case an opened book rests on the nightstand, continuing the association between female learning and female sexuality.

Mercier's Pamela is a combination of innocence and seductiveness, the very quality exhibited by Richardson's tale according to some critics. The anonymous author of *Pamela Censur'd* in particular complains of Richardson's deceptiveness, his posture as editor, not author of inflammatory scenes he calls moral. Pamela herself, according to this author, "instead of being artless and innocent sets out at first with as much Knowledge of the Arts of the Town, as if she had been born and bred in *Covent Garden*."[21] Eliza Haywood, too, asserts the deliberate subterfuge and hidden motives masked by Pamela's innocence. Her examination is a fully developed narrative, centered on the use and abuse of female wit.

For Haywood's anti-Pamela, Syrena Tricksy, motive is simple and comprehensive. This young woman, as her mother puts it, is to make her fortune "either by Marriage or Settlement equal to it" (26). To this end, Syrena "had both a Genius and Inclination to make the most of her Men" (48), and the subterfuge she employs to do so is ensured by her improbable face, her one true gift:

> what was most to be admired in her was, that the Innocence which is inseparable from Infancy, and which is so charming, even in the plainest Children, never forsook her Countenance; but continued to dwell in every little Turn and Gesture long after she came to Maturity, and had been guilty of Things, which one would think should have given her the boldest and most audacious Air. (1–2)

Her letters of course reveal her to be anything but innocent, though the narrative does chronicle a growth of sorts—increasing interpretive and manipulative skills. In the beginning, Syrena is a bit naive, using her power over her first lover to "wheedle

---

19   The engravings after Highmore are by Antoine Benoit and Louis Truchy. See Tom Keymer and Peter Sabor (eds), *The Pamela Controversy: Criticisms and Adaptations of Samuel Richardson's "Pamela" 1740–50* (6 vols, London, 2001), vol. 2, pp. 335–48.

20   This painting exists in two states. Peter Sabor discusses the visual representations of *Pamela* in his contribution to *Prose Criticism and Visual Representations*, vol. 2 of *The Pamela Controversy*, pp. xxxiv–xli.

21   *Pamela Censured: in a Letter to the Editor: Shewing that under the Specious Pretence of Cultivating the Principles of Virtue in the Minds of the Youth of both Sexes, the Most Artful and Alluring Amorous Ideas are convey'd* (London, 1741), pp. 21–2; reprinted in *The Pamela Controversy*, vol. 2, pp. 35–6. See Tom Keymer's remarks on the various ways one can read this anonymous work: as a "moralizing attack on *Pamela*'s eroticism . . . as an opportunistic work of pornography . . . as perhaps the most ingenious of the marketing ploys surrounding *Pamela*" (p. xv).

out of him" "a very genteel Snuff-Box . . . of *Pinchbeck*'s Metal, which she mistook for Gold" (39), but when she presses her luck, demanding that he pawn his watch in order to give her five guineas, he abandons her (40–5).

Syrena manages subsequent affairs more skillfully, carefully weighing what each lover has to offer and which offer is most advantageous to her. She and her mother "work" together, plotting, scheming, interpreting, revising each other's accounts and judgments, collaborating on new plans to seduce a fortune. Their letters explore the possibilities, lay out the strategies, speculate on the consequences. These letters also undermine their projects, as "having trusted the Secret of their Design to Pen and Paper" (107) from time to time reveals their connivances and contrivances to those they would impose upon. Syrena eventually learns enough to take the possibility of discovery into account when writing or receiving letters.[22] But she cannot develop an innocence that would truly protect her; it is not in her nature to do so (is it in anyone's?). She is cunning and her intelligence combined with her gender, her social class, and her aspirations make her a danger to men.

It would be difficult to argue, however, that Haywood's *Anti-Pamela* seriously condemns female intelligence. In fact, just the opposite seems to be the case. The men in the narrative are duped by Syrena's beauty, their desire for her, and their own need to see innocence in woman's form, but the women she encounters are not so befuddled by her or their responses to her. In the final episode, Syrena is outwitted by "a Woman no less cunning, tho' more virtuous than herself" (270) who successfully intercedes when her husband forms an attachment to Syrena. She does so by contriving to raise the jealousy of another married woman—a plot that eventuates in Syrena's arrest and deportation to Wales "where what befel her, must be the Subject of future Entertainment" (281). The fact that Syrena remains unrepentant is the moral point of this ending, but in making the point Haywood is careful to separate motive from means. Contrivance and design are not themselves immoral. It is the use to which they are put that defines them as such.

Haywood's effort to separate female wit from illegitimate forms of female desire echoes Richardson's own gestures in the same direction. But his novels reveal a steady preoccupation with the "problem" of such a separation, a problem that is centered on the notion of women's writing. In *Sir Charles Grandison* the hero articulates a philosophical position on the matter that would have been anathema to Eliza Haywood, that, in fact, seems to allude obliquely to her career in its invocation of Pope's *Dunciad* and the women writers among the scribbling tribe Pope castigates in that poem. In commenting on his ward Emily Jervois's literary talents (she has translated an Italian sonnet), Sir Charles solemnly intones: "Nor would I have my Emily distinguished by any name but that of a discreet, an ingenious and an amiable young woman. The title of *Wit* and *Poetess*, has been disgraced too often by Sappho's and Corinna's ancient and modern. . . . But do not be disturbed, my Emily.....I mean no check to liveliness and modest ingenuity. The easy productions of a fine fancy,

---

22 In the midst of a scheme to become the wife of an old man, Syrena indulges a purely physical passion for a young man whom she instructs to address her by the name "Harriot Manly" (209), a great "Proof of her Cunning" (209), according to the narrator in that it places her "beyond a Possibility of Discovery" (210).

not made the business of life, or its boast, confer no denomination that is disgraceful, but very much the contrary."[23] Emily responds to this edict—essentially the directive to be but not to be a woman of literary accomplishment—with anxious equivocation. She expresses relief that she has not attempted poetry, contenting herself instead with "plain prose," and she hopes to evade the censure of both Sir Charles and his sister Charlotte who has dubbed Emily "the Poetess" with a gentle derision designed to garner approval from both Grandison and the other moral arbiter of the set, Dr. Bartlett.[24] The Doctor, however, further confuses things by declaring poetry an inoffensive, even admirable, occupation for young ladies: "Sir Charles is an admirer of good poetry; And Miss Grandison would have recollected the Philomela's and Orinda's, and other excellent names among her own sex, whose fine genius does it honour" (431).

Walking the fine lines of behavioral acceptability set up in this and other passages in *Clarissa* and *Sir Charles Grandison* in particular would be difficult for any woman of wit and talent who felt compelled or coerced into doing so; we can conclude from the sheer bulk of Eliza Haywood's published canon that she, for one, never felt such compulsion, whatever coercive measures were brought to bear. Nor, as discussed in the previous chapter, did she feel the need to explain herself or her motives to her readership or to posterity. Nevertheless, her work from 1741 on reveals a fascination with the relationship between empirical observation and penetrative interpretation—what seems to be, what really is, and the power that accrues to those who can either manipulate appearances or discover the truth that hides beneath the surface of things. As a novelist, of course, Haywood lays claim to both talents; Fielding did the same thing, as did Richardson. In fact, one could say that all novelists, all artists of any sort, trade off of the interplay between empirical representation and interpretive possibilities. But in the wake of *Pamela* and in the face of the considerable number of women writers in the marketplace of the 1740s, this interplay assumes a cultural importance that is tied to anxieties about material desire of all sorts—sexual, economic, and empirical. To see, to know, to want, to possess is the general trajectory of material desire, and the ramifications of this path for women is a mid-century preoccupation, discovered most potently by Richardson's *Pamela*.

I use "discovered" in the theatrical sense, as in a scene discovered, for the ramifications of female desire is not the subject Richardson sets out to explain in either *Pamela* or *Clarissa*. In fact, it would seem that his subject in both cases is the potentially ravaging effect of male desire, but as he writes about seduction to readers familiar with the representation of mutual passion in romance narratives and

---

23 *The History of Sir Charles Grandison*, ed. Jocelyn Harris, The World's Classics (Oxford, 1986), p. 431. Further references will be cited parenthetically.

24 At this point in the tale, Charlotte is dependent on her brother to help her deal with Captain Anderson to whom she has made a rash promise—not to marry anyone else while he is single. She did so without talking it over with Sir Charles in the first place (though the relationship seems to have occurred during the time the girls were prohibited from writing to their brother by their father). She has "stood trial" for not telling him, been "forgiven" and is now waiting through the process of Sir Charles's dealing with things for her.

comedies of manners, he finds himself at odds with certain representative readers who recognize in his heroines evidence of desires and designs he would not admit.

In fact, the very idea of "designing" is offensive to Richardson, as witnessed by his famous exchange with Lady Dorothy Bradshaigh concerning the Hampstead episode early in volume 5 of *Clarissa*. Lady Bradshaigh recorded her responses to *Clarissa* in the margins of her first edition copy of the novel presented her by the author. At some point she let Richardson see her marginalia, and he wrote back—also in the margins—creating what Janine Barchas has termed "an almost Talmudic array of glosses upon glosses."[25] Barchas argues that Richardson's changes to the text in the second and third editions of *Clarissa* reflect his concerns about misinterpretation of his narrative, concerns he developed at least partly from his reading of Lady Bradshaigh's annotations. As a representative reader, she struck him as sometimes perverse, sometimes inattentive, sometimes insightful, sometimes astute. In cases where he felt her wrong, he corrected her in the margins of her copy of *Clarissa*; he commented less often when he approved of her responses; when he felt himself justly chastened (usually on matters of social propriety) he would sometimes tacitly acknowledge as much by corrections to the next edition.[26] Of the many exchanges between this author and reader, the Hampstead episode is most notable for the intensity—Richardson's—provoked by the casual use—Lady Bradshaigh's—of a single word—"device."

Clarissa has been traced to Hampstead after escaping from Lovelace in London. He has used a variety of ruses to obtain access to the house in which she has taken refuge, and he eventually manages to gain admittance to her apartment under the guise of a servant seeking appropriate quarters for his master and mistress. There he reveals himself to Clarissa, and the two characters begin anew the struggle for control that has characterized their relationship from the start. Clarissa appeals to the female proprietors of the inn, moral women whose confusion results not from evil intent toward Clarissa, but from uncertainty about the situation in which they find her, a wife or almost a wife, whose husband or husband-to-be, has come to make up a quarrel, resolve a perplexity about the legal status of the marriage, in some way behave honorably to end her distress and anxiety. Clarissa appeals to them, then, to no avail: "Deliver me from this dangerous man; and direct me!—I know not what I do; what I can do; nor what I ought to do!—" Lady Bradshaigh sees no point in the appeal for yet another reason. It is just not a very good plan: "This was a poor device, for she must think he wou'd have follow'd her, and perhaps have forced her into a coach & carry'd her where he had a mind." Richardson is outraged that his heroine

---

25   Janine Barchas with Gordon D. Fulton, *The Annotations in Lady Bradshaigh's Copy of Clarissa*, English Literary Studies, University of Victoria (Victoria, Canada, 1998), p. 9.

26   Barchas observes that "the links between the third-edition changes and Richardson's responses to Lady Bradshaigh's annotations—in which he repeatedly 'corrects' her interpretation of Clarissa's and/or Lovelace's behaviour or character—suggest that Lady Bradshaigh's annotations may have acted as a template for Richardson's later changes to the novel." Ibid., p. 22. On Richardson's probable response to "advice," in terms of "small touches he introduced" in later editions of *Clarissa* "to make the writing throughout more 'noble' and 'correct,'" see Angus Ross, Introduction to *Clarissa, or The History of a Young Lady* (Harmondsworth, 1985), p. 17.

should be seen as a plotter and schemer on any level, insisting that her response to the situation is instinctive, not calculated:

> *Device*, does your Ladiship call it? Cl. Was above all Devices!—In such a distressed Situation, and with a vile Fellow, who had convinced her of his Vileness, she had nothing in her Head or Heart but once more to get from him. She might be in hope to raise the Country upon him, as she once threaten'd. Such a lovely young Creature, pursued by so rakish a young Fellow . . . cast into the Protection of a sensible man, would not have been imposed upon so easily as the two foolish women were, whose Curiosity and Inquisitiveness was more than their Fellow-feeling for one of their own Sex; who was *only* running away from a handsome Rake, no hated Character with women in general, as Lovelace had often experienced: *Device*! I don't love your Ladiship just here! Poor Clarissa! To be classed with a Lovelace as if—But no more—[27]

This episode marks the beginning of the end of the struggle between Lovelace and Clarissa as the opposing paradoxes of their individual fates attest the effect each character has had upon the other. Lovelace's defeat in victory (his psychological dissolution following his physical domination of Clarissa) and Clarissa's triumph in death (her increasing spiritual wholeness as her body disintegrates) offer arguments for readers to pursue. After Hampstead, the characters themselves can best be described as discrete points of reference, representative of the effects of libertinism, on the one hand, and the efficacy of Christian virtue, on the other. The argument is certainly weighted in Christian virtue's favor by the end of volume five. Lovelace's contrivances toward and execution of the rape of Clarissa see to that. But, as Lady Bradshaigh's comments reveal, in the beginning of the volume the characters seem more evenly matched. In fact, in one way, they seem interchangeable. To Lady Bradshaigh, Clarissa, like Lovelace, is a character of devices and desires.

Richardson's impatience with Lady Bradshaigh's assumptions about Clarissa's motives in Hampstead Heath is notable for both its intensity and its unyielding insistence on interpretive control. Richardson exercises his authority just at the place in the narrative where, from Clarissa's point of view, interpretive fluidity (her openness to the possibility that evidence will yield readings in favor of her union with Lovelace) is on the verge of being replaced by interpretive rigidity (her recognition, even before the rape, that marriage to Lovelace and her own virtue are irreconcilable). After his first marginal outburst taking issue with the word "device," Richardson restricts himself to textual underlinings and vertical markings and occasional finger pointings, as if to draw attention to the fact that there is only one valid interpretation, that any notion of Clarissa's "devices" must depend on an absolute disregard of the too-obvious fact that she is at this point in the narrative a victim of Lovelace's machinations, that only a female Lovelace, one whose "curiosity and inquisitiveness" supersede "fellow-feeling for one of her own sex" could interpret her as a contriver.[28]

---

27 Barchas, p. 85.

28 Richardson underscores Lovelace's characterization of Clarissa's "*home-push'd questions on that head*" (i.e., the subject of marriage). See Barchas, p. 90. Mostly, though, Richardson's underlinings suggest that even a Lovelace recognizes Clarissa's innocence.

Lady Bradshaigh's reaction to Richardson's side of the conversation is unrecorded, but there is no reason to think that she would have calmly capitulated to his disciplinary tactics. As Barchas points out, Bradshaigh finds various ways of "declaring her ownership of the text," ranging from her marginal quarrels with the author to her penning of a revised ending to the novel. In a symbolic gesture, in fact, Bradshaigh superinscribes her name over Richardson's dedicatory inscription in the gift copy he presented her. His "From the Author" can be seen faintly under her "Do. Bradshaigh" on the flyleaf of each of the seven volumes of her copy of the novel, constituting, as Barchas points out, "a metonym for the dialogue between text, author and reader that takes place in this copy . . . [as] Richardson and Lady Bradshaigh do battle over the interpretation of the novel, each attempting to impose his or her will upon the other."[29] But Bradshaigh's position in this quarrel is symbolic of another sort of tension as well. For, in a sense she is empowered by Clarissa in terms of asserting her interpretive authority and denied that authority by the same character's relationship to various forms of patriarchal control—from her creator who insists on her chaste simplicity of motive, to her Creator who endorses her denial of sensual pleasure, to her father who curses her and exerts such negative power over her mind and action. In other words, Clarissa's interpretive skill has somehow to be purged of the associations it might have with sexual knowledge, superiority of intelligence, and independence of thought and action. If virtuous female wit must shun knowingness, intellectual dominance, and independent novelty, what remains that still qualifies as wit?

Nature to Advantage Dressed

In the seventeenth and eighteenth centuries, beginning with Locke, wit and judgment were set up as oppositional categories.[30] Wit was celebrated as the ability to see and formulate the similarity between two unlike things whereas judgment manifested itself in the opposite mental activity, discriminating the subtle differences between things that on the surface seem similar. The pairing of wit and judgment in the literature of the time (one thinks specifically of Pope's famous marital metaphor in *Essay on Criticism*) invokes the contrast of surface and depth, emanation and penetration, feminine charm and masculine authority. This gendering is not, however, systematic so much as it is systemic; the habit of dividing the world into male and female is not an old one by this point in the history of western culture, but it is already showing strains that will continue to plague the definition of sexual

---

29 Barchas, p. 34.

30 Locke explained wit as "the assemblage of *Ideas*, and putting those together with quickness and variety, wherein can be found any resemblance or congruity." Judgment, he explains, "lies quite on the other side, in separating carefully, one from another, *Ideas*, wherein can be found the least difference." Metaphor and allusion are the property of wit, which is the lesser of the two mental capacities in Locke's scheme (as it would be in Pope's rendition of the oppositional pair in *Essay on Criticism*). See Locke, *An Essay Concerning Human Understanding*, ed. Peter H. Nidditch (Oxford, 1975), p. 156.

difference and the differentiation of sexual roles and responsibilities on into the twentieth and twenty-first centuries.

The problem lies in the nature of differentiation. If we understand difference to mean simply the occupation of the subject position, the shifting of perspective, the movement of chiastic desire, we understand it as relational, not hierarchical, not categorical. The assertion of difference in this context is an assertion of female subjectivity (as male subjectivity is a privileged category that needs no argument in a world defined by patriarchal prerogatives). Aphra Behn, Delarivier Manley, and Eliza Haywood, like the writer of the Song of Songs, equate female subjectivity with female sexual desire. Richardson distances himself from the overt examination of female desire, as we have seen, but his preoccupation with his culture's strictures against the operation of female wit and his efforts to create an alternate mythology of feminine intelligence find him time and again in murky sexual territory.

In a sense, the feminine/masculine matrix represents in the eighteenth century qualities associated less with sexual than with national or political concerns. The need for a modifier when talking of "female wits" exists due to the fact that the noun "wit" was customarily reserved for men. Obviously most "wits" were male, not female, but the realm in which they excelled in the Restoration and early eighteenth century was the realm of social interaction, the feminine round of fashionable activity, the domain of life where women's sensibilities were to be attended. Wits, beaus, and rakes all partake of Restoration hedonism, each emphasizing the material—rakes in terms of their preoccupation with sexual conquest, beaus in their overattentiveness to dress, manners, and other marks of politeness, and wits in their emphasis on the formulation of well-turned phrases in which sound (rhythm, syncopated enunciation) is at least as important as sense, if not more so. The early eighteenth century witnesses not so much a renunciation of these "types," as an attempt to "civilize" them by various means—to tame the rake's passion for conquest into a monogamous, uxorial devotion, to synthesize politeness with satisfying social interaction, and to bolster the frivolity of wit with a substratum of judgment. Sir Charles Grandison is the model of the would-be rake whose moral sensibility makes him instead a paragon of virtue. He is a meticulous observer of all social forms, a quality that, in him, indicates sensibility rather than self-centeredness. He is also an eloquent and witty speaker. He is the model of manliness that has assimilated all the female virtues.

His female counterpart is less easily imagined, however; her desires, less smoothly accommodated to new moral concerns. To accord her subjectivity at all is to imply a knowingness that is sexual as well as intellectual. After *Pamela*, Richardson adopted the strategy of creating a female foil for his heroine in a character whose morality was unquestioned, but whose wit was gendered masculine by its penetrative insight and caustic, assertive expression. Critics were quick to see the "political" implications of female wits such as Anna Howe and Charlotte Grandison. The anonymous author of *Critical Remarks on Sir Charles Grandison, Clarissa, and Pamela* (1754) elaborates those implications in his description of the characters. They both, he says,

> have . . . high notions of female prerogative, and the preeminence of their own sex over the other; they had both like to have run away with too worthless fellows, and both afterwards treated too honest well-meaning men, during the time of their courtship, like

dogs; and both, I imagine, for all these reasons, will be great favourites with the female part of your readers.[31]

Richardson's own ambivalence about female wit permeates both *Clarissa* and *Sir Charles Grandison*, and each narrative's disciplinary treatment of the representatives of such feminine power (Anna Howe and Charlotte Grandison) is set in opposition to the glorification of the mental habits of Clarissa Harlowe and Harriet Byron respectively. Clarissa's interpretive dominance over Lovelace is demonstrated in the famous letter in which she tells him she will set out for her father's house, deliberately deceiving him in what Joseph Addison would complain of as an example of false wit—the pun—only if we remain in Lovelace's register, conversant with his habits of mind.[32] Indeed, Clarissa realizes she will be misinterpreted, but for all that her use of the pun is not false wit so much as an indication of her complete renunciation of the world, its referents and its linguistic habits. Her metaphorical language refers to a realm she cannot know experientially. That she speaks in parables is therefore understandable and appropriate. This redeemed wit is just one of the many ways Richardson links Clarissa to Christ in the last third of the novel.

Harriet Byron, however, is of this world, or at least of the world centered around Sir Charles Grandison, a world in which goodness prevails. From the beginning, even before she meets the Grandisons, she is depicted as a pattern of goodness whose intelligence and refinement mark her as of the same ilk as Richardson's other heroines. She is known to her family as having "a satirical vein" which is executed in the first few pages of the novel on her suitors Mr. Orme, Mr. Greville, and Mr. Pollexfen and in descriptions of various would-be wits, would-be beaus, and would-be rakes she meets at her cousin Reeves's home in London.[33] When she falls victim, however, to an attempted rape by Sir Hargrave Pollexfen and is rescued by Sir Charles Grandison, Harriet undergoes a period of linguistic distress, similar in kind, though not as severe in degree, to the aphasia and fragmentation Clarissa experiences after she is raped by Lovelace.

Richardson's association of verbal control with sexual subjectivity (and its consequent loss as the result of sexual objectification) is an astute psychological and political insight, as has been pointed out by various critics, most notably Terry Castle.[34] But the heroine's loss of speech is also a telling ethical moment in both *Clarissa* and *Sir Charles Grandison*. In each novel it marks the point at which the heroine begins to define for herself a model of wit that allows for chiastic exchange with a masculine counterpart and that consequently leads to the fulfillment of the spiritual as well as the sexual self. *Clarissa*'s counterpart is the reformed rake Belford, not Lovelace, and her sexual fulfillment is the resumption of her virginal purity despite the rape. She reasserts control over her own body and insists upon her

---

31 *Critical Remarks on Sir Charles Grandison, Clarissa, And Pamela, Enquiring Whether they have a Tendency to corrupt or improve the Public Taste and Morals*, by a Lover of Virtue (London, 1754), p. 25. Further references will be cited parenthetically.

32 *Clarissa*, p. 1233. Addison's comments on the pun are in *Spectator* 61.

33 *Sir Charles Grandison*, p. 48.

34 See Castle, *Clarissa's Ciphers: Meaning and Disruption in Richardson's 'Clarissa'* (Ithaca, 1982).

own sexual as well as spiritual subjectivity. The sexualizing of her death represents a merging of the spiritual and sexual that can be read as the tragic manifestation of the chiasmus of double desire, a physical love that provides the means of spiritual transcendence for the lover-beloved / beloved-lover.[35]

Richardson's project in *Sir Charles Grandison* is to formulate a model of mutual fulfillment in this world; therefore, Harriet's aphasia is followed by a less dramatic, though no less ethically significant, redefinition—or, we might as well say, redemption—of female wit. Harriet's early triumph in the debate about modern learning has alerted us to the sexual ambiguities attendant on her victory. Although the debate marks her as learned and capable of intellectually dominating a discussion about current topics of concern—the ancients and the moderns in this case—she finds herself at the conclusion of the discussion an object of desire without sufficient subjective status. Her defense of English poetry, modern languages, and the education of women earns her the applause of the masculine Miss Barnevelt whose raucous, virile demeanor ("she is a loud and fearless laugher" [58]) Harriet finds disconcerting. Mrs. Barnevelt's reaction to Harriet's triumph is recounted as a sexual attraction: "She profess'd I was able to bring *her own sex* into reputation with her. Wisdom, as I call it, said she, notwithstanding what you have modestly alleged to depreciate your own, proceeding thro' teeth of ivory, and lips of coral; give a grace to every word. And then clasping one of her mannish arms round me, she kissed my cheek" (57). Miss Barnevelt's embarrassing display is seconded by Sir Hargrave Pollexfen who declares his intention to kiss Harriet in turn, "since merit was to be approved in that manner." In other words, Harriet's intellectual triumph renders her sexually appealing to both men and women, not through chiastic exchange but through the self-centered need to appropriate the power she has demonstrated. Her wit in this instance increases the self-consequence of Miss Barnevelt through gender identification and provokes Sir Hargrave's need to reassert his gender's physical power over a woman who has revealed intellectual superiority.

Even at this stage, before her meeting with Sir Charles Grandison, Harriet refuses to define herself as a "learned lady." In fact, the thrust of her argument is to justify the neglect of philological study in favor of the perusal of modern literature written in modern languages. She does however define herself as a "Bible scholar," mistress of a realm of knowledge deemed by Richardson as appropriate for female minds as the author of *Critical Remarks* points out: "you have not only shewn yourself a pious Christian, and a good *Bible-scholar*, but you have made all your heroines the same. . . For these things . . . you cannot be more than enough applauded" (7–8). But such scholarship does not fully occupy the mind of Harriet Byron. Indeed, she is a less pious woman than her rival, the Roman Catholic Clementina, whose biblical scholarship is never asserted (as it would ill suit the Catholic tradition as Richardson wished to portray it—that is, as autocratic, oppressive, and uncompromising). Harriet is driven by curiosity, especially following her "conversion" from witty self-

---

35 For pertinent readings of *Clarissa*'s position within Christian discourse about suffering and transcendence, see Margaret Anne Doody, "The Gnostic Clarissa," *Eighteenth-Century Fiction* 11 (1998): 49–78 and Peggy Thompson, "Abuse and Atonement: The Passion of Clarissa Harlowe," *Eighteenth-Century Fiction* 11 (1999): 255–70.

possession to Grandisonian acolytism. And the object of her curiosity is the secular god himself, the paragon of virtue whom she has come to love.

The author of *Critical Remarks* demonstrates his own skill at biblical exegesis in a commentary on the moral thrust of Richardson's fiction. While his insights are not unique in their contention that Richardson parades prurience under the cover of morality, his invocation of the Genesis account of the fall casts the charge in terms that paradoxically point to Richardson's fundamental project—the redemption of female wit—and the difficulty of achieving it. The *Remarks* begin with an account of the conventional interpretation of the Fall of Man. "It is said, that by Adam we are to understand the mind or reason of man; by Eve, the flesh or outward senses; and by the serpent, lust or pleasure" (42). These allegorical equivalences render the narrative's meaning thus: "the true causes of man's fall and degeneracy, when his mind, through the weakness and treachery of his senses, became captivated and seduced by the allurements of lust and pleasure, he was driven by God out of Paradise" (42). In other words, the "masculine" mind, seduced by the "feminine" body, lost its innocence through indulgence in sensual pleasures.

Alternatively, the author proposes that the allegory is "intended to warn men against, and shew them the dangerous consequences of, an idle curiosity and researches into vain and useless Things, and to make them sensible, that all they could acquire thereby would be pain and misery, the necessary consequences of the loss of virtue and innocence, and a shameful sense of their own nakedness; that is, the corruption and depravity of human nature" (42–3). In this interpretation, Adam is the mind; Eve, idle curiosity—and various entities, including Richardson himself, serve as the tempter who sets curiosity going: "He not only raises the passions," the author complains, "but kindly points out the readiest and the easiest way to lay them" (46). This interpretation insists that curiosity is, like the body, focused on the stimulation and potential satisfaction of sensual pleasures; descriptive language that excites lust is but one step removed from the physical act of sexual gratification itself.

Harriet Byron, motivated by her desire to be married to Grandison, is similarly focused, in part at least, on the gratification of sensual pleasure. Although her impulses and methods are sanitized by displacement and ennobled by behavioral constraints and the merging of sexual, social, and spiritual goals, she, like all of Richardson's heroines, experiences the glows and throbs of physical desire. It is this desire that leads her to wonder about Grandison's past, to analyze his speeches, to try to discover his secrets. Her native wit and curiosity are redeemed by her focus on Grandison, knowing him in an intellectual sense, before knowing him in the "biblical" sense. She builds a narrative of the pieces of his life that she puts together from discussions with his sisters and his mentor Dr. Bartlett, from letters, and from his own conversation. Her purpose is ostensibly to determine for herself whether or not he is free to return the love she has begun to feel for him. Of course, by the time she finds he is not free, she has become emotionally involved, and she does suffer while Grandison completes the "story" he has begun with Clementina. But in piecing together his story she also protects herself from the pain attendant on constructing a story for herself and a man who does not or cannot love her in return. Olivia and Clementina are examples of women who invest themselves too heavily emotionally because, in essence, they fail to recognize Grandison's "otherness" and that his desires—sexual and spiritual—are in direct conflict with their own. Harriet is a sexual subject who acknowledges her own desires, but who also says to the other in the sense that Levinas invokes the term: "here I am; send me."

Sarah Fielding and the Domestication of Desire

Critical Remarks on Sir Charles Grandison, Clarissa, and Pamela includes a facetious description of the intense focusing of attention on sexual desire characteristic not only of Richardson's fiction but of the literature of his age in general, according to this author. The passage is amusing, and for that reason, and for its unintentional wisdom as well, it is worth quoting in full.

> Love, eternal Love, is the subject, the burthen of all your writings; it is the poignant sauce, which so richly seasons Pamela, Clarissa and Grandison, and makes their flimzy nonsense pass so glibly down. Love, eternal love, not only seasons all our other numerous compositions of the same kind, but likewise engrosses our theatres and all our dramatic performances, which were originally calculated to give examples of nobler passions. From this situation of affairs among our authors, one would be apt to imagine, that the propagation of the species was at a stand, and that, not to talk of marrying and giving in marriage, there was hardly any such thing as fornication going forward among us, and that therefore our publick-spirited penmen, to prevent the world from coming to an end, employ'd all their art and eloquence to keep people in remembrance, that they were composed of different sexes. (38–9)

Perhaps it was the case that authors of the mid-eighteenth century felt peculiarly compelled to remind readers of the fact that there is such a thing as sexual difference. But if we accept the motive, we must acknowledge that by and large they failed to maintain their focus on such difference. Patricia Meyer Spacks has termed the fiction of this period "novels of phallic power" which she describes as driven by plots of male sexual conquest.[36] And plots of male sexual conquest, by definition, deny or attempt to discipline the fact and force of female desire.

As Alexander Pettit has pointed out, mid-century novelist Sarah Fielding does not write novels that pursue plots of phallic power.[37] Although he would not have put it that way, the insight is perhaps what provokes the author of *Critical Remarks* to invoke Fielding as a moral exemplar whose novels do not, as Richardson's allegedly do, incite lasciviousness in the guise of morality. In fact, he writes in address to Richardson, "none of your brother romancers are, in my opinion, entirely free from

---

36 *Desire and Truth: Functions of Plot in Eighteenth-Century English Novels* (Chicago, 1990), pp. 6–7 and 55–84; cited by Alexander Petit, "*David Simple* and the Attenuation of 'Phallic Power,'" *Eighteenth-Century Fiction* 11 (1999): 169 n.1.

37 He calls David Simple a "male protagonist unmotivated by phallic desire" (169). Also pertinent is Betty A. Schellenberg's discussion of both *David Simple* and *Sir Charles Grandison* as novels that eschew plots focused on "individualistic desire" in favor of "a plot structure that models a community of consensus as the ideal unit from which a stable society is constructed." *The Conversational Circle: Rereading the English Novel, 1740–1775* (Lexington, 1996), pp. 4, 22–35, 51–68.

. . . [lasciviousness], except the moral and ingenious authoress of David Simple"
(39).[38] Yet, Sarah Fielding's own commentary on Richardson suggests that she finds
his emphasis on love laudable in novels which are, like *Clarissa*, centered on women,
for, as Miss Gibson puts it, "Love is the only Passion I should wish to be harboured
in the gentle Bosom of a good Woman; Ambition, with all the Train of turbulent
Passions the World is infested with, I would leave to Men."[39]

Female desire is the subject of Sarah Fielding's novels as much as it is the subject
of Richardson's *Pamela*, *Clarissa*, and *Sir Charles Grandison*. And, like Richardson,
Fielding explores the operations of desire through a concentration on the operations
of the mind. She no doubt seems more "moral" to the author of *Critical Remarks*
(and less emotionally powerful to the twenty-first-century reader) because she differs
from Richardson in that she does not fetishize the relationship between thought and
physical feeling. Her work is absent the glows and throbs that in Richardson's canon
signify the physical manifestations of love as they conflict with or emanate from
intellectual pursuit in conjunction with psychosexual instinct. Yet Fielding's project,
her focus of concern, is no less than Richardson's "Love, eternal love," that is, love
between "beings wholly otherwise" that provides an access to spiritual knowledge
through sexual exchange.

Like Eliza Haywood before her, Sarah Fielding creates hieroglyphic fables that
both mask and reveal longing for the other. To an even greater degree than Haywood,
Fielding embraces the schematic abstractions of allegory. Her characters are less
breathing human forms than ideational constructs, and she prefers theoretical speech
to symbolic gesture. In Fielding's fiction, there is a decided movement away from
the physicality of sexual response which seems at odds with the preoccupation on
love that her fiction shares with other novels of the time. But this kind of perversity
is forced on the woman writer from mid-century on by what G.J. Barker Benfield
has convincingly described as the movement of libertine focus on the body to the
age of sensibility.[40]

Fielding's approach is to deny the binarism behind much eighteenth-century
thought, to drive, as it were, the figure of chiasmus into the essence of being rather
than to see it as the result of essential definitions. The most decided evidence of this
strategy is in Fielding's creation of character in *David Simple* in which, as Felicity
Nussbaum has put it, the presence of "the manly woman and the feminine man . . .
argue that the novel refuses a strictly symmetrical understanding or simple reversal
of sexual difference."[41] For Nussbaum, *David Simple* is exemplary of mid-century
attitudes toward gender and the relationship between rigid definitions of "masculine"

---

38   Earlier, the anonymous author praises *David Simple* as "perhaps the best moral
romance that we have, in which there is not one loose expression, one impure, one unchaste
idea from the perusal of which, no man can rise unimproved." Moreover, in David, simplicity
makes sense as he is "ignorant of the ways of the world" (19).

39   Sarah Fielding, *Remarks on Clarissa, Addressed to the Author Occasioned by Some
Critical Conversation on the Characters and Conduct of that Work* (London, 1749), p. 18.

40   Barker Benfield, *The Culture of Sensibility: Sex and Society in Eighteenth-Century
Britain* (Chicago, 1996), pp. 1–36.

41   Nussbaum, "Effeminacy and Femininity: Domestic Prose Satire and *David Simple*,"
Eighteenth-Century Fiction 11 (1999): 425.

and "feminine," for while, as she points out, the age witnessed the emergence of "relatively fixed masculine and feminine sexual identities," it is also true that "gendered hybridity is everywhere manifest" in the literature of the period.[42] In Sarah Fielding's fiction, I would argue, the hybridity is particularly prominent, a deliberate strategy that undermines essentialism in pursuit of difference.

Nussbaum has discussed the way gendered hybridity functions in *David Simple* to dislocate assumptions about masculinity and femininity, friendship and love, wit and libertine sexuality. Cynthia is defined as a wit, and she is accused of libertinism as a result, but, as Nussbaum points out, the narrative does not treat her as an object of satire (as is the case with characters of her ilk in *Evelina*, *Tom Jones*, etc.).[43] Indeed, she is the center of a group of friends and lovers bound together by respect for one another's strengths, sympathy for one another's weaknesses, a group sustained by Cynthia's penetrative wit and David Simple's innocent sensibility, traits which do not render the individuals inappropriately masculine or feminine but which simply provide essential aspects of community life. Conventionally defined male and female qualities exist in the group, but they are not necessarily the property of men and women respectively. Neither is the most significant love relationship in this group a sexual one. David and Cynthia are friends, and their friendship represents the most important meeting of opposites, beings wholly otherwise. David and Cynthia offer just one example of the ethical ideal, however. The friendships between brother and sister, Camilla and Valentine, and between woman and woman, Cynthia and Camilla, and man and man, David and Valentine, are also founded on a difference that—within the group—provokes ethical wonder and acceptance, rather than political frustration and attempts to conquer or control: "they . . . often talked over the Difference of their Capacities and Dispositions with the same Freedom as if they had been mentioning the Difference of their Height or Size."[44] Outside of the group is another matter. The charge of incest against Camilla and Valentine is just one example of the misreadings possible when conventionality comes into contact with true chiastic exchange. That these misreadings can be dangerous and ultimately destructive of the ethical idea is clear from Volume the Last which chronicles the dissolution of the group, effected by what Fielding herself often terms "Vanity," what we might denominate arrant self-interest—individual and national alike.

Sarah Fielding's ethical world is constructed around, in a sense, opposition to opposition. In *The Cry*, she has Portia explain the coerciveness of binary thought in definitions of wit in particular:

---

42   Ibid., p. 425. Nussbaum links the emergence of fixed categories to the growth of British nationalism (425–9).

43   Nussbaum, p. 435. Nussbaum points out that Henry Fielding in all earnestness treats his sister's wit with respect, not contempt, though he does chastise her for her want of learning—with some disingenuousness, as Sarah Fielding did know Greek and "was considered a bluestocking" (436–7; 437 n.1).

44   *The Adventures of David Simple, Volume the Last*, ed. Peter Sabor, Eighteenth-Century Novels by Women, (Lexington,1998), p. 258; quoted by Nussbaum, "Effeminacy," p. 442.

When mankind are forced to acknowledge another possessed of any particular excellence, the great pains they take in endeavouring to tack on to the excellence some necessary defect, is a contrivance invented by envy, in order to prevent bursting with inward spleen at so hateful a sight. And it brings to my remembrance a practice I have heard of one of our former sovereigns, who, when he wanted money, would never sign any useful bill in parliament, without tacking on another for his own supplies. Thus to make *wit* pass current in the world, malice tacks on to it *want of judgment*, to *sound judgment* is tack'd *want of invention*; to *learning* in men, *pedantry*; in women, *want of every domestic virtue*; to *vivacity*, *levity*; to *gravity*, *dullness*; but above all, to a *lively imagination, madness.*[45]

Thinking in terms of essential definitions, as Fielding has Portia point out, is really a political ploy. The strategy of attaching a rider to a bill illustrates the point of self-interest clearly. The sovereign becomes an example of the expression of political vanity, incapable of disinterested support for positions or policies that do not answer his own needs. In her following illustration, Fielding shifts her focus. The self-interested "world" cannot allow for excellence without attaching to any gift or accomplishment the idea of an attendant weakness or failing.

Fielding herself would seem to privilege a certain kind of opposition, for all of her fictions explore the difference between, as she puts it in *The History of the Countess of Dellwyn*, "the Efficacy of religious Principles towards extracting the sharpest Sting from the highest Adversity" and "the Power of Vanity to bring to nothing every real Advantage."[46] However, in the course of that novel Fielding reveals that self-interest, like wit, can be satisfied more fully in a life led according to religious principles than one driven by vanity. The paradox is explored through the negative experiences of the Countess, a woman of wit and penetration, driven by vanity to pursue courses of action that in the end thwart the happiness she would procure.

The problem with vanity is that it defines the other not as a being of difference but as an object of envy, a target of appropriative, coercive ambition. Miss Lucum is persuaded to marry Lord Dellwyn through an affront to her vanity. She cares little about the proposed union until she is led to fear the Count might marry Lady Fanny Fashion (a stratagem concocted by the Lord and her father). To triumph over her rival, Miss Lucum enters into a loveless marriage, "a Dupe to her own ungovernable Vanity" (1: 120). Her behavior afterwards is similarly driven by self-regard. Even when she allows her husband to direct her actions in the early years of their marriage, she does so from motives of "Self-admiration" (1: 121), not from the opening of herself to the demands of the other, not from vulnerability to love and its mysteries. Her self-defined sacrifice to his will leads her to overvalue herself at her husband's expense:

Lady *Dellwyn* now delighted her Fancy with erecting a Pair of mental Scales; in One Balance placing her own newly-discovered Merits, and in the other *all* such Virtues

---

45   *The Cry: A New Dramatic Fable* (3 vols, London, 1754), vol. 1, pp. 158–9. Further references are cited parenthetically.

46   *The History of the Countess of Dellwyn* (2 vols, London, 1759), vol 1, p. 215. Further references are cited parenthetically.

as she *allowed* her Lord to be possessed of. Her Memory was faithful to the minutest Circumstance that could give Weight to her own Side and, when this last Compliance with her Husband was added to the other numerous Articles, the Balance which contained the whole Load of her Virtues struck the Ground with its Force; whilst that in which her Fancy had placed *Lord Dellwyn*'s Merit, flew upwards with its Lightness; and all the Trifles therein, like Half the Prayer to *Jupiter*, in *Homer*, were lost and scattered in the Air. (1: 122)

This "self-flattery" makes the Countess happy for a time—"one of the gayest Figures in Creation" (1: 123), but this happiness does not last, of course, founded as it is on envy and driven by vanity. "In real Fact," the narrator tells us late in Volume 1, "all that is capable of bestowing any solid Satisfaction in this World, is so easily attained by every Individual, that were the Envious endued with the Power of discerning, they must be cured of that painful mental Distemper, in spite of their Teeth" (1: 242). But Lady Dellwyn's vanity leads her into further competition with Lady Fanny Fashion (now Lady Chlegen), a competition for "Admiration" that in turn opens her to the seductions of Lord Clermont. Without the excuse of real passion for her lover, Lady Dellwyn is drawn into an adulterous affair with Clermont that eventuates in her divorce.

Her husband, though wronged, is no less to blame for the demise of the marriage. He too is motivated by a vanity which disallows difference: "When Lord *Dellwyn* determined to make Miss *Lucum* his Countess, he had not once suffered the Possibility of her desiring any Pleasures separate from his to approach his Thoughts" (1: 138). He too discovers the truth of the following sentiment applied by the narrator to the Countess's weakness: "When Vanity becomes . . . predominant, it brings us into Subjection, and makes us the most abject Slaves to every human Being with whom we converse, who have any Inclination to play the Tyrant" (2: 42–3). The Count is manipulated by Captain Drummond into suing the Countess for divorce, but the Captain's schemes are also motivated by self-interest: he wants to ingratiate himself to the Count in order to partake of his fortune. In the end, the Captain too is foiled when the Count remarries, another example of the inefficacy of founding schemes of happiness on envy motivated by vanity.

Lady Dellwyn is a true wit, but as in the case of the similarly vain Cry (representative of "the world") this is a "trifling advantage" with her because she "want[s] the uprightness of heart which alone could enable . . . a proper use of that capacity" (*The Cry* 2: 230). Indeed, once she marries, the Countess turns away from the productions of wit that might stimulate her own skills of penetration. She avoids in particular "those Authors who have penetrated deeply into the intricate Paths of Vanity in the human Mind," as provoking "a very unpleasing Sensation" (1: 102). Reading challenges her sense of self worth by "setting a Glass before her, which represented her to herself in so many deformed Lights, that she could not bear the disagreeable View" (1: 103). In general, Fielding notes in the preface to *The Countess of Dellwyn*, readers share with Lady Dellwyn a preference for literature that confirms self-definition and self-importance. They seek evidence of others' weaknesses in reading satire as specific attack, thereby missing (as Swift might have told them) the criticism of general human weaknesses from which they might profit.

They thumb and rethumb books that flatter and soothe them in the paths they have chosen: military men prefer heroic tales and a lover's copy of *The Aeneid* is most likely to open at the story of Dido (1: xxxiv).

Mrs. Bilson is every bit as witty as the Countess of Dellwyn, but she, unlike her counterpart, uses her wit to advantage. Having married for love, she finds herself disappointed in her husband's behavior. Yet, instead of pursuing self-interested schemes of revenge or love affairs to bolster her vanity in the face of his neglect, she turns her attention to other duties, the rearing of their children, the care of their home. She does not upbraid her husband, though neither does she praise him, for failing to fulfill the duties of their mutual love. Her goodness leads her to friendship with a wealthy woman who wants to support the family Mr. Bilson treats so carelessly. She asks Mrs. Bilson to bring her family to live with her, but she conditions the invitation by excepting Mr. Bilson from the general offer. Mrs. Bilson refuses; her husband, she says, is good, just misguided, an assessment later confirmed by his repentance and reformation. The wealthy patron leaves the Bilsons her fortune which they spend in the exercise of general charity.

This utopian vision is supported, as is that in *David Simple*, by the wit of a woman—Mrs. Bilson, in this case—who has the skill to see and judge her husband's worth and behavior, both the good and the bad, and who has the principled love necessary to effect reform. Vanity, self-regard, individual ambition will not serve the fundamental ethical purpose which is to achieve happiness. That can come only from chiastic relationships which in Fielding's view merge the interests of self with those of community so completely that the figure is not to be broken down into the individual terms that comprise it. True Wit is differentiated from "humbugging" (2: 17), Fielding's term for malicious wit exercised at the expense of others' feelings. True Wit is "sprightly Humour . . . to enliven and amuse, but never to give mental Pain, or expose any . . . to Derision." The Bilsons "laughed *with*, but never *at*, one another" (2: 288). Underwritten by a sense of religion that accepts "natural Infirmities" as a part of life, this kind of wit serves to join the community in laughter not born of vanity and envy but "of truly gladdened and happy Hearts" (2: 289).

Wit, moreover, allows for an accuracy of perception, penetration that is necessary to the forming of a happy community. It determines the worthiness of the members of the community before one allows oneself the luxury of openness and vulnerability to the demands of the other. Once that is allowed, separate schemes of happiness make no sense. Identity has been fused; the meeting with the other at the heart of the chiasmus has transformed the identity of each.

Central to Fielding's ethical vision is an expression of sexual difference she holds in common with Richardson—the voicing of female desire. In Fielding's fiction, as in *Sir Charles Grandison*, this desire manifests itself in an unselfconscious admission of love and ethical obligation (though as we will see, Fielding rejects the term "obligation" itself). In *The Lives of Cleopatra and Octavia*, Octavia articulates the ideal that Fielding's exemplary female characters pursue:

My predominant Passion was Love, and the highest Notion I could form of Happiness, was a private Life, with a Husband who was agreeable to my Inclinations, and capable of reciprocal Affection. But this Opinion which I had formed of Happiness with such a Husband, rendered me the more cautious of giving way to my Affections, till my Approbation of the Object made such an Indulgence reasonable . . . . [I]t was requisite for my Peace of Mind, that I should be united to a Man who was the Object of my Inclinations, and whose Disposition would make an artful Behaviour on my Part totally needless to obtain good Usage, or to secure his Esteem.[47]

Octavia's occupation of the subject position is reinforced by her depiction of Marcellus as one who more than answers her desires. She likens herself to Pygmalion, "for he was the Portrait I had drawn, animated with Life and Motion" (184). She enjoys with Marcellus a love "unmixed with Vanity," an "Affection . . . so perfectly mutual . . . that our Thoughts were known to each other, before the Tongue could express them" (184). This perfect union is succeeded by its opposite; after Marcellus's death, Octavia is married to Anthony whose experience of love with Fulvia and Cleopatra has led him to form very different ideas of marriage. Octavia endeavors to put Anthony's needs and concerns at the center of her life; she employs her wit to seek his advantage, but her intelligence is a source of pain to him: "when once *Anthony* was convinced in himself that I imagined his Understanding was inferior to mine, all my Compliance with his Will and Submission to his Judgment, appeared to him so many Artifices to recommend my own" (202). Octavia's marriage to Anthony, determined by political necessity (to forge a reconciliation between her brother and the general), is political in nature as well. Competition, founded on the notion of individual ambition, cannot produce the happy effects of love described in the Bilson episodes of *The History of the Countess of Dellwyn* or chronicled in the depiction of Octavia's brief but happy marriage to Marcellus.

Fielding's meditations on the nature of female desire echo Richardson's similar meditations in *Sir Charles Grandison*. Harriet Byron is forthcoming about her esteem and love for Charles Grandison. She identifies him as the object of her desire without compunction or restraint. But she defines desire as desire for his happiness, and when it appears that his happiness lies in love for another woman, Clementina, Harriet withdraws physically from his presence, symbolically signifying resignation of the demands her desire would place on him. Olivia, of course, does the opposite, pursuing Sir Charles, brandishing a poinard, threatening him with violence if he does not return her love. Her actions are motivated by vanity and self-regard; she illustrates a point that Fielding will make in *The Cry*: "Fury and love . . . never inhabited the same breast towards the same object; and whenever we fancy they meet, let us but examine them a little nearer, and we shall easily distinguish pride piqued from disappointed love" (1: 53). Harriet's suffering is the suffering of disappointed love. She loses no esteem for the object of her desire; indeed, her approbation and affection increase as he fulfills his ethical responsibilities to the woman he loved first. Harriet's happiness is, however, dependent on Sir Charles; her desire being thwarted, she finds herself in a depleted condition, physically and emotionally.

In *The Cry*, Portia explains the nature of her desire to a disbelieving, cynical audience. She admits to being in love: "It would, I confess, be the highest joy of my life, to know myself instrumental to . . . [Ferdinand's] happiness." If that is not to be,

---

47   *The Lives of Cleopatra and Octavia* (London, 1757), p. 179. Further references are cited parenthetically.

however, she "would take care that by [her] behaviour [she] became not the cause [of] his misery" (1: 51). She claims that were he to marry another, she could not hate her rival, and when the Cry ridicules her, she explains: "I might indeed be grieved for the disappointment of my love, but I could not be angry that he had exerted his undoubted right of chusing" (1: 52). The Cry satirically remarks that her lover would be under "obligations to *Portia*, for her fantastic generosity; he would thank her highly for her disinterested love, in desiring him to marry another woman" (1: 54). Their perverse interpretation of Portia's words is like Anthony's perverse reading of Octavia's behavior toward him. Portia patiently explains that she does not define love in terms of "obligation," by which she disavows the kind of love that is constantly looking toward the demands of the self, requiring of the other certain behaviors and addresses before yielding to affection and regard. Her recognition of her lover's otherness is recognition of her ethical obligation to him, however, a contextual shift in register that Fielding herself is not suggesting (that sense of "obligation" would be foreign to her) but that fits with her own perception that ethical communities transform words, concepts, and identities through the reciprocity of mutual love.

When Portia is faced with the possibility that Ferdinand does not return her love in full measure, she too suffers, though—had his infidelity been proved her suffering would be less acute than Harriet's because he would prove himself unworthy her esteem and therefore incapable of the kind of mutual exchange these fictions set up as requisite to the highest human happiness. Her disappointment is more philosophical than Harriet's because she feels that Ferdinand is acting against his own self-interest as well as her happiness in choosing to love someone other than herself—"for I verily believe that I am the only one of his acquaintance who hath truly penetrated his character; and, consequently, the only one who can properly be said truly to love him" (2: 227).

Portia ends her meditation on true love with valorization of female wit:

> without reciprocally understanding each other, there can be no true love. A man who chuses a companion, whose capacity doth not reach high enough to comprehend any of his ideas might (as far as regards that single companion) be as well struck dumb; for the utility of language is to him entirely vanished. (2: 227–8)

Without a woman to hear and to understand, male speech is meaningless—man is deprived of the one trait that distinguishes him from other animals. He is, in essence, reduced to his senses. In a paradox worthy the subtlest wit, Fielding has asserted that without a woman of wit—both (i.e. women and wit) traditionally associated with the senses, the surface, not the mind—man is reduced to senses, surface, absence of thought. He needs sense to avoid nonsense; he needs the female in order to be male. The logic is indisputable, but Fielding's argument certainly turns the traditional devaluation of women on its head. What she has given voice to here is the essential binarism of every definition wherein the figures are so dependent on one another they can no longer be—cannot exist—without the opposing force of difference.

The assumption at the heart of sentimentalism is the centrality of marriage and the resulting importance of the marital unit as the site of happiness. The rise of sentimentalism involves the domestication of virtue, that is the shift from public to private life and the accordant valorization of spousal fidelity and parental care over public demonstrations of courage and conviction in support of the state. Such a shift increases the significance of the female. That Richardson and Fielding place such an emphasis on the woman's duty or right to speak her desire is revolutionary, as is the movement of virtue into the individual home. If the state is formed of units of desiring subjects who assure each other's happiness through ethical treatment of one another, political stability is all but guaranteed as the locus and objective of desire has moved into the private realm. That this shift occurs during the mid-century, during the last serious effort of the Jacobites to gain the throne, is no coincidence. The Catholic/Protestant tension that drives the plot of *Sir Charles Grandison* is reflective of the cultural clash between public effeminacy and private manliness, between nonsense and sense, between the outmoded national paradigm of phallic power and the emergent nation defined by women's wit spoken in the voices of men.

The Figure of Wit[48]

Emergent forms of wit, Addison opines, must be "manly," and as such they must eschew the obvious materiality of anagram, acrostic, pun, mere rhyme (doggerel, echo, bouts rimes, etc.), image, lipogram, and chronogram. Addison reflects the conventional construction of such materiality as feminine by associating it with women's pastimes, clothing, and accessories. At the end of *Spectator* 58, for example, he assumes the voice of a projector, recommending that "modern Smatterers in Poetry" imitate the ancients by trying to excel in patterned verses. He praises a "young Poetical Lover" for writing verses in the shape of his mistress's fan and proposing to write another set of verses that will form a ring that "shall exactly fit" her finger. He equates such experiments with other fashionable "Female Ornaments."[49] Echo, of course, is female according to mythology, the nymph who pines for Narcissus, and that she lends her name to a kind of wit Addison disavows in Essay 59 reinforces both the gendering of false wit begun in the first essay of the series and the nature of emergent forms of true wit (self-reflective and self-absorbed) that the series endorses and encodes as "manly." Essay 60 associates the false wit of wordplay, such as a book-length poem on the Virgin Mary consisting of only eight words in various combinations, with monkish learning; but as the essay continues, Addison once more compares such labors to courtship rituals:

> When the Anagrammatist takes a Name to work upon, he considers it at first as a Mine not broken up, which will not shew the Treasure it contains till he shall have spent many Hours in the Search of it: For it is his Business to find out one Word that conceals itself in another, and to examine the Letters in all the Variety of Stations in which they can

---

48   This section originally appeared as part of a longer study entitled "Wit and *The Spectator*'s Ethics of Desire." Reprinted with permission from *Studies in English Literature 1500–1900* 45, 3 (Summer 2005).

49   *The Spectator*, ed. Donald F. Bond (5 vols, Oxford, 1965), vol. 1, p. 248. Further references will be to this volume and cited parenthetically by page number.

possibly be ranged. I have heard of a Gentleman who, when this Kind of Wit was in fashion, endeavoured to gain his Mistress's Heart by it.[50]

Bouts rimes are also associated with female frivolity; Addison traces their origin to "Tasks which the *French* Ladies used to impose on their Lovers" (1: 258). Though he defines them as "excusable" in light of their original purpose, their relationship to both female whim and French fashion renders them suspect. True wit can be tested by translation alone, Addison explains in *Spectator* 61: "[I]f it bears the Test you may pronounce it true; but if it vanishes in the Experiment, you may conclude it to have been a Punn" (1: 263). True Wit, Addison explains, is like Aristinetus's description of a fine woman: "When she is *dress'd* she is Beautiful, when she is *undress'd* she is Beautiful" (1: 263). The image is a significant reminder of traditional associations between wit and desire, associations the *Spectator*, in the end, would rather redeem than condemn. The thrust of the series seems an attack on false wit, a fleshing out—as it were—of the principles adumbrated at the end of Edward Bysshe's *Art of English Poetry* (1702) which itself can be seen as part of a larger cultural project establishing the values associated with the heroic couplet—balance, antithesis, control, tension, the satisfaction of rhyme.[51] Predictably, the examples of false wit mentioned by Bysshe, like those elaborated by Addison, are resonant with what from the Anglican view was regarded as the "superstition" of Catholicism, and, in the general political atmosphere of 1710, this resonance would have been particularly acute, due to the notoriety of violently "high Church" Henry Sacheverell. In fact, the country had been preoccupied for at least six months by questions of Anglicanism's relationship to dissenters, Whigs, and moderates on the one hand, and Catholics on the other.[52]

---

50   Mary Bohun, to her credit, is unimpressed with her lover's efforts to turn her name into an anagram. He mistook her last name for Boon, and when informed of his mistake, "lost his Senses, which indeed had been very much impaired by that continual Application he had given to his Anagram" (1: 255).

51   See, for example, Bysshe's chapter "Rules for Making English Verse," in *The Art of English Poetry*, 1702, ed. R. C. Alston, English Linguistics 1500–1800: A Collection of Facsimile Reprints 75 (Menston, 1968), pp. 1–36. J. Paul Hunter's work on the heroic couplet is pertinent here. See, for example, his "Sleeping Beauties: Are Historical Aesthetics Worth Recovering?" *Eighteenth-Century Studies* 24 (2000): 1–20.

52   Sacheverell's anti-toleration campaign began in the early eighteenth century and consisted of sermons and pamphlets in which he "violently abused dissenters, low churchmen, latitudinarians, and Whigs" (DNB). His rhetoric famously prompted Defoe's satire, *The Shortest Way with Dissenters* (1702) and other negative responses, but through the early part of the eighteenth century, his church career flourished, fueled by general approval of high church sentiment and by his own charisma and oratorical power. After a sermon preached at the Derby assizes on August 15, 1709, leading Whigs initiated an impeachment in the House of Commons which ended in a three-year suspension of preaching for Sacheverell and, more disastrously for the Whigs, a rise in his popularity (especially among women as *Spectator* 57 suggests) and the ultimate fall of the Whig government in August 1710. Addison writes his series on wit after Sacheverell's sentencing (regarded as a victory for the Tories because of its relative benignity) but before the fall of Godolphin's government and a Tory victory in the November 1710 general election.

Even without the explicit association of symbolic language and Roman Catholicism, however, the very idea of wit would have recalled to some minds of 1710 the general atmosphere of the Restoration court and by extension would have led to concerns about threats to political stability posed by the exiled Catholic king and his heir. Addison seems intent on forging those connections and linking them to a broader cultural criticism of a certain kind of materiality. For by the early eighteenth century, "wit" had accrued connotations that—to some minds—explicitly linked it to libertine thought, not Catholicism but free-thinking at best, atheism at worst. Wit, to these minds, represented a materialism that emanated from and stimulated desires of the flesh. Mary Astell's was one such mind.

Those of us accustomed to thinking of the *Tatler* and the *Spectator* as the engines of moral reform they claimed to be need reminding occasionally that in their own time these papers were associated, by the Tories anyway, with a very different kind of reform. Even discounting for the exaggerations of political rhetoric, it seems clear that contemporaries would bring a set of associations to the papers that would color their reading of the ideas and arguments therein in a way different from our own. For one thing, these works were clearly the product of the Kit-Cat Club, reflecting the known attitudes of that group of famous and influential Whigs. And what was known of those attitudes was that they were, in two separate senses, libertine.

The Kit-Cat Club was a toasting club, proposing and voting on the "reigning beauties" of the time, determining for a season the one who stood foremost among the many. The competition was serious and the honor at being chosen was real. Verses honoring the "toasts" were inscribed on wine glasses by the members of the club and recorded for posterity in John Nichols's *Select Collection of Poems* (1782).[53] The "candidates" were supposedly virgins, not mistresses, real or potential. The point was to nominate and celebrate beauty, and the conventional wisdom was that the "happy Virgin who is receiv'd and drank to at their Meetings has no more to do in this Life, but to judge and accept of the first good Offer."[54] Of course, the reality may have been otherwise. Tory satirists certainly suggest that the "toasts" were at least sometimes women of questionable virtue. And, in any event, the notion of Whig statesmen, writers, and booksellers electing themselves the arbiters of taste, in essence defining desire, is ominous—perhaps more so than if there had been personal interest involved. What gives them the right? Whence derives their authority?

Certainly, that is Mary Astell's question. She alludes to the toasting as an example of the luxury, free-thinking, and voluptuousness of the "most Illustrious Society of the Kit-Cats," which she styles a self-appointed and oppressive cultural authority: "When an Ill-bred Fellow endeavours to protect a Wife, or Daughter, or

---

53   See "On the Toasting Glasses of the Kit-Cat Club" (1703) in *A Select Collection of Poems with Notes Biographical and Historical*, ed. John Nichols (8 vols, London, 1782; New York, 1969), vol. 5, pp. 168–76. For the Kit-Cats' link to and difference from the Knights of the Toast, see Robert J. Allen, *The Clubs of Augustan London* (Cambridge, 1933), pp. 39–41.

54   From *Tatler* 24. *The Tatler*, ed. Donald F. Bond, (3 vols, Oxford, 1987), vol. 1, p. 188. Further references will be to this volume and will be cited parenthetically.

other vertuous Woman, from your very Civil Addresses, your noble Courage never fails of being rous'd upon such great Provocations, and if the vile Offender don't sneak out of your way, unarm'd as he is, you know how to whip him thro' the Lungs most valiantly."[55] Her prefatory dedication to the Kit-Cats implies that the wit she describes in the following essay typifies their rhetoric of raillery and ridicule. Her particular target in the *Enquiry After Wit* is Shaftesbury's "Letter Concerning Enthusiasm" in which he asserts that subjecting religion to the "rule of ridicule" is an appropriate, even necessary test of truth. Shaftesbury, combating the kind of zeal characteristic of both Sacheverell and some dissenting sects, reflects the general urbanity of the Whig response to earnest religious debate, rhetoric Astell deems inappropriate but characteristic: "Improperly and Inconsistently do our Men of Wit talk of GOD and Religion . . . For the Subjects are *really too Grave*, to suffer a Man of Sense to divert himself with their Foolish, as well as Prophane and Impious way of treating them" (33). The *Spectator* papers, of course, eschewed direct religious controversy, but in locating the site of cultural authority in the coffee house rather than the sanctuary, taking as its typical subject matter the material experience of everyday life rather than the concerns of eternity, these papers would seem to Astell the products of *"lovers of Pleasure more than lovers of GOD"* (82), what Astell says of wit in general. Wit, to her, is nothing more than a "wallow[ing] in Sensual Delights," and she "esteem[s] it beneath the Dignity of a Rational Nature to dwell upon the Pleasures of Sense" (31).

Florence Smith reads *Tatler* 32 as a direct response to Astell's antisensualist pamphlet.[56] "Platonic," intellectual women, *Tatler* 32 asserts, are to be "converted" by men who awaken their passions and thereby teach them to "fall in with the Necessities of mortal Life, and condescend to look with Pity upon an unhappy Man, imprison'd in so much Body, and urg'd by such violent Desires" (1: 241). The *Tatler* posits against Astell the "naturalness" of erotic desire and the falseness of intellectual schemes that seek to deny or divert that desire, distinctions that Joseph Addison draws on later, in the *Spectator* series on wit. Here he links false wit to overly clever (and ineffective) courtship rituals and true wit to the actual (natural) arousal of sexual desire. In choosing to compare true wit to female beauty that pleases whether clothed or naked, Addison invokes what could be considered a libertine aesthetic. He does, after all, encourage readers to imagine and admire the nude female form as he teases them with the prospect of a situation in which desire can be aroused and gratified—the vision of a beautiful woman dressed, and the act of unclothing her to reveal the beauty that has already been perceived and acknowledged. But because Addison obscures the difference between the naked and the clothed, the analogy probably did not strike most readers as libertine in 1710 any more than it strikes most of us that way today. There is nothing clandestine or lascivious or transgressive about Addison's frank admission that a beautiful woman will be beautiful whether

55 *Bart'lemy Fair: Or, an Enquiry after Wit* (London, 1709), p. 6. Further references will be cited parenthetically.

56 See Allen, p. 48, who cites Smith's *Mary Astell* (New York, 1916), p. 25, for the view that in *Tatler* 32 "Mary Astell's educational theories are roughly handled" in retaliation for Astell's attack on the Kit-Cats in *Bart'lemy Fair*.

dressed or undressed. In fact, the figure of speech functions by aestheticizing the erotic impulse. By "figuring" "true wit" as a dressed and undressed woman, Addison suggests that one of the most important functions of wit is to construct aesthetic pleasure from the impulses of material desire.[57] In its very nature, Julia Kristeva has observed, "[t]he figure of speech is amatory: as condensation and displacement of semantic features it points to an uncertainty, not concerning the *object* of love . . . but an uncertainty concerning the bond, the attitude of the loving subject toward the other."[58] How appropriate that Addison would figure wit as the object of masculine erotic desire.

The idealizing and aestheticizing of women and wit obviously dematerializes them and by that means regulates them—denying them the status of desiring subjects with aims and objectives other than the aims and objectives of men and judgment. But Addison is, in the last analysis, a materialist himself, and in the fetishizing of the papers in which he presents his version of true wit, in his general fascination with the materiality of contemporary life, in his focus on the here and now rather than the eternal, he makes provision for differences he would theoretically obscure. In his *Spectator* papers, Addison replaces one kind of materialism with another; he, in essence, constructs manliness out of what had been traditionally gendered female. Like Moses before him and Richardson after, Addison sings his sisters' songs, and in the very act of appropriation leaves traces of difference, echoes of the voices of women who once spoke their own desires.

---

57   See Erin Mackie who reads the passage as "[t]he imposition on woman's body of the male critic's aesthetic ideal." *Market á la Mode: Fashion, Commodity, and Gender in "The Tatler" and "The Spectator"* (Baltimore, 1997), p. 230.

58   *Tales of Love*, trans. Leon S. Roudiez (New York, 1987), p. 91.

Chapter 6

The Forgotten Woman

In her preface to her 1798 novel *The Young Philosopher*, Charlotte Smith declares her credentials for delineating "all the evils arising from oppression, from fraud and chicane": "If a Writer can best describe who has suffered . . . I am above almost any person qualified."[1] Legal chicanery, domestic cruelty, painful personal loss resonate loudly when they appear in the fictional world of Charlotte Smith. *The Young Philosopher*, like most of her works, offers a scathing indictment of both legal corruption and familial abuse, and it also features scenes of domestic tragedy. In this novel, the middle-aged Laura Glenmorris doubles for Smith as the author enacts her own anxieties and the anxieties of her historical moment, anxieties born, in large part, of the sense of liminality that the age of sensibility had conferred on women.

Laura's suffering replicates Smith's painful personal history in its source—frustrations with obtaining legal justice—and in its effect—severance from a beloved child. Laura's response to these trials, however, is condemned by Smith in the novel's preface wherein she states that part of her moral purpose is to show that "too acute sensibility, too hastily indulged, is the source of much unhappiness" (6). Daughter Medora's kidnapping catapults Laura into, first, a restless terror, then, madness and confinement in a private madhouse. Although she is rescued from this space and reunited with husband and daughter, Laura seems permanently damaged: "I feel," she says, "that my mind is hurt, my temper embittered" (350). At the novel's close, Laura pleads for return to America where she will not be "haunted by the images of lawyers [and] the dread of persecution." "[W]hile I stay in England," she poignantly opines, "I am sure I shall be incapable of happiness" (350).

In a didactic flourish toward the end of the novel, the narrator ascribes Laura's unhappy history in large part to the psychological excess of dwelling on "imaginary miseries" (349), underscoring, as it were, the author's prefatory disavowal of sensibility. In the novel proper, however, as Lorraine Fletcher has noted, "sense and sensibility are not clearly differentiated."[2] Her perception is born out in studies by Chris Jones and Markman Ellis which have intelligently theorized the repudiation of sensibility that characterizes much literature of the 1790s, arguing that overt criticism of the mode or movement thinly masked the continued commitment to a notion of community founded on sympathy, feeling, and sentiment.[3] Both recognize, however,

---

1 *The Young Philosopher*, ed. Elizabeth Kraft, Eighteenth-Century Novels by Women, gen. ed. Isobel Grundy (Lexington, 1999), p. 5. Further references will be cited parenthetically in the text.

2 *Charlotte Smith: A Critical Biography* (London, 1998), p. 276.

3 Jones, *Radical Sensibility: Literature and Ideas in the 1790s* (London and New York, 1993) and Ellis, *The Politics of Sensibility: Race, Gender and Commerce in the Sentimental*

that self-consciousness about sensibility had become acute by the last decade of the eighteenth century. Increasingly suspect, as a result, were both the language of feeling and the sentimental novel which codified powerful, and emotionally manipulative, cultural paradigms. Writers who employed such language and wrote such novels did so with an awareness of a sophisticated readership as likely to laugh as to cry at the sensible subject and sentimental situation.[4] As a consequence, novelists developed indirect, or ironic, strategies of fashioning fictional communities from feeling individuals. And, as Jones has pointed out, Charlotte Smith was particularly skilled at discovering and putting into play an irony that preserved sentimental unity in the act of disclaiming it. "As a female author highly conscious of her reception," he notes, Smith "could be seen as progressively cultivating the 'private' authorial persona . . . in a knowing exploitation of literary technique and manipulation of emotional response."[5] Coupled with this focus on the suffering female, however, is the skillful structuring of "parallel situations" in a narrative characterized by the "play of irony and allusive satire which disturbed the expectations of the reader and the conventions of the genre."[6] Jones's point in this analysis is that Smith's indirection confused critics who failed to see that female vulnerability could coexist with committed radicalism. But Smith and other late-century writers—radical and conservative alike—knew that the suffering self can become a powerful unifying force. They demonstrated in various ways that the suffering female self has particular potency in traditionally patriarchal societies under the stress of revolutionary change.[7]

Banished

Who better to illustrate the ethical implications of the suffering woman than Hagar whose wilderness cry provokes the response of God? She is the only individual in the Bible—male or female—to give God a name, and she calls Him "El Roi" which means, literally, "God of seeing" and which signifies both "'God of my seeing,'

Novel, Cambridge Studies in Romanticism, gen. eds Marilyn Butler and James Chandler (Cambridge, 1996).

4 Ellis discusses the repudiation of sensibility as extending to anxieties about the motives and morality of novel-reading itself (pp. 190–221). In a similar vein, Jones observes: "With the disintegration of a widely shared moral consciousness the novelist could no longer have confidence in the reactions of the reader. The didactic art of sensibility relied on the identification of the reader with the character whose emotional and moral responses might refine their own and strengthen the social passions which were hailed as the forces of progress." By the 1790s such didacticism will not work (183).

5 *Radical Sensibility*, p. 184.

6 Ibid., pp. 183–4.

7 Not to be discussed below, but worth remembering, is Edmund Burke's depiction of the suffering Marie Antoinette in *Reflections on the Revolution in France* (1790). Burke, of course, was pursuing a conservative agenda, but most writers committed to social reform also exploited the suffering woman. Mary Wollstonecraft's *Maria; or the Wrongs of Woman* (1798), Eliza Fenwick's *Secresy* (1795), and Mary Hays's *Victim of Prejudice* (1799) come readily to mind, as does William Godwin's controversial emphasis on his deceased wife's emotional travails in *Memoirs of Mary Wollstonecraft* (1798).

that is, whom I have seen; and 'God who sees me.'"[8] We hold these meanings in our minds simultaneously, according to biblical commentators, but we also read a special significance into the second aspect of Hagar's naming: "The God who sees me," is a God "who notices the oppressed, the needy, the marginalized, those of whom human society takes no notice."[9]

The forlorn. The rejected. The dispossessed. The desperate. The exiled. Those seeking refuge and shelter and kindness—amid harshness, torment, and pain. The misunderstood. The homeless. The unloved. The unwashed. The unattractive. The unhealthy. The unknown. The wanderers. The strangers. The oppressed. The hurt and wounded. The mad ones. The bad ones. The ones that do not fit it. Hagar bears their burden. She cries their tears. And God sees.

The story of Hagar is bound up with the story of Sarah (Sarai) and Abraham (Abram). She enters the biblical narrative at the behest of Sarai: "Sarai, Abram's wife, had borne him no children. She had an Egyptian maidservant whose name was Hagar. And Sarai said to Abram: 'Look, the Lord has kept me from bearing. Consort with my maid; perhaps I shall have a son through her'" (Genesis 16: 1–2). Unusual as this arrangement seems to us today, it was standard operating procedure in biblical times—not just in the tribe of Abram, but all over the ancient world. Sarai is doing what any good wife would do. She is ensuring the transmission of her husband's seed and the continuation of his lineage through the means at her disposal—a handmaid turned concubine, a vessel. The strange and wondrous thing in this story is that the vessel speaks.[10]

Often the struggle between Sarai and Hagar is presented as a common episode of jealousy that could have and should have been resolved by Abram so that it did not eventuate in the banishing of Hagar and the disenfranchising of Ishmael. The biblical narrative, to be sure, provides evidence that the progeny of Abram and Hagar, the descendants of Ishmael, define themselves in opposition to the progeny of Abraham and Sarah, the descendants of Isaac. We do not call the Ishmaelites members of the tribe of Abram, and, in fact, in many of the important stories—the story of Joseph, the story of Moses—the oppressors of Israel are linked to the tribe of Ishmael. The peoples, as we know to our continuing pain and sorrow, are seen and see themselves as natural enemies, despite a common paternity, and despite the presence of both Ishmael and Isaac at the grave of Abraham (Genesis 25: 9). Abraham is represented as a loving father in both Islamic and Jewish traditions. The enmity between the people, it is agreed, can be traced back to the bitterness between the mothers of the tribes. Of the two, the burden of responsibility falls on Sarai. She was the one, after all, who insisted on Hagar's banishment. Yet, it was also through Sarai's agency that Hagar became the mother of Ishmael in order that through Hagar's agency Sarai herself could become a mother at all.

---

8   *Etz Hayim*, 88.

9   Ibid.

10   Or, as Tikva Frymer-Kensky puts it, "Hagar, who was supposed to be a neutral body being passed from Sarai to Abram, reacts: This 'womb with legs' is a person with her own viewpoint." *Reading the Women of the Bible*, p. 228.

In a patriarchal society, of course, the "best" men have many women—or can have. Early Hebrew society (as it is represented in the biblical texts) seems to have had some notion of emotional monogamy, and the stories of the meetings between Isaac and Rebekah, Jacob and Rachel, Moses and Zipporah, the lovers in the Song of Songs are emblematic ethical moments of ideal reciprocity and mutual desire. Nevertheless, these special marriages do not preclude other couplings for the husbands. Concubines abound, and their relations with the patriarchs are not represented as episodes of adultery or occasions for jealousy or any other kind of uxorial discord. Generation is desired by all—to the point that it is a matter of Jewish law that a man may put aside a wife to whom he has been married for ten years without issue.

It is also a matter of Jewish law and lore that, while generation is to be desired, marriage is also about companionship and love:

> The story is told of a woman in Sidon who lived ten years with her husband without bearing a child. Deciding to part from each other, the two came to R. Simeon ben Yohai, who said to them, 'By your lives, even as you were paired over food and drink, so should you be separated over food and drink.' They followed his advice and, declaring the day a festal day for themselves, prepared a great feast, during which the wife gave her husband too much to drink. In his resulting good humor, he said to her, 'My dear, pick any fine article you want in my home, and take it with you when you return to your father's house.' What did she do? After he fell asleep, she beckoned to her menservants and maidservants, and said to them, 'Pick him up, with the couch, take him along, and carry him to my father's house.' At midnight, he woke up from his sleep. The effects of the wine had left him, and he asked, 'My dear, where am I?' She replied, 'You are in my father's house.' He: 'But what am I doing in your father's house?' She: 'Did you not say to me last night, Pick any desirable article you like from my house and take it with you when you return to your father's house? There is no fine article in the world I care for more than for you.' They again went to R. Simeon ben Yohai, and he arose and prayed for them, and they were remembered [by God and granted children].[11]

This midrash is associated with the Song of Songs, but it might be said to hearken back as well to the marriage of the first patriarch, for Abram had certainly been married longer than ten years to a barren wife. He seems content to accept their fate. It is Sarai who takes matters into her own hands and decides to provide a surrogate through whom she and Abram can have a child.

In choosing Hagar, she is no doubt selecting someone who reminds her of herself. After all, she does say "I shall have a son through her"—so the notion that there is identification is not farfetched. Indeed, Hagar is an Egyptian, a stranger, and she may remind Sarai of her own brief sojourn as a stranger in the palace of an Egyptian king who desired her. In providing Hagar for Abram, Sarai relives a moment when she was the object of desire—a psychologically understandable thing for a woman who is having to accept barrenness. Perhaps there is something else going on as well. Perhaps between maid and mistress there has been some conversation about Abram and the possibility that he is incapable of fathering a child. Perhaps Sarai had

---

11   Song R. 1: 4, no. 2.

wondered aloud to Hagar, and perhaps Hagar half believed Abram incapable.[12] The arrangement could have begun as a conspiracy between the women to validate their sex and to ensure the status quo. Perhaps it was even a pre-emptive strike on Sarai's part—just in case Abram stopped talking to God long enough to remember that he had the right to put her aside in favor of a woman who could bear his heirs.

It would be more than a matter of common jealousy that would provoke Sarai's anger at the quickly-pregnant Hagar's insolence. In fact, the text tells us that Sarai was "lowered in [Hagar's] esteem" (Genesis 16: 4), suggesting that the handmaid began to exhibit a disdain that was evident, as well as inexplicable, to Sarai. She seems to believe that a confederacy has developed between Abram and Hagar, and so she demands that Abram reject the one she now calls "slave." We noted in Chapter 1, Abram's reaction is dismissive and passive. He does not fight his wife's anger, nor does he object to her harsh treatment of the woman who is carrying his child. Nor does he rush to retrieve Hagar when she flees into the wilderness, toward Egypt, toward home. But God does follow and God does convince Hagar to return. God also names the unborn son, Ishmael (God hears), in commemoration of this encounter, and he describes the people who will emerge from the life growing in Hagar's womb:

'I will greatly increase your offspring,
And they shall be too many to count'
The angel of the Lord said to her further,
'Behold, you are with child
And shall bear a son;
You shall call him Ishmael,
For the Lord has paid heed to your suffering.
He shall be a wild ass of a man;
His hand against everyone,
And everyone's against him;
He shall dwell alongside of all his kinsmen.' (Genesis 16: 10–14)

This prophecy is not simply a forecast about Hagar's progeny. It speaks as well to her deepest desire. In this first instance of God's intervention in her life, she knows only negative need—the need to escape pain. She is "running away" (Genesis 16: 8), so God sends her back to Sarai and Abram. He does not promise her an easy time, but he does tell her to return: "Go back to your mistress, and submit to her harsh treatment" (Genesis 16: 9). If, on the one hand, the reason for her return is for the destiny of her people, it is also for her own comfort, her own emotional well-being, despite the "harsh treatment" she is told to expect. The episode ends by emphasizing Abram's bonding with his infant son and his concubine-wife. The repetition and chiastic arrangement of the three names in the final two verses of Genesis 16 rhetorically emphasize the strength of the bond between the man, woman, and child: "Hagar bore a son to Abram, and Abram gave the son that Hagar bore him the name Ishmael.

---

12 Midrash records references to Abraham as a "barren mule." Gen. R. 53: 10; Deut. R. 1: 25.

Abram was eighty-six years old when Hagar bore Ishmael to Abram" (Genesis 16: 15–16). It is to create this bond that Hagar has returned.

Of course, as we know, this family will not remain together. The substitution of Ishmael for Hagar in the second chiasmus reflects the split that will occur between concubine-wife and husband. After Isaac's birth, Sarai (now Sarah) insists on the expulsion of Hagar and Ishmael, and so they go. Both Jewish and Islamic traditions, however, maintain that ties of affection, particularly between father and son, continue to bind the triad of Abram, Hagar, and Ishmael. A midrash has it that Abraham attaches a "wheeled water tub . . . to Hagar's loins" when he orders her to leave so that he will know which direction she travels with his firstborn son. Jewish legend also has Abraham visiting the newly married Ishmael's home in order to assure himself of his son's well-being. Abraham is met with hostility and suspicion by Ishmael's Moabite wife Aissa, whereupon, the patriarch asks the young woman to tell Ishmael that an old man from Canaan stopped by and said "'the household of this house is not in good repair.'" Hearing the message, Ishmael promptly divorces Aissa, and Hagar contracts another marriage for her son, this time with a woman, Fatima, "from her father's house in the land of Egypt." Three years after the marriage, Abraham again travels to his son's household and again is met by his unknowing daughter-in-law who, unlike her predecessor, responds to his requests for water and bread with willing hospitality (here I am). As a result, "Abraham entreated the Holy One in his son's behalf, and Ishmael's house was filled with all manner of good things." The midrash ends, poignantly, "Then Ishmael realized that his father still loved him."[13]

As for Hagar herself, she remains a source of discomfort for Sarah. In the foregoing midrash, Abraham vows to Sarah that he will not dismount from his camel during his visit to Ishmael, and he does not. In fact, on neither occasion does he see either Ishmael or Hagar as they are away from home collecting fruit the first time and grazing the camels the second. Still, he remains mounted on his camel at Sarah's insistence. She knows the danger inherent in her husband's entering the dwelling of Hagar and Ishmael. Abraham would no doubt feel at home; and he might not return. Indeed, according to Islamic tradition, that is exactly what happens. Abraham follows Hagar and Ishmael to Arabia, and he stays to found the Kaaba in Mecca and to die and be buried there too.[14] Yet, even knowing the dangers, the misrashic Sarah does agree to the visit. To the classical rabbinic mind, anyway, Hagar's expulsion from Canaan was not an erasure or an eradication. It could not be. For one thing, she was the mother of Abraham's first son, who was named by God himself. Secondly, she is, as Tikva Frymer-Kensky puts it, one "of those few women—Samson's mother, Hannah, and Mary in the New Testament—who receive a divine annunciation of the coming birth."[15] And, finally, her story is the story of Israel itself.[16] The brief narrative of Hagar functions as a mise-en-abyme of the story recounted in Exodus of enslavement, abuse, expulsion, and redemption through generation. Sarah is the matriarch of Israel, but Hagar is the prototype. She is the honored stranger in a

---

13   PRE 30; MhG. Gen. pp. 339–40.
14   Plaut, *The Torah: A Modern Commentary*, p. 143.
15   *Reading the Women of the Bible*, p. 230.
16   See *Reading the Women of the Bible*, pp. 232–4.

strange land, the unjustly oppressed, the special concern of God, and the founder (with Abram) of a powerful nation.

In Frymer-Kensky's words, through the story of Hagar, Genesis "integrates Ishmael into Israel's self-understanding as its God-approved alter ego."[17] The conflict between Hagar and Sarah should not, therefore, be construed as a "conflict between 'us' and 'other,' but between 'us' and 'another us.'"[18] There is the domestic us, the us of a stable marriage, an established home, and a lasting commitment; there is the single us, free and unbounded, loved intensely and memorably and perhaps often, but not restricted or constricted by that love. The domestic us fears loss of the things that define us; that us suffers from jealous self-regard. The free us fears the unknown and suffers the uncertainties of unprotected existence, the harms that the world feels compelled to inflict on those who choose or who are forced to lead unconventional lives. The domestic us dreams of freedom. The free us longs for security. And, of course, sometimes we move from a domestic world into a wilderness, and, whether we do so by choice or by force, we find that the definitions that protected us no longer apply. We may eventually embrace the opportunity to explore our freedom, but in the beginning, we all cry out, like Hagar (and Sarah), for succor and comfort and help. In the end, like Sarah (and Hagar), we tend to find a way to establish a home, define ourselves relationally, and participate in the ongoing saga of our part of human history.

National Identity and the Suffering Self[19]

The Young Philosopher's Laura Glenmorris experiences much of Sarah's history and much of Hagar's as well. Like Sarah, she is a beloved wife and mother. Yet she also suffers the pains of exile and madness. Moreover, Laura's suffering, like Hagar's suffering, is born of her sexual nature. Her passion for Glenmorris led Laura to marry against her parents' will, an act that forces her to move to Scotland; her life there brings, first, the happiness of pregnancy, then the severe sadness of the loss of a child, and, finally, exile to a cave in the Highlands where she retreats to evade the evil machinations of her presumably dead husband's relations. As she maps out her own identity against the history and the geography of her country, she finds herself increasingly alienated from England, from Great Britain. A Sarah in the beginning, in the end, Laura is best described as a Hagar, exiled and longing for the birth of a new world.

By the 1790s, Linda Colley has argued, Britain had in essence redrawn its boundaries to absorb within its sense of national identity the regionalisms that had earlier in the century seemed Celtic other to Anglo-Saxon self.[20] By 1790, the elite

---

17 Ibid., p. 237.

18 Ibid. p. 236.

19 Portions of this section first appeared in my article entitled "Encyclopedic Libertinism and 1798: Charlotte Smith's *The Young Philosopher*," in *The Eighteenth-Century Novel*, 2: 239–72 (© AMS Press, Inc., New York, 2002). Used with permission.

20 *Britons: Forging the Nation 1707–1837* (New Haven and London, 1992), pp.155–64.

of the "boundary" regions were working in London, serving in the British military, marrying English heiresses, vying for posts and recognitions and power with their English counterparts. According to Colley, expanding empire and cognizance of others that seemed truly alien (rebelling Americans, colonial populations) made the inhabitants of the British Isles more aware of things they had in common, more content to huddle Scottish, Welsh, and Anglo-Irish identities along with Englishness under the umbrella of "Briton."[21] In a sense, then, the stated goals of various revolutionaries of the time were already being met through rapprochement driven by economic and political necessity.[22]

Episodes of *The Young Philosopher* set in London, Lancashire, the Scottish Highlands, Wales and, briefly, in Ireland and Jamaica examine British identity in all its constituent parts. Smith pursues her exploration of corruption and the need for change chronologically as well as geographically, debunking outmoded beliefs about "Britishness" and revealing in the process the vertiginous instability of individual and communal existence in a world freed from the reassuring errors of the past. Her invocation of the Celtic aspects of Britain in particular suggests that the assimilation and rapprochement Colley describes were not the only cultural responses to the strains England felt during the troubled latter half of the eighteenth century. For if in some quarters and by some formulations, the Celtic regions of Great Britain could be called on to strengthen the definition of Britishness, for other camps and other hypotheses they provided the opposite evidence, evidence of communal identity that transcended and remapped conventional notions of both family and country.

The individual's identity in this vision of reshaping takes on both more and less significance than it had in traditional formulations of community. Glenmorris's justification for leaving England for America calls the entire matter of national identity into question by narrowing and domesticizing community: "'If I have those I love with me . . . is not every part of the globe equally my country?'" (351).[23] A few paragraphs later he redraws the boundaries of communal identity, elaborating a theophilanthropic sympathy that makes a community of the entire world: "'[T]rue philanthropy does not consist in loving John, and Thomas, and George, and James, because they are our brothers, our cousins, our neighbours, our countrymen, but in benevolence to the whole human race . . . . [W]herever a thinking man enjoys the most uninterrupted domestic felicity, and sees his species the most content, *that*

---

21 Ibid., p. 164.

22 I refer to the United Irishmen, in particular, behind whose movement lay a new vision of nation, one that Kevin Whelan has described thus: "[r]ather than seeing religious, ethnic and political diversity as a disabling problem, the United Irishmen saw it as a glorious opportunity to construct a wider, more tolerant and generous vision of Irish identity." Whelan quotes the United Irishmen's declaration of principle: "'We have thought much about our posterity, little about our ancestors. Are we forever to walk like beasts of prey over the fields which these ancestors stained with blood?'" "Reinterpreting the 1798 Rebellion in County Wexford," in Daire Keogh and Nicholas Furlong (eds), *The Mighty Wave: The 1798 Rebellion in Wexford* (Dublin, 1996), pp. 9–10.

23 Eleanor Ty discusses the community built on these principles in *The Young Philosopher* as a group of "ex-centrics," united by their alienation from England and English institutions. See *Unsex'd Revolutionaries: Five Women Novelists of the 1790s* (Toronto, 1993), p. 144.

is his country'" (352). Individual contentment depends on general benevolence and domestic felicity requiring identification with the entire human race and the creation of an intimate circle of friends one calls family. Such an ideal places large demands on the individual who must negotiate the various claims made by intimate responsiveness (roughly aligned with the demands of sensibility) and theophilanthropic benevolence (requiring dispassionate judgment and control, or "fortitude" as Smith puts it in her preface). *The Young Philosopher* reflects the anxieties born of such negotiations.

The very concept of "national identity" is an unstable one in the world of *The Young Philosopher* as the central characters illustrate. All of the Glenmorrises are citizens of the world, self-defined as proudly lacking fixed national affiliation. Laura was born in Florence of a Dutch merchant and his English wife. Although she was reared in England, she was never naturalized she tells Delmont. Born in Scotland, Glenmorris was educated on the continent and employed, for a while, by Laura's father in England. After the two elope to the Highlands and suffer through the tragic events to which I have referred above, they emigrate first to Switzerland where Medora is born and then after the revolution in America is over to that country where they have lived for about fifteen years at the time Laura and Medora come to England to claim Medora's portion of her grandfather's estate. It is in England, then, that Laura tells young George Delmont, her future son-in-law, the story of her marriage to Medora's father, a story which further undermines the idea of "nation" by reinterpretations of history linked to places of ideological significance. Lancashire and Scotland are prominent settings and provide occasion to address the past, the relationship of present to past, and the role of the individual in national history and cultural tradition.

In Lancashire and Scotland, Laura Glenmorris finds herself confronted with the past—a material as well as a narrative past. Laura's mother, proud to be the descendent of an illegitimate child of Geoffrey Plantagenet, keeps armor and other relics as evidence of her connection. Laura's reading of history differs significantly from her mother's; she attaches more opprobrium than honor to the heroic exploits of the past. She says of her mother's family pride: "'Why any one should find delight in fancying that some of the most hateful characters in history were their ancestors, I never could imagine'" (93), a sentiment that echoes what we have been told earlier of George's childhood attitude toward "those who figure in the annals of nations": "[A]fter he was nine or ten years old, [he] never voluntarily sat down to read pages that seemed almost exclusively the annals of fraud and murder, of selfish ambition, or wicked policy, involving millions in misery for the gratification of a few" (30).

Still, when Laura finds it convenient to tap into the legendary power of the Plantagenets, she does not hesitate to do so. Eloping with her lover, Laura provides Glenmorris some of the armor of Geoffrey Plantagenet which he dons for the purpose of frightening and thereby evading the servants who have heard the stories and believe the spirits of the heroes of the past haunt the present. Laura and Glenmorris invoke and impersonate the ghosts of the past in order to escape a restrictive present in which they are limited by family prejudice and notions of aristocratic pride. The future they rush toward, however, is a step further back into the past, in a sense, for in the Highlands of Scotland they enter the feudal world of clan society.

If Laura finds "relationship" to the Plantagenets of merely superstitious value, another aspect of her genealogy strikes both her and her husband as more meaningful, of positive, rather than negative, ideological significance. Laura and Glenmorris are distant relations, we discover. In fact, as Glenmorris complains, "the insolence of high blood, with which [Laura's mother] insults most . . . people, is surely very ill placed when addressed to me, whose family was in fact the original stem from which her own derived its consequence" (89). Laura's mother, Lady Mary de Verdon is ashamed of that originary root, as is England of her Celtic past, Smith would seem to be suggesting. Not least among the reasons that England seeks to dissociate herself from the Celtic tribes of Scotland, Ireland, and Wales is that they are the common ancestors of Britain and France, as Hume, from whom Smith draws her sense of British history, points out. In both *The Young Philosopher* and in *Minor Morals*, also published in 1798, Smith endorses this view of the common heritage of these divided nations. In *Minor Morals*, Mrs. Belmour tells her young protegés: "the island called Britain was peopled from Gaul, as that part of the Continent was then named which we now call France:—so you see we can trace our origin no farther than to the people we despise and hate." Smith goes on in this work to report (though with some skepticism) the "remote tradition . . . that this island . . . was, by some violent concussion of the earth, severed from the Continent, and it must have been precisely from France."[24] In *The Young Philosopher*'s Scottish episode, this thesis is more imaginatively developed.

It is in Scotland that Laura discovers the repressive effect of tyranny, the danger of vesting too much power in a single individual or family—which is, of course, the way clan society is defined. Glenmorris, as head of the clan, is beloved by his people—and rightly so. He uses his autocratic power for their good and their loyalty is as much the result of affection and gratitude as custom and duty. But Smith acknowledges that such power, even in the right hands, is tyranny, and when Glenmorris is abducted by pirates, his wife discovers the dangers of such a political system as the Laird of Kilbrodie (with the help of his diabolical mother) seeks to secure Glenmorris's lairdship for himself. The Lady of Kilbrodie tries to terrorize Laura into miscarrying her unborn child; the Laird himself tries to force Laura to marry him. Laura resists this oppressive despotism during her pregnancy; and, after the death of her infant, she manages to escape.

Although Laura finds succor and support from the loyal members of her husband's clan, the very nature of clan society makes such loyalty disloyal, an act of rebellion against the new chieftain, the Laird of Kilbrodie. Jeannie and Donald who do the "right" thing in helping Laura evade her torturers are revolutionaries, more concerned with human rights than with what really is the equivalent of law in the Highlands. The cave dwelling in which these rebels conceal Laura is in a sense symbolic of a key tenet of radical thought in that it represents a move even further into the past than Laura's journey from Lancashire and the Wars of the Roses to Scotland and

---

24 *Minor Morals, Interspersed with Sketches of Natural History, Historical Anecdotes, and Original Stories* (2 vols, London, 1798), vol. 2, pp. 17–18.

clan society represented.[25] In *Minor Morals* Smith quotes Hume in describing the ancient Britons and life in England prior to the Roman conquest: "Certain it is, that the manners and religion of the Britons . . . were the same as those of their Gallic neighbours. They were almost naked, living in huts or caves."[26] Laura is not so primitive, but her movement from a castle that belonged to Geoffrey Plantagenet to the fortified tower of a Scottish laird to a cave is a movement backwards through history. In the cave, she exists in a space that evokes a time before France and England were separate nations. In the cave, she is a citizen of the world.

When Laura is rescued by a Highland hunter and taken to his modern estate, however, she is ushered back into the present. What she finds there, in his home, is the same kind of suspicion and enmity that marked her life with her parents and her in-laws. Lord Macarden's sister, like Laura's parents and the Laird of Kilbrodie and his mother, is hostile to Laura and the challenge Laura represents to her security, status, and power. If her brother, Lord Macarden, falls in love with Laura (as he, of course, does) and if they marry, his sister and her children stand to lose their share of the family fortune, their place in the family home. In the aftermath of the Reign of Terror, this cyclical narrative pattern serves as a warning to readers hungry for social change. Without some sort of radical shift in perspective, Smith seems to imply, history is destined to repeat itself—not only in terms of the macro-narratives that chronicle international struggles for power but also in terms of the micro-narratives that define and destroy domestic life and individual happiness. The roots of oppression lie buried deep in the past. But so does the possibility for change. After all, if we go back far enough into the past, there is no nation, there is no class distinction that leads to family pride. All Britons, all Frenchmen, were originally cave dwellers, living wandering lives in "small tribes," "their sole property . . . their sword and their cattle."[27]

This anthropological sense of unity is one means by which Smith theorizes a transcendence of national identity, but while it helpfully undermines the authority of national identity and the pride of aristocratic privilege, it does not provide a means of creating a communal identity that is not defined by nation or class. In a third regional episode, Smith suggests that what is needed as the basis for communities that transcend nation and class is a new approach to history—an approach that begins with the individual and that emphasizes the commonality of human desire and human suffering.

Earlier in the eighteenth century, Laurence Sterne had fashioned a narrative around the notion that national and religious divisions can be bridged through sympathy for one another. His *Sentimental Journey* is in essence a rendition of the story of the Good Samaritan, and like that parable Sterne's narrative seems to be suggesting that the answer to social ills lies in the human heart, feeling for one another that prompts

---

25 The next chapter will explore the "cave" as a retreat from ethics into fear of the other. In Smith's novel, however, the cave is a safe haven in which Laura can maintain the vestiges of connection to others through Jeannie and Donald, certainly, but also through interaction with the natural world. See *The Young Philosopher*, pp. 127–9.

26 Ibid., 19 n.

27 Smith, quoting Hume, *Minor Morals*, p. 19 n.

kindness and charity. Charlotte Smith endorses this view in *The Young Philosopher* in several ways. Medora's claim to her grandfather's estate, for example, is never settled by law; instead her cousin who has inherited the whole fortune, simply deeds Medora what should have been her share. This cousin has been touched by the sufferings of Medora and Laura Glenmorris; she, like Jeannie and Donald in Scotland, simply does what is morally right rather than what is legally permissible. In a regional scene set in Wales, Smith ties such behavior to revolutionary politics.

Significantly, George Delmont is in Wales waiting for a ship to Ireland where he is to bail his irresponsible elder brother out of a financial jam. George feels obligated to do this because of traditional attitudes about primogeniture that regard the family fortune as belonging to the eldest son. These are notions that George abhors; even the reviewer for the *Anti-Jacobin* faults him for responding to the demands of the feckless and reckless Adolphus as though such responsibility were the dictate of society rather than an act of his own free will: "The young philosopher conceives a very bad opinion of the government of his country, as if it were the fault of a government . . . that a person foolishly becoming security for another should have to pay for his folly."[28] The novel, however, makes it clear that in so behaving, George is caught up in patterns over which he has no control and of which he never really breaks free. He stops providing financial rescue for his brother only when that brother marries Miss Goldthorp and her fortune along with her. As George waits in Wales for the winds to shift so that he can go to Ireland, however, he has an experience that both asserts the importance of life outside the traditional patterns and suggests the means for escaping those patterns.

This escape comes in the form of sentimental imaginative involvement in the story of a "*misfortunate* young gentlewoman" (182). George occupies himself during his detainment in Wales with reconstructing the history of a young woman called Elizabeth Lisburne through the oral and written fragments that document her existence. Nothing about the history is certain or authoritative; the local fisherman who first tells George about her does not even believe Elizabeth Lisburne "*was* her name" (183). She was in the town, the man supposes, to meet a lover who was to come for her from Ireland. After a month, she committed suicide. Refused burial by the local church, she was consigned to a makeshift grave "in the lee of the great Mavor Crag" by the fisherman, his wife, and son (182). No family ever came to claim her belongings, though the man advertised. He concluded, he tells George, "she had disobliged her friends for this said love" (183). George peruses her papers and books, transcribing one of Elizabeth Lisburne's poems for Mrs. Glenmorris to whom he writes this tale. The last stanza, addressed to her faithless lover, bespeaks Elizabeth Lisburne's despair and her determination:

---

28   Review of *The Young Philosopher*, *The Anti-Jacobin Review and Magazine* 1 (1798): 190.

Yet go forgiven, Hillario, go!
Such anguish may'st thou never know,
  As that which checks my labouring breath;
Pain so severe, not long endures,
And I have still my choice of cures;
    Madness or death. (185)

George's response is the combination of aesthetic detachment and sentimental identification that represents the revolutionary ideal: "The verses are not very good, yet they are surely the language of the heart, and mine aches when I think of what this poor unfortunate must have endured" (185).

George's final commentary on Elizabeth Lisburne reflects a similar bifurcation of judgment and sentiment. "To us in this world, she is now nothing," he comments; but immediately following that rational dismissal, he insists emotionally that her presence is "too strongly before" him to allow him to think clearly or finish transcribing the poems "of poor Elizabeth" that he wishes to send to Mrs. Glenmorris (185). The polarities of significance here underscore the sense of anxiety surrounding questions of identity throughout *The Young Philosopher*, invoking parallel scenes and thematic resonances that intensify and expand the cultural impact of this unknown suicide. Her death and burial at a Celtic seaside recall Laura Glenmorris's cavern exile by the sea in Scotland, her despair at the loss of her husband, the surreptitious burial of her dead infant. Elizabeth Lisburne's suicide over disappointed love invokes the memory of Mary Wollstonecraft, mentioned in Smith's preface and just about to be recalled to the reader's imagination by a scene that parallels Maria's fate. Laura, like Wollstonecraft's Maria and unlike Elizabeth Lisburne, will "choose" madness over death in response to thwarted desire. Other echoic parallels in the pages that follow the Lisburne tale reinforce the sense of Wollstonecraft's presence, as formulated in her memoirs. In Ireland, for example, George will discover a "marriage market" identical to the one he is perennially trying to avoid in England, the same "market" that defined as imprudent Laura's marriage to Glenmorris, that questions George's love for Medora, that rendered Elizabeth Lisburne an outcast, that Wollstonecraft herself disavowed, and that William Godwin and *The Young Philosopher*'s Godwinian Armitage philosophized against.[29] The act of suicide itself links Lisburne to the revolutionary dictum "[e]n me rendent la vie insupportable Dieu m'ordonne de la quitter," Rousseau's words, quoted by Laura Glenmorris in her account of exile in Scotland (122). In the world envisioned by the radical thinkers of the late eighteenth century, individual men and women will be free to define and pursue their own desires—even unto madness or death. These extremities suggest the possible cost of such freedom. From the psychological boundaries of the world newly mapped by a revolutionary politics that includes an insistence on individual sexual agency

---

29 See Godwin's *Political Justice*, ed. H.S. Salt (London, 1890), pp. 101–5 for his argument against cohabitation in general and marriage in particular. *The Young Philosopher*'s Armitage has separated from his wife due to incompatibility of temper—a fact that is presented with understandable sympathy by Smith (52–3); though in general the novel endorses marriage, contemporary courtship customs are one of the primary targets of its criticism.

for both men and women, Laura and Elizabeth reveal the loneliness, isolation, and confusion at the new center of things.

Wandering

What kind of world will form around the nucleus of the desiring, suffering female self? Hagar's world—a world of weeping, silence, and despair. In the century to follow, the speaking female novelistic subject would become the quiet victim whose pain would prompt a Godlike male to ask "what aileth thee" and to "open her eyes" to the fact that water is readily available from a well that only he can reveal to her. He will not receive drink from her hands in the way of Eliezar and Jacob; he will not offer the caress of reciprocity; he will not say "here I am; send me." And he will not ask her to drink, to caress, or to say "here I am." He will assume her inability to meet him face to face; he will assume, that is, the need to care for and sustain her. He will not recognize her desire, but he will legitimize her suffering—and her offspring. She will survive; but she will not thrive.

As Tikva Frymer-Kensky has said, "readers today tend to be angry at Sarah, to castigate her for being insensitive to the plight of someone for whom she should have felt both compassion and solidarity."[30] Indeed, there is much evidence that Hagar and her son are the favored characters in a sentimental reading of the narrative in which they appear. They represent a new kind of ethical possibility—responsiveness without reciprocity, sympathy without exchange, transcendence without desire. To put it more positively, Hagar's inarticulate sorrow evokes compassion, and compassion prompts the relief of suffering. In the place of the people who should have cared for her (i.e. Abraham and especially Sarah), the reader steps in (as God himself did) to protect and defend. The only difference is that God also is the one who required the banishing of Hagar. He wounded and he repaired, whereas readers blame without taking responsibility for the fault they castigate. The fact is that to have the power to aid is to have the power to harm. Whoever is not Hagar is responsible for both the wounding of Hagar and the rescuing of Hagar. Readers today, however, tend to see themselves as rescuers only, in opposition to the wounding force of Sarah.

By "today," I do not mean the beginning of the twenty-first century. I mean the "today" of the long modern era in which we still live, the era that began during the very period of our concern in this book. For Hagar is the heroine of the Romantic age, epitomized nowhere so poignantly as in Frances Burney's final novel, *The Wanderer*. It is not necessary to make a long, detailed case for the association between Ellis and Hagar; after all, Ellis is nameless for the first third of the novel. She is black when we first meet her.[31] She is a "wanderer" an "unprotected female,"

---

30 *Reading the Women of the Bible*, p. 226.

31 Of course, Ellis has no child and in that she is unlike Hagar who was represented in popular literature in the late eighteenth century, both in England and America, as a mourning, outcast mother. See, for example, the two-scene play, *Hagar in the Desert* , 4th ed. (Worcester, 1785). This play was "translated from the French for the Use of Children." In sixteenth- and seventeenth-century European art, as Ruth Mellinkoff has discussed, there is an emphasis on "Hagar's sorrow." "Sarah and Hagar: Laughter and Tears," in Brown and McKendrick,

an "Incognita," a "fugitive." She is more often in tears than not. Ellis's, "other," her Sarah, as it were, is Elinor, who is verbal and angry and active. She "follows her own humor" and "ungoverned inclination." She is a "revolutionary" who speaks in her own voice, and she demands that others do so as well. She is the one who says "here I am, send me"—only no one is asking. She is willing to go, to do, to be, to speak, but no one demands, listens, or hears. In the end, she is a pathetic creature, thoroughly repudiated by the novel's "hero" Harleigh, who rejects her "noble, though . . . masculine spirit," in favor of the "sweet," "blushing," exiled Ellis who spends most of the narrative avoiding the speech that will reveal who she is and what she wants.[32] In the fates of Ellis and Elinor we see the options for women reduced to two alternate routes—the loved victim who never speaks of her desire or the unheard "madwoman" who speaks of nothing else.[33]

The text of Burney's final novel, therefore, can be said to lead us away from the ethics of desire; but the subtext (as in Charlotte Smith's *Young Philosopher*) stands evidence of an undergirding ethical paradigm of mutuality and reciprocity, despite the silence of Ellis and the silencing of Elinor. The novel, after all, begins on the coast of France with "the voice of a woman" crying in "keen distress" from the shore as a small boat full of Englishmen and women prepares to leave a country which is in the throes of bloody revolution (11).[34] The suppliant is given succor in an act of responsiveness couched in the very terms of ethical discourse: "since she is but a woman, and in distress, save her, pilot, in God's name. . . . A woman, a child, and a fallen enemy, are three persons that every true Briton should scorn to misuse" (12). The old sea officer who insists on this responsiveness amid the clamor of those who would harden their hearts turns out, in the end, to be Ellis's uncle. Indeed, as Ellis makes her way, unknown and friendless, through English society from the top of the social scale to the bottom (or below!), she encounters many who respond to her need with generosity, although it must also be said that she meets many more who greet her with indifference, inconsistency, and hostility. Of course, the ethical relation was never asserted to be a common relation. It is by definition special as it provides through human connection access to the divine.

Illuminating the Book, pp. 47–9. On the association of Hagar with "blackness" and the place of the debate about the blackness vs. the "Egyptian-ness" of Hagar in pro and con slavery debates, see Janet Hover-Gabler, *Dreaming Black/Writing White: The Hagar Myth in American Cultural History* (Lexington, 2000), pp. 38–54.

32 *The Wanderer; or Female Difficulties*, ed. Margaret Anne Doody, Robert L. Mack, and Peter Sabor, Oxford World's Classics (Oxford, 1990), p. 862. Further references will be cited parenthetically in the text.

33 It is probably unnecessary to remark that Charlotte Bronte's *Jane Eyre* will be the most powerful statement of these alternative possibilities for women of the nineteenth century. The force of the double-edged myth was substantial—as the generative feminist study by Sandra Gilbert and Susan Gubar suggests. See their *Madwoman in the Attic: The Woman Writer and the Nineteenth-Century Literary Imagination* (New Haven, 1979), p. 53, where they note "it is debilitating to be *any* woman in a society where women are warned that if they do not behave like angels they must be monsters."

34 Margaret Doody notes that Ellis "is at first a voice and nothing else." "Introduction," *The Wanderer*, xv.

The instances of ethical connection in *The Wanderer* seem, on the surface, to fall into one of four categories: 1) disinterested displays of compassion such as we witness from Juliet toward Dame Fairfield's children and, reciprocally, from Dame Fairfield toward Juliet (657–60; 707–22); 2) displays of compassion arising from hopes of companionship or love such as Sir Jaspar and Harleigh both evidence toward Juliet; 3) compassion that seems inexplicably tied to some visceral responsiveness to the mien, demeanor, and circumstances of Juliet but that is, in the end, revealed to be a form of family feeling. The Admiral, Aurora, and Lord Melbury are Juliet's uncle, half-sister, and half-brother respectively. They do not know this fact until late in the novel, but throughout they accept obligation and they demonstrate responsiveness to her, and she, to them; and 4) incidental, almost instinctive acts of kindness that seem as quickly forgotten as spontaneously rendered. Mr. Giles Arbe and Selina and Mr. Tedmond are not mercurial, exactly, but they are also not exactly reliable. Their responsiveness is the response of a moment—of good and generous hearts, but of weak minds, as it were. In fact, Gabriella, who guilelessly reveals Juliet's history to Sir Jaspar before Juliet feels it safe to do so, also falls into the fourth category (640–7). Her love for Juliet is unquestioned, but incomplete because Gabriella, like everyone else in the novel, is cut off from Juliet's full confidence. Juliet explains to the ever-curious Sir Jaspar: "I have not made my situation known . . . to the friend of my heart, the confident of my life, the loved and honoured descendant of the house by which I have been preserved, and from which alone I hope for protection! Judge then, how powerful must be my motives for secrecy! And she, —she submits to my silence!" (649) Voice is acknowledged in *The Wanderer* to be as integral to identity as name; throughout the narrative, Harleigh, in particular, repeatedly pleads for Ellis to reveal the one and speak in the other: "Trust me, then, more generously! be somewhat less suspicious, somewhat more open" (336). But Ellis is skittish: "From the customs . . . of the world, I have been brought up to avoid all obligations with strangers" (281). We do not need a Levinas to remind us, at this point, that without voice, without openness, without obligation, without responsiveness to the stranger, there can be no ethical relation.

Yet there is no sense in which Ellis is blamed for keeping herself to herself. In fact, even before we discover the powerful motive that compels her silence (and Burney does not reveal this motive until quite late in the novel), we trust that she is a character for whom "all disguise was disgusting . . . if not induced by the most imperious necessity" (773). We also trust that Burney will open all to us, eventually; the implicit contract between author and reader sustains our interest in the long novel, and we are not disappointed as the secret that is revealed partakes of dramatic circumstances of both perfidy and loyalty. There are perfectly valid reasons—aesthetic and moral—for withholding information sometimes. One question *The Wanderer* addresses is whether or not ethics can survive in situations requiring secrecy. Late in the novel, the question is answered in the affirmative. Wandering in the New Forest, Juliet is confronted by "an immense dog" who "suddenly made a point at her, and sprang forward" (686). Terrified, but rational, Juliet "knew that flight, to the intelligent, though dumb friend of man, was well seen to be cowardice, and instinctively judged to be guilt" (686). Instead of running, therefore, she faces her wouldbe canine attacker and with a caressing gesture summons the animal to her: "The dog, caught by her confidence, made a grumbling but short resistance; and, having first fiercely, and next attentively, surveyed her, wagged his tail in sign of accommodation, and, gently advancing, stretched himself at her feet" (687). The theoretical lesson Juliet draws from this victory is one of "mild philanthropy": "the kindness of an instant gains you to a stranger" (687); but when the next moments bring additional threats from the human world, she reveals a deeper insight and an ability to apply wisdom to the benefit of herself and others. It is not kindness, but self-possession that staves off the unwanted advances of the cur's masters, distracted from their woodcutting by the presence of "a girl" (688). As the rowdy young men squabble over who saw her and who gets to kiss her "virzt," Juliet becomes increasingly aware of "the danger of personal and brutal insult" (688). Fighting back the instinct to flee, she, instead turns to face her "persecutors . . . with the same assumed firmness, though not with the offered caresses, with which she had just encountered her four-footed pursuer" (689). She disarms the men with "civility and apparent trust," transforming them from enemies to friends who lead her to shelter and safe dwelling (689).

At the end of the novel, these young men are recompensed with "a high price" for their dog who becomes Harleigh's companion on the grounds of Harleigh Hall. Thus, they stand with the others "to whom Juliet . . . owed good office" and who were visited by Juliet and her husband "with gifts and praise" for their kindnesses to the wanderer in her hour of need (872). Had Ellis/Juliet not learned that, in the absence of voice, self-possession will suffice to establish the subjectivity necessary for ethical relation, the woodcutters, following their baser instincts, could not have been so honored. Because of Juliet's sense of her own self-worth, these men can stake a claim to worth as well. Later on in the novel, Juliet will find a need for self-possession that does not establish ethical relation. Accused of thievery by Mrs. Howel, but "certain, whatever might be her ultimate fate, that her birth and family must, inevitably, be soon discovered," Juliet finds it within herself to face down her challenger with steady nerves (814). "There is nothing which so effectually oversets an accusing adversary, as self-possession," the narrator opines (814–15). If not converted, like the woodcutters, to amity by Juliet's self-possession, Mrs. Howel is at least disarmed and reduced "from rage to shame" (815), setting the stage for Juliet's restoration to her rightful place in English society at a Harleigh Hall that can open its doors to the redeemed and exile the irredeemable.

Throwing this lesson into stark relief is the embedded narrative of Juliet's father, Lord Granville, whose unethical behavior has rendered Juliet nameless and voiceless, needing to rely on self-possession for survival because incapable of positioning herself in the world through any other means. In fact, because of Lord Granville's refusal to acknowledge his daughter and establish beyond doubt her legitimacy while he was still living, the revelation of her name when she arrived in England would not have done much to alter her reception as it would have been instantly disputed until the codicil to her father's will was revealed. Granville loved Juliet's mother, but the match was an "unequal" one, and the inequality embarrassed him. As the old Admiral bluntly, but eloquently, puts it, had she married an equal—a "worthy tar," for example, he "would have been proud . . . while your lord was only ashamed of her! for that's the bottom of the story, put what dust you will in your eyes for the top" (843).

Because of this shame, Juliet was banished. Like Ishmael rather than Hagar in this instance, she is cut off from her paternity, violently so by those who champion her siblings, Lord Melbury and Lady Aurora. Lord Denmeath and Mrs. Howel are so blindly prejudiced against Juliet that there is no possibility of reconciliation when, in the end, Juliet's heritage is revealed and confirmed. Lord Denmeath immediately leaves; Mrs. Howel follows shortly thereafter. Her hardness of heart is further punished, however, by explicit instructions to stay away from Harleigh Hall, the Admiral himself serving as the "messenger of positive exile" in a personal visit to her and her likeminded cohorts, Mrs. Ireton and Mrs. Maple (872). The novel comes full circle, therefore—beginning with an exile and ending with the same. It is tempting, of course, to point to the Ishmael/Isaac paradigm as one that maps out intractable difference, difference that disallows ethics. When the exile returns, the occupier must leave. That would certainly speak to the fears driving some of the world's most problematic relationships today. But we must distinguish between the story of Isaac and Ishmael and the story of Sarah and Hagar. The stories are necessarily intertwined, but the ethical message is not the same. The mothers cannot live together, but the children, it turns out, can. And the force that splits one dyad is the very force that draws the other dyad together. It is Abraham over whom the women fight; it is Abraham over whom the brothers unite.

Of course, the unity between Isaac and Ishmael is temporary; the conflict, indeed, rages even as I write. There are periods of respite, calm, and cooperation, but bonds so close they cannot be severed seem destined to provoke an effort to separate, absorb, or eradicate. Burney's novel understands this point as well. Cast against the backdrop of the French Revolution, in which the assertion of identity despite powerlessness figured so prominently, and written in the midst of the Napoleonic wars in which the emperor sought to erase national distinction (identity) by world dominance (power), *The Wanderer* is naturally focused on questions of self and the way the "I" asserts himself or herself—especially herself—in relation to the other.[35] Margaret Doody maintains that Ellis is an everywoman, seeing in the "elle" that she shares with Elinor an assertion of feminine power:

> That name, in a macaronic pun, signifies that elle is, i.e. "she is." Woman lives. (Emily Brontë, significantly, was to choose "Ellis Bell" as her pen name.) Burney is very fond of names for her female characters that have that "elle" or she built into them, and the similarity of "Ellis" and "Elinor" alerts us to the possibility that these two characters may be seen as aspects of each other.[36]

---

35   The d'Arblays had a personal stake in the Napoleonic wars. In 1814, the year *The Wanderer* was published, the 60-year-old d'Arblay was commissioned to serve in the guard of restored monarch Louis XVIII. "D'Arblay was thrilled and honoured, though it is hard to see why: he was ranked only as a Sub-Lieutenant and the pay was derisory, scarcely enough to cover the expenses of his elaborately embroidered new uniform, plumed helmet, weapons and the two warhorses required." His wife, on the other hand, "contemplated his return to military service with horror." Claire Harman, *Fanny Burney: A Biography* (London, 2000), pp. 329, 330.

36   "Introduction," p. xvi.

Aspects of each other, certainly, they are also aspects of another "other" signified by "El." Like Hagar, and like Ishmael himself, these characters speak to and of a God who listens, a God who affirms their right to be and to speak.

Penetrating the Impostor

According to Margaret Anne Doody, Robert L. Mack, and Peter Sabor, the title of Burney's final novel alludes directly to the Christian legend of the Wandering Jew. The mean-spirited, caustic Mrs. Ireton speculates that Ellis, still incognita, "may be a person of another century. A wandering Jewess" (485). Mrs. Ireton goes on to embellish the legend with her characteristic spitefulness: "I never heard that the old Jew had a wife, or a mother, who partook of his longevity; but very likely I may now have the pleasure of seeing one of his family under my own roof? That red and white that you lay on so happily, may just as well hide the wrinkles of two or three grand climacterics, as of only a poor single sixty or seventy years of age. However, these are secrets that I don't presume to enquire into. Every trade has its mystery" (485–6). While Mrs. Ireton's remarks are meant to discredit and embarrass Ellis, the novel's title turns the insult into an honorific. Indeed, as Hyam Maccoby has noted, Romantic writers including Shelley, Monk Lewis, Godwin, and Bulwer Lytton present the Wandering Jew not as a expiatory culprit but as a victim, "one more example of the Romantic hero—a wandering hero, isolated from normal society, expiating some crime which, in the last resort, was a praiseworthy act of rebellion against a tyrannous authority."[37] Of course, the legend, in general, does not honor the Jew who, because he ridiculed (or even crucified) Christ, is doomed to wander in solitude and suffering until the second coming. In fact, the image is a classic form of antisemitism in most contexts, in most times. But the Romantic writers universalized the image. Perhaps, the Jew was "guilty of a real crime, but . . . [it was a crime] that had heroic quality, since it introduced him to a new dimension of knowledge beyond the range of ordinary mankind."[38] "They turn him into an individualist who has sharpened his sense of individuality through sin, while it is the essence of the Wandering Jew in the authentic legend that he is not an individualist, however lonely his suffering, but a figure that has an expiatory role in relation to the Christian community."[39] But are these exclusive categories? A sense of individuality posited against any community strengthens communal resolve, for better or for worse. Ellis experiences this fact of human nature, as does Elinor—Ellis to her empowerment, Elinor to her disenfranchisement.

Ellis is the Wanderer, so it makes some sense that she is most clearly implicated by the legend of the Wandering Jew. In late-eighteenth-century folk legend, in particular, the Jew was associated with various impostors. Indeed, Mrs. Ireton directly alludes to

---

37   "The Wandering Jew as Sacred Executioner," in Galit Hasan-Rokem and Alan Dundes (eds), *The Wandering Jew: Essays in the Interpretation of a Christian Legend* (Bloomington, 1986), pp. 254, 236–60.

38   Maccoby, p. 254.

39   Ibid.

this popular conception, as she is accusing Ellis of that very crime.[40] And Mrs. Ireton is not the only one who levels this charge. Mrs. Howel calls Ellis both "impostor" and "adventurer" (564, 565); she is later widely "stigmatized as a swindler and an impostor" (673); even the Admiral call her "impostor" before the two of them sort out the various complications of her story and their joint history (830). Ellis is quite aware that appearances are all she has and that they do not provide much information for those who want to trust her. Therefore, she is especially grateful for those who accept her innocence on faith: Lady Aurora, who "will not conclude me to be an adventurer, though I dare not tell her even my name!" (136) and Dame Fairfield who rejects the charges because "a person who could be so kind to her children could not have so black a heart" (721).

The fact is, however, that though she is innocent, Ellis is also an impostor. She is well born, and for the bulk of the novel, she is relegated to menial tasks, demeaning treatment, humiliating scorn. One word of her patrimony would have resulted in a hiatus in abuse at the very least. But she persists in her anonymity. She insists on ignominy. How does she expiate her crime of willful deception? She is not wandering still at the end of the narrative. After all of her equivocation and evasion, what does Ellis do to gain admittance to society? And, for that matter, what does Elinor do to earn expulsion? Ellis becomes a part of the landed gentry of England, but Elinor becomes an exile from home and family. Ellis's imposture is thoroughgoing. It drives the narrative for three-quarters of the length of the novel. Elinor puts on one disguise—a slouch hat, some old clothes. Occasionally, she fosters misunderstandings that bring Harleigh into her orbit, and once she even refers to herself as "impostor," but her impostures are occasional (586). They are not thoroughgoing in the way that Ellis's prolonged disguise is. So why the unequal dispensation in the end?

A Wanderer, like the Wandering Jew, separates herself from "the common herd," and "find[s] that she has strayed from the beaten road only to discover all others are pathless!" (873). These words are Elinor's lament about her own fate, but the next paragraph refers to Juliet as "the Wanderer," as we too have been doing throughout this discussion. As Wanderer, Ellis/Juliet is "cast upon herself; a female Robinson Crusoe, as unaided and unprotected, though in the midst of the world, as that imaginary hero in his uninhabited island"—an island apart from the "common herd," the route to and from which is "pathless" and individualistic (873). In other words, as their names suggest, and as Margaret Doody and others have noted, Ellis/Juliet and Elinor do not represent two different female possibilities. They are two versions of the same fate. Like Sarah and Hagar, they are not self and other, but self and another self.

Elinor, like Juliet, is self-possessed. But when she faces danger without flinching, she arms her opponent rather than disarming him. "'Imagine not my courage tarnished by cowardly apprehensions of misinterpretation—suspicion— censoriousness,'" she announces to Harleigh (780), who then proceeds to dismantle

---

40   See G.K. Anderson "Popular Survivals of the Wandering Jew in England," in Hasan-Rokem and Dundes, *The Wandering Jew*, pp. 76–104, esp. 83–92. For an overview of the legend, in general, see Yvonne Glikson, "Wandering Jew" in *Encyclopaedia Judaica*, CD-ROM edition, 2006.

the intellectual framework by which she has come to perceive the world. This framework of philosophical skepticism, materialism, individualism has rendered her so self-possessed that suicide seems not just an option, but an obligation; not an annihilation of self, but an assertion of selfhood. When following their disputation, Elinor agrees to live, "meditate upon religion," and "court resignation," it is a concession, a diminishment, a defeat (796). Moments later, in a speech to Ellis, her former passion blazes forth in an excess of metaphor by which she continues to assert the subjectivity and responsibility that, along with Ellis, we fear will make quiet resignation and peaceful meditation difficult, if not impossible, to achieve:

> I believe you to be good, Ellis!—I exonerate you from all delusory arts; and, internally, I never thought you guilty,—or I had never feared you! Fool! mad fool, that I have been, I am my own executioner! my distracting impatience to learn the depth of my danger, was what put you together! taught you to know, to appreciate one another! With my own precipitate hand, I have dug the gulph into which I am fallen! Your dignified patience, your noble modesty—Oh fatal Ellis!—presented a contrast that plunged a dagger into all my greatest efforts! Rash, eager ideot! I conceived suspense to be my greatest bane!—Oh fool! eternal fool!—self-willed, and self-destroying!—for the single thrill of one poor moment's returning doubt—I would now suffer martyrdom! (796)

If we put this speech into our own colloquial language, we can see more clearly the ethical core. Essentially, Elinor says to Ellis/Juliet:

> I know you are not an impostor. And I know you aren't guilty, even though I said you were. I am just afraid of you. And, in fact, in my fear, look what I've done: I've set myself up for pain and annihilation. If I have suffered loss, it's because I put you in the position of suffering victim by which you have won love and approval. While wanting those very things for myself, I have lost them.

> If I could even for a minute doubt this loss, I'd make myself a victim and maybe as a victim/martyr I would be loved. But I know I have been so self-willed and so self-focused that I've lost hope of love and approbation—even from myself.

Hagar laughed at Sarah out of self-possession and fear; Sarah cast Hagar out in an act of self-assertion and fear. The Christian legend that relegated the Jew to wander the world did so out of a sense of self-approval and fear. The descendants of Ishmael and those of Isaac lash out in fear, banish one another in assertions of possession. France was engaged in a global act of self-possession as Burney wrote *The Wanderer*, but France would not obliterate otherness, and would find herself cast out, dispossessed, and fearful in her turn.

   In fact, that a cyclical sense of history informs *The Wanderer*, as it does *The Young Philosopher*, is made explicit in a scene set in the mansion of the Earl of Pembroke at Wilton. Here, Juliet pauses in front of the Vandyke portrait of the children of Charles I. This portrait calls to mind the revolution, the deposing and death of the king, and the exile of his family. It also brings to mind the restoration of the house of Stuart, the Glorious Revolution, the Act of Settlement, and the establishment of the House of Hanover. The heated controversies that surrounded the children upon whose likenesses Juliet gazes are no longer the source of volatile unrest, discord, and danger. In fact, the Admiral himself glosses over the fractiousness of Protestant/ Catholic conflict by asserting his own "respect for a parson, whether he be of the true religion, or only a Papist" (858). This magnanimous verbal gesture might seem patronizing were it not voiced in the midst of an episode in which Juliet is preparing to sacrifice her life for the sake of the Roman Catholic Bishop who has nurtured and sustained her in exile. The "natural enmities" between France and England, between Protestant and Catholic are simply forgotten in light of the threat posed to both by Robespierre's Reign of Terror, in the historical present of the narrative, and by Napoleon's campaign in the present of the novel's writer and first readers. As the Admiral puts it, "my enemy in distress is my friend" (854). Even the secular, materialistic view that Elinor rejects after her debate with Harleigh is not so much repudiated as redeemed. In Harleigh's argument, the very worms that prove the materiality of our bodies become evidence for the immortality of the soul. If there is no difference between body and soul, he says to Elinor, why may we not imagine that "those wretched reptiles" "formed from the human frame, may partake of and retain human consciousness?" (786) Likewise, mere pages after Elinor's determination to commit suicide has been repudiated, Juliet embraces self-annihilation as a noble end.

If all entities, including individual identity, are subject to these revolutions of contextual meaning—that is, if suicide is noble in one context and ignoble in another, if Protestantism is the same as Catholicism when both are under attack, if a Juliet with no money and no friends must live the life of an Ellis, if self-possession slides so easily into self-destruction, if self is so unstable that every version is in a sense an imposture—how can we establish ethical relation? Without subjectivity, as this study has argued, there can be no ethics. In a world shaken by revolution that seems to demand repeated re-definitions of self, however, how does one maintain a stable subject position? Drawing on the Sarah/Hagar paradigm, we might posit that the only way to do so is to approach the other as self, not in order to absorb the other in an act of unethical assimilation, but in order to know the other from the other's point of view which becomes, temporarily, your own. It is an act of possession, to be sure, but a chiastic act in which the coming together is always followed by a moving apart.

In *The Wanderer* such moments are usually moments of sexual or sexualized exchange. Harleigh, frustrated by Ellis's secrecy, cries "why must I find you for ever thus, impenetrable, thus incomprehensible?" (337). To fully comprehend, one must penetrate. The word has psychological, intellectual, and sexual force. Elinor longs for Harleigh to "penetrate [her] with his own notions" (781). Harleigh, who himself has longed for "sweet reciprocation" with Juliet (578), is finally rewarded when she admits that her most difficult role to play had been the one that required her "seeming always impenetrable—where most I was sensitive" (861). To some degree the most powerful and the most erotic use of the word, however, occurs in the description of Juliet's response to her half-sister, Aurora, who in a moment of intense emotionality, "with eyes glistening, and arms opening, gently ejaculated, 'My sister!' and fell, weeping upon her neck" (817). The highly charged language continues for several paragraphs as Juliet "nearly ceased to breathe" until "the almost too powerful delight of her bosom, found some vent in a violent burst of tears" (817).

She is the "penetrated Juliet," weeping in her sister's arms, asking if the Lady Aurora can possibly bear not "turn[ing] away from . . . so helpless, —so desolate an object?" (817). Lady Aurora places "her hand upon the mouth of Juliet" and encircles her with her "white arms." Lady Aurora "would have kissed" Juliet's tears "from her cheeks" were it not for the fact that "her own mingled with them so copiously, that it was not possible." The two sisters "shewed their sensibility to be but fulness of happiness, the meeting, the acknowledgment, with the throbbing recollection of all that was passed, so touched each gentle heart, that they could but weep and embrace, embrace and weep, alternately" (818). The language is conventional for such scenes of emotional intensity, but it is also language that speaks to the essence of the ethical paradigm under examination here. Recognition of self in other is a moment of such power and such satisfaction, it is no wonder that it is also a moment of great erotic intensity. Juliet's love for her brother, Lord Melbury, is framed as platonic. His attraction to Juliet is sexual, but she repels his advances and keeps him at a physical distance she does not impose on Lady Aurora. Juliet's attraction to her sister is a self-referential (or auto-erotic) attraction. It is also highly ethical. She loves her sister as she loves herself.

How to Talk to God

When Juliet embraces Aurora, she, in essence, embraces herself. The act seems symbolic of the self-knowledge necessary to a life of moral purpose and ethical relation. Other biblical versions of the Sarah/Hagar paradigm make this point quite clear. The Leah/Rachel narrative is one such version in which Rachel, like Sarah, is denied children, even as she watches her husband's other wife thrive in fecundity. Here, there is no enmity between the women, but Rachel is in despair and "envious" of her sister. She says to Jacob: "Give me children, or I shall die" (Genesis 30: 1). Jacob is "incensed" (Genesis 30: 2), as well he should be. Rachel is threatening self-annihilation, and she is putting the blame on him. She is the Genesis proto-type of Elinor. Unlike Harleigh, however, Jacob does not try to reason with a suicidal woman; instead, he says, in effect, you are talking to the wrong person: "Can I take the place of God, who has denied you fruit of the womb?" (Genesis 30: 2). At this point, Rachel concedes and names a surrogate wife, her maid Bilhah. Bilhah conceives, and Rachel is "vindicated" by God who has, in Rachel's words, "heeded my plea and given me a son" (Genesis 30: 6).

Unlike Sarah, Rachel is content with the arrangement, and Jacob fathers a second son by Bilhah. Rachel sees this son as a sign of "prevail[ing]" over Leah in a "fateful contest" (Genesis 30: 8), a healthy kind of competition, as it turns out, since the tribal fathers are multiplying at a steady rate. Leah herself is spurred to competition and denominates a surrogate of her own. Zilpah bears two more sons for the house of Jacob. The friendly rivalry continues until God finally "remembered Rachel" and "heeded her and opened her womb" (Genesis 30: 22). In the end, there are twelve sons, and the house of Israel is firmly established, though the nation will take a bit longer.

Rachel is the beloved wife of Jacob. He fathers children by several women, but Rachel is the woman he loves. The love is reciprocal, but complicated by the fact of Leah's imposture on the day of Jacob's presumed marriage to Rachel. Awaking to find himself groom of the wrong sister, Jacob nevertheless proves a good husband to Leah who "was hated" but who did not know she was hated. She had compensatory delights—her many children. Rachel does not resent the imposture. In fact, commentary suggests she aided and abetted Leah who had been promised to Esau and who deserved better. Yet, without resentment, there can also be jealousy, and jealousy, if managed correctly, can actually be a good thing. Jacob is smarter than Abraham with regard to the women of his tribe. When they have complaints, he does not attempt to negotiate or adjudicate. He tells them to talk to God.

There is no evidence in the text, however, that Rachel actually does talk to God. That evidence comes from a later instantiation of the Sarah/Hagar ethical paradigm— this one concerning Hannah, the mother of Samuel. Hannah is married to Elkanah who loves her deeply. But, like Sarah and Rachel before her, she is barren. Her husband has another wife, Peninnah who has children and who, in the way of some women, finds it necessary to gloat. Peninnah, unlike Hagar, does not gloat about being able to conceive; she does not teach her children to "fool" in an offensive way. She is not guilelessly offensive like Leah, however. She does jeer, and when she does, she gets to the heart of the matter: "to make [Hannah] miserable, [Peninnah] would taunt her that the Lord had closed her womb" (1 Samuel 1: 6). Of course, it is perhaps true that Hagar knew Sarah well enough to know that she would not be hurt by reference to God's lack of concern. Sarah was focused on life and the men in her life. It is likely, too, that Leah knew the way to spur Rachel to procreative energy was to simply ignore her. In each case, the biblical text affirms that God is the one who finally relieves the state of barrenness, but only in Hannah's case is he the one who is asked to do so.

Elkanah tries to reassure Hannah. Children are fine, but marriage is not just about procreation. "Why are you so sad?" he asks her. "Am I not more devoted to you than ten sons?" (1 Samuel 1: 8). Hannah does not answer him. She knows the fault is not in him or in her, really. Somehow, she has to get God's attention. So she goes to "the temple of the Lord" to pray: "In her wretchedness, she prayed to the Lord, weeping all the while. And she made the vow: 'O Lord of Hosts, if You will look upon the suffering of Your maidservant and will remember me and not forget Your maidservant, and if You will grant Your maidservant a male child, I will dedicate him to the Lord for all the days of his life; and no razor shall ever touch his head'" (1 Samuel 1: 9–11). She humbles herself; she suffers; she speaks to God. In fact, her lips move while she prays, and a priest notices. He assumes that she is drunk, talking to herself. He says, "Sober up!" (1 Samuel 1: 14) She does not get defensive, though she seems to be praying in a way that is not recognizable as prayer to the priest. Nonetheless, she is capable of explaining her behavior to him in clear, precise language: "I have been pouring out my heart to the Lord. Do not take your maidservant for a worthless woman; I have only been speaking all this time out of my great anguish and distress" (1 Samuel 1: 15–16). For some reason, not stated in the text, the priest believes her. He simply believes her innocence, he credits her sincerity, he acknowledges her integrity. Without probing, he states: "Then go in peace . . . and may the God of Israel grant you what you have asked of Him" (1 Samuel 1: 17). And he does.

So, we come back to the question with which we began: what kind of world will form around the nucleus of the suffering woman? Hagar's world. Sarah's world. Rachel's world. Leah's world. Penninah's world. Hannah's world. Female difficulties, as Frances Burney and Charlotte Smith both knew, abound. But so does kindness. So does succor. So does hospitality and relief. The voice of the woman crying in the wilderness of pain, of exile, of barrenness, of despair is a voice that can be heard and that has been heard—by the men who love them and by the God they love. But, as importantly, it is a voice they themselves hear, a voice like their own, speaking to perennial needs, not least of which is the need to be heard.

Chapter 7

The Lot Motif and the Redaction of Double Desire

Frances Burney deploys a metaphorical arsenal in the dedicatory poem to her first, anonymously published, novel *Evelina* that maps out and secures, as it were, the emotional territory of late-century fiction by women. The poem is brief, so I quote it in full:

> Oh author of my being!—far more dear
>   To me than light, than nourishment, or rest,
> Hygicia's blessings, Rapture's burning tear,
>   Or the life blood that mantles in my breast!
>
> If in my heart the love of Virtue glows,
>   'Twas planted there by an unerring rule;
> From thy example the pure flame arose,
>   Thy life, my precept—thy good works, my school.
>
> Could my weak pow'rs thy num'rous virtues trace,
>   By filial love each fear should be repress'd;
> The blush of Incapacity I'd chace,
>   And stand, recorder of thy worth, confess'd:
>
> But since my niggard stars that gift refuse,
>   Concealment is the only boon I claim;
> Obscure be still the unsuccessful Muse,
>   Who cannot raise, but would not sink, your fame.
>
> Oh! of my life at once the source and joy!
>   If e'er thy eyes these feeble lines survey,
> Let not their folly their intent destroy;
>   Accept the tribute—but forget the lay.[1]

In this poem, Burney invokes some familiar images and themes. Most interesting for the present discussion is her self-construction in terms of garden, political subject, and hieroglyph, for these images recall the central motifs of the early fiction of female desire, motifs that we examined in Chapters 2, 3, and 4 of this book. The speaker's heart "glows" with "Virtue" "planted" by her father. She is a kind of garden, her body's blood and heart comprise the soil tilled by her father's example,

---

1   *Evelina, or the History of a Young Lady's Entrance into the World*, ed. Edward A. Bloom and Lillian D. Bloom, Oxford World's Classics (Oxford, 2002), p. 1.

life, and works. Her own works are paid in "tribute" to him, in exchange for the "boon" of concealment; she is a vassal in a sense, attending on her lord, her master-father, her king. Her identity is hidden, however; his identity is secret as well. The poem is addressed to ------ ------; after all, to reveal his name is to reveal her own, so if she is the "recorder of [his] worth," she is so in a cryptic, private language, in hieroglyph, as it were. He is the "author of [her] being," and in the poem she would also be the author of his; but the mutuality of their love and their mutual obligation is unspoken and, significantly, unacknowledged between the two of them. The secrecy of ethical love, and a sense of its complicated relationship to cultural power and natural fecundity are as old as the Song of Songs. But here we see a difference in that the female lover speaks, but her male father-lover is not allowed to hear and to respond. Her longing is voiced but unacknowledged and unrequited.

Brian McCrea has examined the impotent father figure in eighteenth-century fiction, arguing that the years 1650–1740 witnessed in England a "demographic crisis" in the failure of many landowners (about half of them) to produce male heirs.[2] This crisis resulted in a novelistic preoccupation with fathers and father-figures. In fact, McCrea's reading complicates the typical feminist analysis of eighteenth-century fiction which posits a strong and oppressive patriarchy. According to McCrea, the opposite is actually true of much of the fiction of the time:

> Rather than portraying the patriarch as a powerful figure who either silences or violates the female spirit, Richardson, Lennox, Inchbald, and Burney offer us patriarchs who are absent, impaired, or dead. This weakened patriarch creates difficulties for female characters, but difficulties that have less to do with oppression than with the uncertainty created in families by the absence of a commanding father.[3]

In fact, the desire for the father leads to the "naturalizing" of father/daughter relations that would otherwise seem suspect. McCrea's discussion of Inchbald's *A Simple Story* focuses in part on the rather odd passage in which Miss Milner comes to terms with her passion for her guardian, the Catholic priest, Dorriforth. Her desire exists, according to the narrator, only because of the "early difference, in their systems of divine faith." Had she been reared in the Roman Catholic church, Miss Milner would have realized that his office as priest represented an insurmountable barrier, like the "barrier which divides a sister from a brother."[4] As McCrea notes, the fact that he is a guardian/father is never formulated as a problem. On the contrary, as it turns out, that makes him an appropriate object of desire.

The brother/sister motif of early fiction has yielded to the father/daughter motif that begins to dominate late-century depictions of female desire. Both relational models, of course, assert the intensity of erotic and emotional longing through the

---

2   *Impotent Fathers: Patriarchy and Demographic Crisis in the Eighteenth-Century Novel* (Newark, 1998), p. 15. McCrea draws on Lawrence and Jeanne C. Fawtier Stone's study *An Open Elite? England 1540–1880* (Oxford, 1984) to establish the fact of this demographic crisis.

3   Ibid., p. 28.

4   *A Simple Story*, ed. J.M.S. Tompkins, The World's Classics (Oxford, 1988), p. 74. Further references will be cited parenthetically.

invocation of incestuous urges. The authority for the brother/sister model hearkens back, as we saw in Chapter two, to the Song of Songs. The love implied by the brother/sister pattern of address is one of mutuality and equality. Father/daughter incest—metaphorically as well as literally—has very different cultural connotations and very different ethical implications, as we shall see.

Lot's Women

The story of Lot and his daughters is part of the larger narrative about Abraham and the establishing of the covenant between God and the Hebrew people, the covenant that will time and again prompt the "here am I" response. While Levinas concentrates on that responsiveness as a general ethical paradigm, I have narrowed the focus to insist throughout this study that it is particularly necessary for lovers to recognize obligation not as duty but as a part of desire. Just as Abraham and Isaiah respond to God's presence with eagerness to act and to serve on his behalf, so do lovers eagerly accept the demands placed on them by the other. Desire is fulfilled in the recognition of ethical obligation. It is distinct from duty and different from need. It is holy and it points us toward God.

Lot, however, stands as an example of weak patriarchy and a warning of the cultural cost of an attenuated masculine authority. Some rabbinic commentary on the incest episode in Genesis, in fact, focuses on Lot's deficiencies as the cause of his daughters' improper desire. The daughters do not arbitrarily turn to incest—their doing so is predetermined, first by Lot's own condoning of incestuous love in Sodom and second by his complicity in his daughters' scheme to become impregnated by him. After all, Lot repeats his pattern of drunkenness on the second night, even after he realizes what occurred during his period of besottedness the night before. His weakness is in turning away from the acceptance of full responsibility by refusing to see and acknowledge the other. Lot renounces responsibility even as he participates in creating the psycho-sexual conditions in which the incestuous relationship occurs.

Lot's culpability exists alongside his daughters' ennobled motives. Lot's daughters are convinced that the destruction of Sodom and Gomorrah is indicative of a universal conflagration. Consequently, their desire is less for their father than for the preservation of the human race, and while they are mistaken in the assumption on which they found their behavior, in the end, the children they conceive are indeed important to the preservation of the Hebrew people and religion. Confused, also, are the ethical nuances of even this reading of the narrative, for the elder daughter names her son Moab (of my father), a blatant, even brazen, acknowledgment of her sin (however justly committed); the younger daughter chooses the name "Ammon" (of my people), a denomination which speaks only to the ennobled motive and suggests to commentators that her sin is less than her elder sister's sin. Yet it is through the Moabites that the Hebrew people and religion will survive later on, for it is Ruth the Moabite woman who will marry Boaz and give birth to Obed, the father of Jesse, the grandfather of David, the great grandfather of Solomon. And so the elder daughter of Lot whose sin is greater than her sister's sin is ancestress of the Hebrew kings and is therefore responsible for not only the survival but also the greatness of the descendants of Abraham.

Lot's daughters, like other of the matriarchs, act according to principles that are open to misinterpretation, but that are in the end justified by the events that follow. Their instincts are validated, not so much by their own behavior, but by the chain of events that their behavior sets off. These women are tricksters. As their machinations serve the divine purpose, they can also be described as nobler and more ethical than the circumstances would seem to warrant.[5] The same cannot be said of Lot's wife. She does not stand as a positive example in either Jewish or Christian thought. In fact, the opposite is true. Rabbinic commentator Rashi emphasizes her wrongdoing, explaining her metamorphosis into a pillar of salt as punishment, not for turning around to watch the destruction of Sodom and Gomorrah, but for an earlier sin. The logic is dependent on a midrash, a story of Lot and his wife receiving guests into their home: "When Lot asked her for a little salt for their guests, she replied, 'Do you wish to introduce this evil custom of hospitality here too?'" "She had sinned through salt and was punished through salt," Rashi informs us.[6]

Jesus saw it differently—albeit also midrashicly. Lot's wife was, in his view, indeed punished for her backward glance which signified (paradoxically) a wish to save her life. Speaking of the "second coming," or the "rapture," Jesus informs his followers that the end of time will bear resemblance to the "days of Lot," not necessarily in its depravity but in its focus on the quotidian. In Lot's time, "they did eat, they drank, they bought, they sold, they planted, they builded" (Luke 17: 28). But the day Lot left Sodom, Jesus observes, "it rained fire and brimstone from heaven, and destroyed them all" (Luke 17: 29). So, the lesson of Sodom and Gomorrah that Jesus wishes to impart is the need to leave when the time comes to leave: "In that day, he which shall be upon the house top, and his stuff in the house, let him not come down to take it away: and he that is in the field, let him likewise not return back" (Luke 17: 31). And then, in one of the shortest verses in the Gospels, Jesus delivers the warning: "Remember Lot's wife" (Luke 17: 32). The next verse elaborates: "Whosoever shall seek to save his life shall lose it, and whosoever shall lose his life shall preserve it" (Luke 17: 33). The confusions of the text are compounded by the commentary. I will spend the next few pages explaining just what those confusions are, after which I will turn to Elizabeth Inchbald's own pillar of salt, Miss Milner, whose crimes are similarly difficult to decipher and whose punishment is likewise cryptically emblematic.

The problem with Lot's wife's briney punishment is that it strikes us as excessive. After all, she does not seem to have violated an express commandment. She was not actually around to hear God tell Lot that he must not look back, or at least

---

5   Indeed, Robert M. Polhemus has articulated a profound and compelling history of what he calls the "Lot complex" and what he describes as "a dynamic configuration of wishes, sexual fantasies, fears, and symbolic imagery that has worked to form generational relationships and structure personality, gender identity, religious faith, and social organization"— *Lot's Daughters: Sex, Redemption, and Women's Quest for Authority* (Stanford, 2005), p. 4.

6   *The Soncino Chumash*, ed. Rabbi Dr. A. Cohen and Rev. Rabbi A. J. Rosenberg (London, 1947), Gen. 19.

there is no record that she was. And we do not know that she has been ordered explicitly by Lot to keep her eyes focused ahead, nor do we know that she has been informed as to what the punishment will be if she fails to comply. I suppose most readers assume that she knows she is not to look back, but nowhere in the text are we told that she is specifically instructed not to do so. A careful commentator cannot make assumptions that the text does not support; therefore, Rashi, obviously, sought explanation elsewhere. This episode cannot be construed as a simple instance of cause and effect, so there must be significance in the kind of punishment, the nature of the act that precedes the punishment and the reason that Lot himself is saved despite his many shortcomings.

To break the analysis into its constituent parts, we will begin with the kind of punishment Lot's wife endures—her metamorphosis into a pillar of salt. A pillar is a signpost or a monument. One might erect a pillar as a marker to indicate place (to give direction to travelers) or as a statue to commemorate some worthy event, some occurrence worth documenting. Indeed, even Jesus' injunction suggests that Lot's wife is to be remembered. She is to serve as a sign to point us in the right direction. For Jesus, what she illustrates is God's ability to cut us off short, freeze us in death during a moment in time. She proves that our will is nothing compared to God's power.

For other rabbinical commentators, she demands remembrance too, and the commentary is less cryptic than the Gospels as to why. In the Babylonian Talmud, Berakoth 54b, we read: "Our Rabbis taught: If one sees the place of the crossing of the Red Sea, or the fords of the Jordan, or the fords of the streams of Arnon, or hail stones in the descent of Beth Horon, or the stone which Og king of Bashan wanted to throw at Israel, or the stone on which Moses sat when Joshua fought with Amalek, or [the pillar of salt of] Lot's wife, or the wall of Jericho which sank into the ground, for all of these he should give thanksgiving and praise to the Almighty." Respondents say, "We understand [why this blessing should be said over] all the others, because they are miracles, but the transformation of Lot's wife was a punishment." Still, they are told, "one should say on seeing it, Blessed be the true Judge." Why? " R. Johanan said: Even in the hour of His anger the Holy One, blessed be He, remembers the righteous, as it says, And it came to pass when God destroyed the cities of the Plain, that God remembered Abraham and sent Lot out of the midst of the overthrow." The blessing acknowledges God's intervention into human life, sometimes in miraculous ways. The pillar is a sign of that intervention and as such is honored.

Some commentary puzzles over the question as to why a sin would be punished by salt which plays a positive role in temple worship and in other rituals associated with Judeo-Christian culture signifying values absorbed into western culture in general. Salt is a preservative, and it is also associated with hospitality, generally—not simply in the midrashic gloss on Lot's wife's failings as a hostess. Salt is a traditional sign of welcoming care for the guest. And as such it brings us to the central significance of Lot's story and the key characteristic of his daughters—at least one of them whose kindness to a stranger is part of rabbinic lore. There is a midrash that tells of the way beggars were treated in Sodom during Lot's time. They were allowed to come into the town—encouraged to do so, even—and the denizens therein were free with their gifts of money, heaping coins upon them. But the coins were useless as there was no food to be bought. Eventually, the beggars died and the Sodomites, waiting for the inevitable to occur, were quick on the scene to retrieve their coins. One of Lot's daughters was moved by the deplorable condition of one beggar to give him bread instead of money. The Sodomites, impatient to see the story unfold in the way it always unfolded, became suspicious at the unusual length of time it was taking the beggar to die. Setting up spies to find out why, they pinned the blame on Lot's daughter, captured her, lathered her with honey, and strapped her to a pillar in order for the bees to find her. The stings of the insects made her scream so loudly she was heard beyond the city walls.

Lot and his daughters, the ones he saves, are associated with hospitality in the Torah itself. In Genesis 19, angels appear to Lot, disguised as men. They have been sent by God in compliance to Abraham's request that Lot be saved from the planned destruction of Sodom and Gomorrah. In a number of ways, the angels serve to test Lot—and through Lot, Abraham as well. In Genesis 18, in the same conversation that reveals the planned annihilation of the wicked cities, God promises Abraham and Sarah a son through whom "Abraham is to become a great and populous nation" (Genesis 18: 18). God also gives a reason for his choosing of Abraham: "For I have singled him out, that he may instruct his children and his posterity to keep the way of the Lord by doing what is just and right" (Genesis 18: 19). Lot had been of Abraham's household, and by this logic, though he and Abraham had been long separated, Lot should retain some of the goodness he had acquired through close association with his kinsman. Abraham himself counts on that; after all, he bargains with God using the formula "[w]ill You sweep away the innocent along with the guilty . . . and not forgive it for the sake of the innocent . . . who are in it?" (Genesis 18: 23–4). There are not enough innocent to save the city, as it turns out, but Lot's righteousness is determined when he welcomes the strangers/angels into his home and makes "a feast for them" with "unleavened bread." More importantly, he denies the men of Sodom access to his guests, even when they storm the house insisting that Lot send the strangers out "that we may be intimate with them" (Genesis 19: 5). Lot offers his daughters as substitutes (possibly assuming they would be rejected)[7] but the men of Sodom are furious and press in on Lot, vowing to do him harm. The angels solve the problem by smiting the ruffians with blindness.

Lot's protective care of his guests demonstrates his goodness, as does his willingness to sacrifice something of his own to preserve the strangers' lives. The gesture of offering to send his daughters into the raucous crowd may not impress us with regard to Lot's ethics; nevertheless, as the story plays out, it seems to me that the daughters themselves would have agreed with the stratagem, even if it had ended with their being abused by the Sodomites in their guests' stead. For in welcoming the stranger, Lot is not merely demonstrating the goodness of his own heart; he is

---

7   In fact, Richard Elliott Friedman says that's exactly the point, as to him "it is not the Near Eastern tradition of hospitality but of *bargaining* that accounts for what is going on here . . . Lot is supposed to make an extraordinary gesture. . . . But no one is supposed to take him up on it." *Commentary on the Torah*, Genesis 19: 8 n.

acting in accord with the laws of Abraham, the way Abraham governs his people and household, the "evil" custom to which Lot's wife so objects.[8]

There is hope for Lot's wife, though. Unlike Lot's sons-in-law who scoff at Lot's insistence that they leave before the city is engulfed in conflagration, Lot's wife does escape. She allows herself to be led with her husband and daughters by the angels who take her by the hand and lead her "outside the city" (Genesis 19: 16). But in looking back, she loses her life, the life she could have saved. Two questions beg to be answered regarding this part of the story. Why does she look back? And what does it mean that she is denied life beyond Sodom? The first question has been answered in various ways. She looks back from a longing for the past, from an addiction to the ways of Sodom that she really does not wish to leave, from an irresistible and mean-spirited curiosity that wishes to witness her triumph over the people with whom she has lived, from concern for the daughters she has had to leave behind with her scoffing sons-in-law. All of these are plausible explanations, some speaking to her moral worth, some to her moral degradation.

Significantly, however, her motive does not really matter, for having witnessed the destruction, she cannot live to tell about it. That was what the angel meant in the first place by ordering Lot to keep his eyes focused ahead as he left the city. It seems to me, in other words, that the second question is easier to answer than the first. Lot's wife cannot live not because of what she has done but because of what she has seen. The sight of Sodom and Gomorrah burning renders her mute, lifeless, a cipher to be understood only through the interpretation of others, never through her own words, in her own voice. Lot's wife is an occasion from this point on for exegesis that eludes explanation.

Not so the daughters. The daughters have their eyes focused ahead both literally and metaphorically. They do not look behind as they leave Sodom, and their behavior in the cave outside of Joar is driven by a desire for generation. What they do is predicated on their belief that they alone, with their father, have survived the destruction of the rest of the world's population: "And the older one said to the younger, 'Our father is old, and there is not a man on earth to consort with us in the way of all the world.'" (Genesis 19: 31). But, more importantly they approach the problem and its solution with an ethical sensitivity that seems to derive from the tribe of Abraham. Knowing what they have to do and understanding the degradation to which Lot would have to sink to be willing accessory to the deed, they create conditions that will mitigate his guilt; they make him drunk: "'Come,'" says the eldest to the youngest, "'let us make our father drink wine, and let us lie with him, that we may maintain life through our father'" (Genesis 19: 32). And twice we are told "he did not know when she lay down or when she rose" (Genesis 19: 33, 35).

---

8   As Plaut notes, "Lot's offer of his daughters to protect his guests may seem fantastically disproportionate. The implication in the text, however, is that Lot is a model host who will go to extreme lengths to honor the hospitality code." *The Torah: A Modern Commentary*, Genesis 19: 8 n. Alter disagrees, seeing the offer as "rash" and justly punished by the demeaning episode of incest that follows Lot's expulsion from Sodom. *Five Books of Moses*, p. 92.

His behavior is instinctual, not deliberate. The daughters preserve both their father's seed and his moral integrity.

Or so they intend. Commentary does not exonerate Lot, and (as noted above) history itself bears witness to a problem with the girls' solution to their dilemma as their offspring became the Moabites and the Ammonites, traditional enemies of the Hebrew people, the tribe of Abraham. Moreover, in denying Lot knowledge of their plan, the daughters also rob him of the opportunity to demonstrate his ethical sensibility, his true moral worth. He knows there are other living human beings. Presented with the option of incest, Lot would have had to face his fears. He had chosen to live in a cave outside of Joar because of anxiety as to how he would be received by the people of that city. After all, Joar might be reluctant to welcome a stranger, to extend hospitality to the straggling survivors of a city so wicked. Lot does not take the chance, and because he does not, his daughters conclude they are all alone, and because they do not present him with the chance to say yes or no to their scheme of survival Lot cannot choose between the difficult choices that are his to make.

When the angels appeared to him in Sodom, Lot did the right thing. He took them in, as the law of hospitality would have him do, in spite of the furor attendant on that choice. When the men of Sodom clamored at his door, demanding the strangers, Lot took another chance and offered his daughters instead. In reward for his moral clarity and ethical commitment to the stranger/other, Lot preserved both himself (and the purity of his daughters) and his guests. Outside of Joar, the situation is different. Lot and his daughters have survived the destruction of Sodom, but they are damaged. They are no longer capable of ethical behavior, not because of their selfishness, but because of their fear. They retain a sense of their own ability to respond to the other, but they cannot do so because they will not give themselves the chance to hear that other's demand. More important perhaps is their inability to adjust to being the stranger who asks rather than the host who gives. In ethical exchange, we must from time to time assume each role. Lot and his daughters, for all their moral worth, fail in the end to behave ethically because they refuse to assume the role of stranger and allow another to say "here I am; send me."

On a purely commonsense level (to say nothing of philosophy), fear is obviously an emotion that prevents social interaction and impedes the forming of interpersonal bonds. As the ethical operates within the field of social relations, fear is, again obviously, an impediment to ethical thought and action. Fear derives from the self and turns the self inward. Fear prevents the individual from seeing the other's face, but also it prevents the individual from turning toward the other in order to allow his (or her) face to be seen. Fear of this sort is the condition of modern life; it is a condition of life that emerged as a cultural norm in the eighteenth century. In a sense, from the eighteenth century on, we have witnessed the triumph of Lot over his uncle Abraham. Fear has been the cause, and the failure of ethics has been the consequence.

I am talking about Lot in his latter days, of course, for as we have seen Lot is associated early on with hospitality, the bond between host and stranger, a fundamentally ethical relation. In fact, even when he lived and traveled with Abraham, Lot's primary characteristic was an innate understanding of the importance of hospitality and the roles of both host and stranger which he demonstrated by strategic silence as the tribe passed through Egypt on its way to Canaan. Here Abraham (still Abram at this point) introduces Sarai (later Sarah), his wife, to his Egyptian hosts as his sister. He instructs Sarah: "'Please say that you are my sister, that it may go well with me because of you, and that I may remain alive thanks to you'" (Genesis 12: 13). The Egyptians will honor the brother/sister relation; they will not, however, honor laws of possession. At least that is Abraham's suspicion, as he explains to Sarah: "'If the Egyptians see you, and think, "She is his wife," they will kill me and let you live'" (Genesis 12: 13). He turns out to be right, though the Egyptians chastise him for lying and causing plagues to be visited on them as a result of the Pharaoh's taking Sarai, the wife, when he thought he had Sarai, the sister. They quickly return her to her husband to relieve themselves from God's fury, and Abram, Sarai, Lot and the tribes make their way out of Egypt on their journey to Canaan.

Lot parts company with Abram shortly thereafter; nephew and uncle love each other, but there is dissension between their tribes. In the interest of peace, brotherhood, they go their separate ways. In Abram's words: "Let there be no strife between you and me . . . for we are kinsmen" (Genesis 13: 8). Abram gives Lot the choice, and Lot chooses Jordan, which includes the cities of Sodom and Gomorrah, attracted, despite the influence of Abram, to the urban evils and temptations that would ultimately prove his undoing. What he retained, however, was a hospitable nature; he stood ready to welcome the stranger, even in the midst of depravity. Lot truly was an upright man. But he was also weak; and in the end it takes both strength and moral rectitude to open oneself to the ethical demands of the other.

Nature's Child

When fathers in late-eighteenth-century fiction exhibit post-destruction Lot-like fears of the stranger, daughters are the ones who suffer damage and hurt of various kinds. To Mary Wollstonecraft, the primary wrong done to women by faulty fathers is that they " render women . . . artificial, weak characters . . . and consequently . . . useless members of society."[9] Some actual fathers do so, of course, but Wollstonecraft's analysis focuses on the fathers of culture—writers who instruct through compellingly written guidebooks or engaging philosophical narratives as do John Gregory and Jean-Jacques Rousseau. Both Gregory's *Legacy to his Daughter* and Rousseau's *Emile* insist that pleasing a man is both the core of a woman's existence and the aim of her education. Such a reading of woman's "sexual character" obviously denies the fact of female desire. Women become mere objects of "voluptuous reveries." *Emile*'s Sophie provokes Wollstonecraft's "indignation" at creator Rousseau—as she herself first confesses and then demonstrates in a series of rhetorical questions: "Is this the man who, in his ardour for virtue, would banish all the soft arts of peace, and almost carry us back to Spartan discipline? Is this the man who delights to paint the useful

---

9   *Vindication of the Rights of Woman*, ed. Miriam Brody (London, 1982), p. 103. Further references are cited parenthetically.

struggles of passion, the triumphs of good dispositions, and the heroic flights which carry the glowing soul out of itself? How are these mighty sentiments lowered when he describes the pretty foot and enticing airs of his little favourite!" (107)

Rousseau subscribes to a notion of sexual difference that is really no difference at all. If "the whole education of women ought to relate to men," as he suggests, a woman like Sophie becomes nothing more than an embodiment of masculine desire.[10] "To be a woman means to be coquettish," Rousseau asserts, adding that "dependence is a condition natural to women" and that "guile is a natural talent with the fair sex."[11] The cultivation of a woman's physical self is to be aimed toward the development of attractiveness as opposed to the strength young men need to acquire. Girls enjoy dressing up, adorning themselves or their dolls as surrogates of themselves, and "as for holding a needle, that they always learn gladly."[12] To this series of proclamations tending to a definition of sexual character, Wollstonecraft responds curtly: "What nonsense!" (108)

Still, Wollstonecraft admits a certain attractiveness in Rousseau's ideal:

> to reason on Rousseau's ground, if man did attain a degree of perfection of mind when his body arrived at maturity, it might be proper, in order to make a man and his wife *one*, that she should rely entirely on his understanding; and the graceful ivy, clasping the oak that supported it, would form a whole in which strength and beauty would be equally conspicuous. (104)

That is not the way things are, however: "husbands, as well as their helpmates, are often only overgrown children; nay, thanks to early debauchery, scarcely men in their outward form—and if the blind lead the blind, one need not come from heaven to tell us the consequence" (104). Nevertheless, in imagining what would be the ideal case, Wollstonecraft reveals her own distance from late-seventeenth- and early-eighteenth-century women writers. The curve in the image of the ivy on an oak tree is a fitting emblem for even the most positive view of heterosexual love in the late eighteenth century, and it is, significantly, not a chiastic image. Wollstonecraft is critical of Rousseau, but even her own imagery is infused with the myth of Britain, the stalwart oak signifying the manly strength that she feels should ideally characterize the nation, particularly the aristocracy. Were the aristocracy as strong and whole as it should be, women could buttress that strength in a gracefully conjoined state. This ideal, summoned to criticize the men who fail to live up to it, is itself not a model of ethical love.

In fact, Wollstonecraft's musings on heterosexual love emphasize the obliteration of sexual difference as much as do Rousseau's. For Wollstonecraft, as for (interestingly) Samuel Johnson as well, the perfect marriage, the perfect love is a condition of "perpetual friendship," a conversation, to be sure, but a conversation that elevates the intellectual meeting of two minds over the sensual meeting of two bodies.[13]

---

10   *Emile or On Education*, trans. Alan Bloom (New York, 1979), p. 365.

11   Ibid., pp. 365, 370.

12   Ibid., p. 368.

13   See Johnson, *Rambler* no. 167 in which he defines marriage as "the most solemn league of perpetual friendship."

While late-seventeenth- and early-eighteenth-century women writers certainly figured heterosexual love as discourse, they grounded talk between their loving (and, admittedly, often doomed) pairs in moments of mutual physical responsiveness. In the severing of erotic attraction and ethical commitment, late-century moralists and novelists indicate a fissure has occurred in society, one that has yet to be repaired. For her own part, Wollstonecraft certainly pursued love as a combination of erotic and intellectual attraction, but she suffered as a consequence—as acutely as Behn's Silvia or Manley's Rivella or Haywood's Alovisa ever did. In the midst of a social revolution as intense as the one that characterized the late seventeenth century, she, along with other visionaries, sought to mitigate the pains caused by socially constructed inequalities. That was the purpose of philosophical speculation in the late eighteenth century just as the imagining of freedom from social restraint, regardless of the pains suffered as a consequence, was the purpose of philosophical thought a century before. Further, as we have seen, during the intervening years, the imputation of immorality has attached itself to erotic desire. It becomes problematic to return to the garden with unalloyed delight. Hence, garden episodes in which young lovers enjoy unfettered passion become in several significant novels of the 1790s precursors to scenes of horrific social violence, precipitated and presided over, interestingly, by the father who reared his daughter to be a "child of nature."

Like Wollstonecraft, other women writers of the 1790s were both intrigued and repelled by the idea of the naturally educated man and the woman (educated naturally too) formed to please and complete him. Mary Hays's *The Victim of Prejudice* and Eliza Fenwick's *Secresy*, for example, reflect the influence of Emile and Sophie in depictions of young lovers who learn to love by nature's laws, not society's rules. The natural man and woman are upheld as ideals, just as Rousseau presented them; yet in testing the ideal against the realities of the time they live in, the women novelists endorse Wollstonecraft's perception that as long as nature's law and society's rules are in conflict with one another, masculine strength will not answer the demands of feminine weakness.

While a preoccupation with frail fathers and weak male lovers characterizes much late-century fiction by women, no one narrative so completely examines the ethical ramifications of male weakness, truncated female desire, and the attendant failure of ethics as Elizabeth Inchbald's 1791 novel, *A Simple Story*. Since the mid-1980s this novel has been regarded as a classic, achieving canonical status in the emergent field of the Romantic novel (Romanticism until that time having defined itself primarily through the genre of poetry). Eighteenth-century scholars such as Patricia Meyer Spacks have also recognized in Inchbald's tale a powerful articulation of the problematics of female desire.[14] For my purposes, I find the narrative an apt illustration of the Lot motif, telling evidence that by the end of the eighteenth century the ethics of the cave threaten to replace the ethics of the face-to-face encounter in heterosexual relationships as in most social relations characterizing the emergent individualism of western culture.

Inchbald's title somewhat belies the point I have just made. Instead of titling her novel "Miss Milner and Matilda" and thereby emphasizing the focus on this mother

---

14 See Spacks, *Desire and Truth* (Chicago, 1990), pp. 195–202.

and daughter, Inchbald directs our attention to the fabular nature of the two-generation tale. We see this sort of diversion in Smith's misleading title of her mother-daughter narrative (*The Young Philosopher*), in Hays's use of a descriptive phrase rather than a proper name (*The Victim of Prejudice*), and in Fenwick's thematic title (*Secresy*) as well. This shift in the convention of entitling narratives that continue to be focused on the experiences of a single protagonist or a few protagonists seems almost a retreat—a turning away from the implications of ennobling the individual life to the extent that the novel seems to have emerged in order to do. The title itself, then, may be our first sign of a retreat into a kind of darkness, obscurity, secrecy—a cave too dimly lit for the face-to-face encounter. But the title page also holds out the wistful hope of ethical clarity, a hope that will be frustrated in the pages that follow.

The novel begins with news of a guardianship, bequeathed by a Mr. Milner on his friend Dorriforth, a Roman Catholic priest. The child, a daughter, is eighteen. We are given a brief history of her parents' marriage and the religious circumstances that defined it. Mr. Milner was Roman Catholic; his wife, Protestant, and "they mutually agreed their sons should be educated in the religious opinion of their father, and their daughters in that of their mother" (4). Although as J.M.S. Tompkins points out, this circumstance is hardly unusual for interfaith marriages of the time and Miss Milner's Protestantism is in fact never presented as a source of concern to either her father or her guardian/lover/husband, the gendering of denominational preference is significant. Inchbald herself was a Roman Catholic, but I think that fact less important than the association of Protestantism with British nationality and free-thinking with French nationality. In the cultural categories prevalent at the time of *A Simple Story*'s composition and publication, Dorriforth's Roman Catholicism links him to the past—both in Europe in general and in the British Isles in particular. Miss Milner is associated with the present, with Protestantism and, significantly, with both nature and art.

The child of Mr. and Mrs. Milner receives a Protestant education in which she learned "merely such sentiments of religion as young ladies of fashion mostly imbibe." At the age of eighteen, her mind remains "without one ornament, except those which nature gave" (4–5). But this natural child is also a child of fashion, her natural inclinations "not wholly preserved from the ravages made by its rival, *Art*" (5). With this early introduction, Inchbald establishes a tripartite division of the individual ethical character—there is Nature, which is a somewhat reliable guide, there is Art (or social convention and fashionable dictates), a destructive and misleading guide, and there is Religion, itself a corrective to the ravages of Art, but as practiced in society (Protestant boarding schools, for example) a guide which has abdicated and abnegated responsibility. Miss Milner, in other words, has not been ethically enhanced by the encounter with God provided by her Protestant upbringing. She is ill-prepared for what awaits her as she moves into the home and comes under the tutelage of Dorriforth.

Her father has the best intentions in consigning her to Dorriforth's guardianship. In fact, he seems supremely ethical in honoring both his commitment to his wife, i.e., his promise to rear his daughter in the faith of her mother, and his commitment to his daughter, i.e., concern for her moral character and emotional well-being. He chooses Dorriforth because his friend unites "every moral virtue to those of religion, and native honour to pious faith" (5). Uncorrupted by society, buttressing natural goodness with religious precepts and discipline, Dorriforth will make an ideal teacher for his daughter, respecting her as an other to be encountered, not a second self to mold, to assimilate, to force into compliance . Dorriforth, Milner trusts, "will protect without controlling, instruct without tyrannizing, comfort without flattering, and perhaps in time make good by choice rather than by constraint, the dear object of his dying friend's sole care" (5). The one codicil Milner attaches is that Dorriforth resist the impulse to instruct Miss Milner "in one religious opinion contrary to those her mother had professed, and in which she herself had been educated" (5). This requirement seems fair enough, right, even, given the pledge Milner has made to his wife; but the words which he uses to reinforce the point expose the ethical problems such a caveat introduces: "'Never perplex her mind,'" he instructs Dorriforth, "'with an idea that may disturb, but cannot reform'" (5–6). Without disturbance, there is no reform, of course. Which ideas will disturb and reform? Which will disturb without reforming? To leave the determination to the father/guardian is to ask him to play God, rather than to lead to God. The face-to-face encounter allows disturbances the consequences of which cannot be foreseen and must be left to the divine. Milner, for all his effort, has created a situation in which his daughter and his friend cannot sustain the occasional glimpses they get of one another's face, and because they cannot, the ethical which is the foundation of their relationship cannot survive the exigencies that come to define their existence.

What should be a simple story of an erotic encounter that leads to personal fulfillment and spiritual insight becomes through fear of self and other a tortured tale of misunderstanding, mistaken assumptions, misguided action. Yet, in another sense, this story is indeed a simple one—a familiar one, anyway—for it is the story of all broken hearts and fractured relationships. Miss Milner and her guardian/lover are intensely affected by one another from the moment of their first meeting. When Miss Milner's name is announced upon her arrival at Dorriforth's London home, Dorriforth "turned pale—something like a foreboding of disaster trembled at his heart, and consequently darted over all his face" (13). Miss Milner is similarly stricken: "The instant Dorriforth was introduced to her by Miss Woodley as her 'Guardian, and her deceased father's most beloved friend,' she burst into a flood of tears, knelt down to him for a moment, and promised ever to obey him as her father" (13). Dorriforth cannot respond to her because he has "his handkerchief to his face" shielding his visage or else she "would have beheld the agitation of his heart—the remotest sensations of his soul" (13). Here, of course, is the problem. These two are capable of loving one another in the most profound sense. Both erotic and spiritual impulses drive them toward one another; they respond to one another in emotional registers denied everyone else in Volume 1 of the novel. But most of the time, they hide behind disguises, emotional or literal masks that prevent them from recognizing one another as an other.

Yet Miss Milner and Dorriforth do experience genuine "here I am" moments. Miss Milner, in particular, undergoes dramatic changes in her personality and demeanor in response to Dorriforth's demands. These are literal demands, as in the instance recorded in Chapter 7 of the first volume: "'I command you to stay at home this evening'" (29). Miss Milner is crushed. She had planned to attend a ball;

she is young and vain; the evening had promised pleasure and for some arbitrary reason, her guardian sees fit to deny her. Granted, he insists that she stay at home because when he asked if she planned to do so, she thoughtlessly replied "yes," though she had planned to go out all along. Still, her assumption that "what she had said to Mr. Dorriforth might be excused as a slight mistake, the lapse of memory, or some other trifling fault" (28) certainly seems a reasonable assumption as indeed her "yes" does seem to have been just that—a trifling negligence. Dorriforth, however, feels otherwise. One's word is one's word. Having given it, Miss Milner must honor it. In the end, she does. She stays home in compliance to her guardian's will, and Dorriforth responds with an act of mercy. In ethical terms, he is very like the God of Abraham at Mount Moriah. If he does not find a lamb to substitute for Miss Milner, he at least lets her live: "Keep your appointment," he says to his tearfully subdued ward; "and be assured I shall issue my commands with greater circumspection for the future, as I find how strictly they are complied with" (33). All he wanted was demonstration of the willingness to obey; his commands will not be severe as long as Miss Milner says, as Abraham said, "here I am."

Without explicitly acknowledging as much, Inchbald seems drawn to the moment of ethical transcendence inspired by human love. Miss Milner, discovers time and again the power of such moments. In fact, one could say, and Inchbald's narrator indeed suggests, that Miss Milner is addicted to these moments. In Bath, separated from her guardian for the first time since he became such, Miss Milner languishes without hope of—or hoping for—recovery: "Thus, does the lover consider the extinction of his passion with the same horror as the libertine looks upon annihilation; the one would rather live hereafter (though in all the tortures with which his future state is described) than cease to exist; so there are no tortures a lover would not suffer, rather than cease to love" (94). Love is her God, the God whom Miss Milner apprehends through Dorriforth.

Like Levinas, however, Inchbald is dissatisfied with the notion of a purely spiritual transcendence. Indeed, the point of God's covenant with Abraham is generation, the creation of a nation of people committed to the one God but living out their existence most importantly in history, in the presence of one another, in the time and space that define life on earth. Ethics is about human relationships; as long as Dorriforth is a celibate priest, and not fully man, his love for Miss Milner cannot be ethical and hers for him is unnatural and perverse, as attested to by Miss Woodley's reaction when Miss Milner confesses her feelings: "she was white as ashes and deprived of speech" (73). But when, at the death of his brother, Dorriforth inherits his family's wealth and position and the title of "Lord," even the Pope recognizes that he is more valuable as a man than as a representative of God. As a Mr. Fleetmond, himself a Roman Catholic, puts it: "certainly it is for the honour of the catholics, that this earldom should continue in a catholic family!" (101) Dorriforth, now Lord Elmwood, travels to Italy where he is released from his vows and "no longer bound to a single life, but *enjoined* to marry" (103). The sacredness of the duty of generation and fulfillment of family obligation is signified first by Miss Woodley, whose horror has turned to pleasure and anticipatory jubilation. She says to Miss Milner, "I no longer condemn, but congratulate you on your passion; and will assist you with all my advice and earnest wishes, that you may obtain a return" (102). It is, in fact, Miss Woodley who eventually reveals Miss Milner's love to Lord Elmwood. It is she who provokes him to cry out: "For God's sake take care what you are doing—you are destroying my prospects for futurity—you are making this world too dear to me" (130), a telling comment, for the love of another human being does indeed draw one's mind and heart from the contemplation of God. Ethically, in the face of the other, one sees God, but Elmwood is not used to thinking thus. Having been awakened, however, to the power of mutual love, Elmwood proves himself an apt pupil, hovering with concern about Miss Milner whose appetite suffers due to what she believes is an impending marriage between her guardian and the near perfect Miss Fenton. By the time of the scene in question, Elmwood has resolved to break off the engagement with Miss Fenton, but Miss Milner does not know that. She tries repeatedly to force food into her mouth, but she cannot bring herself to eat. When Elmwood "saw by her struggles she could not eat, he took her plate from her; gave her something else; and all with a care and watchfulness in his looks, as if he had been a tender-hearted boy, and she his darling bird" (134).

This eating scene is significant and suggests a care and domestic concern on Elmwood's part to provide for his beloved. Her willingness to be provided for is requisite to the couple's future happiness, so it is with some disappointment and inevitable foreboding that we read in the following chapter that Miss Milner is no sooner the professed beloved of Lord Elmwood than she is regretting the fact that she "did . . . not keep him longer in suspense." "[M]y power over him might have been greater still" (138).

She becomes resolute in her efforts to prove his love—prove that his love will triumph over his judgment, that he will yield to her even when he disapproves of her behavior. Elmwood himself embarks on a trial of Miss Milner. Discovering that he loves her in opposition to Sandford and afraid that Sandford's opposition is in fact what is fueling his love, Dorriforth vows to watch and wait a few months, and then "'marry or—*banish me from her for ever*'" (142). These two, then, replace the language and behavior of care and concern with that of trial, force, and power. The result is predictable. Miss Milner accepts food from Lord Elmwood, they converse, but she "condescend[s] to eat," they speak "with a reserve that appeared as if they had been quarrelling, and so felt to themselves, though no such circumstance had happened" (150).

And then comes the masquerade. Significantly, the episode is prefaced by a "here I am" moment. Miss Milner has for a long time felt pain on behalf of Rushbrook, a nephew of Lord Elmwood's, to whom he refuses admittance due to the transgressions of the child's mother, Elmwood's sister. As Miss Milner and Lord Elmwood approach marriage, she tries again to intercede on Rushbrook's behalf. Lord Elmwood readily relents: "Go for him then to-morrow . . . and bring him home. . . . [T]his shall be his home—you shall be a mother, and I will, henceforward, be a father to him" (150–1). The moment is extraordinary, a "high token of his lordship's regard to Miss Milner" (151). It is an ethically sublime instance of the redemptive, ameliorative power of erotic love. It is followed, however, by a "great incident . . . [that] totally reversed the prospect of all future accommodation" (151)—the masquerade.

This is a repeated motif, and, in fact, we are witnessing a parallel structure here as recognition—disobedience—reconciliation / recognition—disobedience—

reconciliation describes the pattern of the first half of *A Simple Story*—simplicity, itself, as the title suggests. The pattern has been established, and the movement is clearly forecast in the pattern. Miss Milner thoughtlessly assumes that if she wishes to go to the masquerade, she may do so without opposition. Lord Elmwood peremptorily says no. The denial reinforces her desire; she engages in a battle of will. She tells Miss Woodley: "'As my guardian, I certainly did obey him; and I could obey him as a husband; but as a lover, I will not'" (154). Miss Woodley warns that disobedience means she will never have him as a husband, but Miss Milner is obdurate. Besides, Lord Elmwood will not be home; he is going on a hunt. Almost as a tribute to him, it seems, Miss Milner goes to the masquerade accompanied by a "group of wood-nymphs and huntresses" (156), but her costume, the goddess of Chastity, is provocative. The contradictions in her life, her desires, her character are acutely evident in this scene. She has no fun in the woods; but the fact that she goes there does bode dire consequences, both for herself and for her nation.

The masquerade escapade results in the estrangement of Miss Milner and Lord Elmwood. Their engagement is broken off. At first, Miss Milner thinks she is playing a lovers' game, but eventually she becomes convinced that Lord Elmwood's disappointment is not a game, and she again loses her appetite—the one sure sign that she is on the verge of saying "here I am." The significance of her doing so is that in acknowledging her fault and her obligation, she prevents Lord Elmwood from taking a "foreign wife" (178). It is Sandford who recognizes the danger. He sees the couple standing, silent and tearful, as Lord Elmwood prepares to depart for the Continent. Suddenly convinced of their mutual sincerity, he steps in—a Deus ex Machina—and he marries them.

In this marriage is the allegorical salvation of England. The English Catholics could join with Europe in a religious nation as opposed to a geographical one, but at what psychic cost? It is simpler and better to stay home. But there is a price to pay. This marriage, founded on mutual attraction, founders on different desires. The "here I am" moment is not enough to seal the bond between a Miss Milner whose vanity seeks the gratifications of power and a Lord Elmwood whose sense of entitlement seeks the same thing by a different name. The struggle between these two people will play itself out at large over the course of the next century, with the Miss Milners of the world emerging in real life—as opposed to the life of the novel—the victors to whom go the spoils. The problem is, of course, that no one—not even victors—really desire spoils. Miss Milner wants more. When her husband must leave her for three years to attend to his interest in the West Indies, she does not put her desires on hold. She indulges herself in the addiction he helped her develop—the addiction to love. As a result, her child, Matilda, is left to fashion an ethics based not on the "here I am," face-to-face encounter with an other, but an ethics derived from the world of Lot and based on the word of the father. Miss Milner's is the simple story as it is founded and as it founders on purity of intention. Matilda's is the complicated result of such simplicity. Her story is the story of redacted desire.

Matilda's Story

The daughter's story begins with the mother's decision to return to the father, at least to speak to him from beyond the grave. She does so in a sense twice—first in a strange obituary in which she is commemorated for her failings. She stands a print pillar of salt for all who care to learn the lesson of her life:

> On Wednesday last died, at Dring Park, a village in Northumberland, the right honourable Countess Elmwood—This lady, who has not been heard of for many years in the fashionable world, was a rich heiress, and of extreme beauty; but although she received overtures from many men of the first rank, she preferred her guardian, the present Lord Elmwood (then the humble Mr. Dorriforth) to them all—and it is said, they enjoyed an uncommon share of felicity, till his lordship going abroad, and remaining there some time, the consequences (to a most captivating young woman left without a protector) were such, as to cause a separation on his return.—Her ladyship has left one child, a daughter, about fifteen. (204)

This obituary is a recapitulation of the simple story of the first two volumes of the novel, and it serves as an official warning that pretty young wives should not be left without protectors, guardians, father-figures lest their desires overwhelm their judgment and cause some sort of impropriety. It is not the same lesson that we learn from Lot's wife, but it is of the same sort—a cautionary tale.

These words are in print; Lady Elmwood leaves another document in her own handwriting, a letter addressed to her husband in which she outlines conditions by which her daughter can enjoy the protection of a father without violating the father's will. For, of course, it is a violation of Lord Elmwood's determination to never see his daughter to ask that he give her succor and shelter in her orphaned state. She is not alone; with her mother's banishment, she has inherited members of the Elmwood household, Miss Woodley and Sandford, who stand between her and the unkindnesses of the world. But Lady Elmwood asks that her father play a role in her life as well. And, interestingly resonant with the story of Lot, the role she defines for Elmwood is that of "host." Lady Elmwood further leaves no will, "no will at all" (207). As Sandford explains to her estranged husband, "she wished every thing to be as you willed" (207). She is even buried as an exile of sorts, not next to her father, as Elmwood assumes, but on her own. Sandford again explains: "she expressed no . . . desire; and as that was the case, I did not think it necessary to carry the corpse so far" (209). Her voice is silent, except for the one epistolary request concerning her daughter: "Be her host; I remit the tie of being her parent.—Never see her—but let her sometimes live under the same roof with you" (211).

Prior to reading the letter, Elmwood obligates Sandford to a rigid behavioral law: "You have full power to act in regard to the persons you have mentioned [Miss Woodley and Matilda]. . . but be sure, you never let them be named before me, from this moment" (208). He relents later with regard to Miss Woodley, but Matilda, though allowed to occupy rooms in one of his homes, is never to be seen, heard, or spoken of on pain of severe resentment, emotional and physical exile—her own if she violates the conditions, her interlocutor's, if a second party chooses to intervene. Elmwood sees himself as "comply[ing] with [his lady's] desires" (214) in taking this resolution. But hospitality begins with naming; he is not complying in an ethically valid sense.[15]

Throughout most of Volumes 3 and 4, Matilda futilely longs for acknowledgment from her father. When they finally do meet inadvertently face-to-face, she faints, uttering the words "'Save me.'" At that point, Elmwood does speak a name—but the name of "'Miss Milner—Dear Miss Milner,'" not the name of his daughter (274). In fact, Matilda is banished by her father as the result of this emotional meeting. It is later, when she is abducted by a licentious, overeager nobleman, that Lord Elmwood answers her demand and does indeed "save" her. But, in a more significant sense, it is she who saves him.

When Lot leaves Sodom, he attempts to save his wife and daughters. His wife, for reasons we can never know but that we can suppose are driven by fear, looks back and thereby rejects salvation. His daughters are saved but only to be betrayed by the silence and darkness of their father's fears into actions that are noble in intent and devastating in effect. We see in the union of Miss Milner, the Protestant, with Lord Elmwood, the Roman Catholic, a coming together of strangers who learn to love one another but who cannot open themselves to the astonishment of the unknowable, who, instead, cloak themselves in selfishness, defensiveness, rigidity, coldness when faced with the strangeness of one another. Indeed they never call one another by their given names. Miss Milner, like Lot's wife, rejects the salvation that has come her way through the love of and for her guardian and protector. Lord Elmwood, like Lot in turn, refuses to open himself to the face of his daughter; he provides without hospitality, illustrating what Jacques Derrida describes as *"the opposite of nearness."*[16]

Lady Elmwood astutely perceives that her estranged husband is incapable of being a father to his child, so she asks, instead, that he welcome the stranger into his home. Of course, the host has a right to choose to whom his home will be opened. Indeed, the central problem of hospitality, as Derrida observes, has to do with "distinguish[ing] between a guest and a parasite": "Not all new arrivals are received as guests if they don't have the benefit of the right to hospitality or the right of asylum. . . . Without this right, a new arrival can only be introduced 'in my home,' in the host's 'at home,' as a parasite, a guest who is wrong, illegitimate, clandestine, liable to expulsion or arrest."[17] Does Matilda have this benefit of the right to hospitality? Does she have the right of asylum? Her mother thinks so, but her father is less sure.

When Matilda takes up residence on her father's estate, she finds another already ensconced there. Rushbrook is a member of Lord Elmwood's household, placed there, we recall, by Lady Elmwood herself. That Lord Elmwood continues to honor the relationship he so long resisted suggests that, residually anyway, he has respect for the ethical acuity of his morally flawed wife. Still, he does not treat Matilda with

---

15 On naming and hospitality, see Anne Dufourmantelle, *Of Hospitality: Anne Dufourmantelle Invites Jacques Derrida to Respond*, trans. Rachel Bowlby, Cultural Memory in the Present, gen. eds Mieke Bal and Hent de Vries, (Stanford, 2000), p. 12.

16 Anne Dufourmantelle's language, ibid., p. 52.

17 Derrida, in Dufourmantelle, *Of Hospitality*, pp. 59, 61.

hospitality. And, in fact, even Rushbrook is regarded as a "parasite." Indeed, Matilda calls him that in a fit of justifiable jealousy (232); but, more to the point, Elmwood treats him as such, for Rushbrook, like all in Elmwood's household, is liable to sudden expulsion. Elmwood has welcomed no one into his home; he treats no one as guest; he recognizes no one, with the possible exception of Sandford, as family. Elmwood is walled off from guests and family alike, cloaked in a fear that will not allow him to see the face of the other, to respond to the other's demands, to demand from the other the willingness to serve. He is not the Lot of Sodom, offering the best of what he has to the guests who enter. He is the Lot of Joar weak, frightened, and blind. His daughter, like Lot's daughters, must provide the way into the future from the past—and she does.

The Chiasmus of Double Desire

Inchbald's simple story is far from simple in terms of thematic resonance and narrative strategy, as many critics have pointed out.[18] And, though the second half of the novel focuses on the daughter, the mother continues to dominate. For even after her death has rendered Miss Milner/Lady Elmwood absent and silent, there are those who hear the echoes of her voice and feel the traces of her existence. Significantly, the ghost of maternal presence is described by Derrida as the linkage between hospitality and madness, and it evokes the fear of the unknown in a palpable way. Miss Milner, like all good mothers, creates a secure home for her child, but in doing so—in establishing the norms and patterns of a life that cannot be sustained— she creates the condition of fear and anxiety once the child is faced with other norms and patterns, once the child becomes an adult and encounters the stranger or indeed becomes the stranger.

Miss Milner's first function is to disrupt a home the home of Dorriforth. For that she is scorned and feared by Sandford, who is also the first to open himself to her as a stranger whose voice he will attend. He resists so long because he, unlike the rest of the novel's populace, understands that to listen is to become transformed, to lose some of his self-possession, to encounter the unknown and the unknowable. Sandford's role as adversary of Miss Milner, friend to Elmwood, and protector and friend of Matilda is based on his clear conception of justice and righteousness, but these categories are not rigidly attached to person, religion, or place. Sandford's resolute stability is a source of strength for everyone in the novel, but he represents the opposite of fundamentalist, nationalist principles, the kind to which an indiscriminate hospitality often lead. As Jacques Derrida has put it "[w]herever the 'home' is violated, wherever at any rate a violation is felt as such, you can foresee a privatizing and even familialist reaction, by widening the ethnocentric and nationalist, and thus

---

18 See, for instance, Terry Castle, *Masquerade and Civilization: The Carnivalesque in Eighteenth-Century English Culture and Fiction* (Stanford, 1986), pp. 290–330; Patricia Meyer Spacks, *Desire and Truth*, pp. 195–201; and Diana Pérez Edelman-Young, "Cloistering and Fragmentation: The (Re)construction of Female Subjectivity in Elizabeth Inchbald's *A Simple Story* and Mary Shelley's *Mathilda*," unpublished M.A. thesis, University of Georgia, 1997.

xenophobic circle."[19] Choosing guests carefully is necessary because once they are welcomed, the commitment is a lasting one, and must be (to be ethical) a reciprocal one.

In exile, Miss Milner creates a home for Matilda defined not by place but by community—Miss Woodley and Sandford—and community values—love of father and mother and resentment of Rushbrook, the usurper. (The resentment is a development that happens after the death of Miss Milner, but it grows from the community she creates.) It is Matilda, in her father's home, who first sees the fissures in the world—both in terms of her father's character and in terms of Rushbrook's value. Her first response is fear, or at least tears, which in another novel might betoken an overdeveloped sensibility and prefigure the heroine's dissolution or even death. Matilda, however, is a tougher spirit. She is of the order of Eliza Fenwick's and Mary Hays's and Charlotte Smith's young heroines. She can face difficult truths without flinching—and, fear notwithstanding, she opens her "home." Rushbrook is welcomed into Matilda's community in exile. She, broken and ill, nevertheless acts as hostess to Rushbrook whose vague, unstable, unfixed personality becomes increasingly defined through concern for his cousin.

Matilda's kindness toward Rushbrook is the equivalent of the drink offered Eliezer by Rebekah or that given Jacob by Rachel. Rushbrook finds himself affected by Matilda. He pities her emotional isolation and physical infirmity. Gradually, he recognizes these feelings to be deeper than mere sympathy, indeed to be "genuine love": "With a strict scrutiny into his heart he sought this knowledge, but arrived at it with a regret that amounted to despair" (250). His despair is the equivalent of fear, and in another, it could be paralyzing. But like Matilda whose tears precede an act of hospitality, Rushbrook transforms his fear into an act of bravery. In full knowledge of the possible repercussions, but with awareness as well that estrangement between father and daughter cannot serve the ends of anyone's happiness, Rushbrook disrupts Elmwood's home with a reference to Miss Milner: "'It was the mother of Lady Matilda . . . who was . . . friend to me; nor will I ever think of marriage, or any other joyful prospect, while you abandon the only child of my beloved patroness, and load me with the rights, which belong to her'" (290).

With the face-to-face encounter between father and daughter, obstacles between Rushbrook and Matilda loom less formidably, but the Lot motif continues to hover over their relationship in certain ways. Indeed the narrator remarks that Elmwood's reconciliation with his daughter "might give Rushbrook a pang at this dangerous rival in his love and fortune" (333). And we are also told that Rushbrook is content to come second in Matilda's affections for he "loved . . . [her] too sincerely; he loved her father's happiness, and her mother's memory too faithfully, not to be rejoiced at all he was witness of." We are further informed that secret hopes that "[t]heir every blessing might one day be mutual" do not "increase the pleasure he found, in beholding Matilda happy" (333). All of these comments could lead us to read the ending of Inchbald's narrative as an assertion that the father-daughter bond has displaced the bond between lovers who are to become husband and wife. That would be, after all, but to end where this fable began. *A Simple Story*, however, is not that

---

19 *Of Hospitality*, p. 53.

simplistic, and, ultimately, the narrative trades the ethics of the cave, the love of the broken, fearful father, for the face-to-face encounter between "beings wholly otherwise." It is Elmwood who appropriately shifts attention from himself and his thwarted desires to the young lovers and the possibility of reciprocal fulfillment. He does so by doing the one thing that Miss Milner's own father could not bring himself to do. Elmwood allows his daughter to hear and speak for herself.

When Rushbrook asks for Matilda's hand in marriage, Elmwood will not answer for his daughter. He insists that Matilda be asked in person and that she be allowed to answer in her own voice: "go to him in the library, and hear what he has to say;—for on your will his fate shall depend" (336). Matilda repeats this edict to Rushbrook in words that emphasize that her prerogative and desire will determine the outcome of the courtship. Her father will not intervene: "his lordship has told me it *shall* be in my power: and has desired me to give, or to refuse it you, at my own pleasure" (337). The novel coyly denies us the gratification of hearing Matilda's clear response to the question once it is put to her, but in a sense it is appropriate that we remain outside this private conversation. The novel's lesson has been conveyed through Elmwood. Through his story we have been taught that it is possible to overcome fear simply by learning to listen. Elmwood attends to his daughter, and, by doing so, responds most profoundly to the echo of her mother's voice. More like Abraham than Lot at this point, Elmwood is finally listening to his wife.

Matilda's story is the story of reparation and recovery. As such, it is a lesson for a broken world, a world in which the bonds between human beings, even those of the same family and nation, are uncertain and unreliable because the languages they speak are unknown to each other, their cultures foreign, their assumptions and interpretations unexpected, incomprehensible, and frightening. But, as Matilda and Rushbrook and ultimately Elmwood illustrate, fear does not have to be the failure of ethics if, despite reservations and anxieties, Protestant and Catholic, male and female, young and old will come out of the caves in which they dwell to encounter one another face-to-face in the place they all call home.

It was a strengthening act for Dorriforth to renounce his vows of celibacy in order to marry Miss Milner, but not in the terms posited by the Pope or the English Catholics. The strength resided in looking into the face of another without fear, in welcoming the stranger, in being a lover, a father, and a host whose concern for the other emanates from and leads to a reverence for God that transcends the sectarian and, in doing so, sustains the nation. Elmwood's marriage ended in ignominy, but it also resulted in generation. It is the paradox of the Lot motif, after all, that the shame of a Moabite birth yields the glory of a Davidic kingship. And as Matilda implies in her speech to Rushbrook, woman's desire defined the past, and woman's desire ensures the future. Her mother, after all, has told her so.

Miss Milner's voice, the voice of the writer who created her, the voices of all the novelists we have considered, the voices of the Shulamite woman, Deborah, Jael, Esther, Sarah, Rebekah, Rachel, Hagar, and Lot's daughters are voices that cannot be silenced for those who wish to hear them. The echoes of their spoken words, the effects of their actions, the ways they shaped history, thought, and texts—these traces persist in our culture as evidence that women have always had voice, desire, subjectivity. Women have always had and have always exercised the ability to love, to wound, to heal, to respond, to demand. We can pretend otherwise, by simply refusing to acknowledge their presences—and we have done so in the past, partially through coercion or sometimes violence, but partially too by our own complicity. Yet, in spite of the fact that for many years no one particularly wanted to hear of or from eighteenth-century women writers, they kept speaking in volumes on dusty library shelves. Once in a while, someone would listen. Montague Summers, for example, heard Aphra Behn. Florence Hilbish listened to Charlotte Smith. Joyce Hemlow attended to Fanny Burney. Today, in large numbers, scholars, teachers, theologians, historians, literary critics, philosophers, and readers of all types, answer the demand of the women of the past by acknowledging obligation, by accepting responsibility, by looking into their faces and repeating the mantra of ethical relation: "Here I am; send me." I hope that this volume will stand among the works of these others as an acknowledgment of a face-to-face encounter, a monument to a meeting "in the heart of a chiasmus."[20]

---

20 Derrida, "At this very moment," p. 8.

Conclusion

The Last Word

At the end of the book of Exodus, the Israelites complete the building of the tabernacle or mishkan. The master craftsman, Bezalel, fashions the altar and its accoutrements, including a basin and stand for ritual washing. This laver and receptacle he forms "from the mirrors of the women who performed tasks at the entrance of the Tent of Meeting" (Exodus 38: 8). It struck early commentators as a paradox worth exploring that the mirrors of women would be used for the construction of a sacred object. One commentator, Ibn Ezra, explained that the point must be the rejection of vanity: "they overcame worldly temptations and found no more need to beautify themselves."[1] Rashi, however, has a different explanation, based on a midrashic reading of the text. He sees the mirrors as appropriately sacred—not in their rejection of the carnal interest in beauty, but in their very ability to awaken desire:

> The daughters of Israel came along with the mirrors they gazed into to adorn themselves. Even those they did not withhold from bringing as an offering to the Tabernacle. But Moses rejected them because *they were made to satisfy the evil inclination*. Whereupon the Holy One Blessed be He said to him: Accept! For these are dearer to me than everything else, because through them the women raised up countless hosts in Egypt. When their husbands were weary from the hard labour, they would go along and bring them food and drink, give them to eat and take the mirrors. Each one would look into the mirror together with her husband and egg him on with words saying: 'I am more comely than you.' In the course of this they would arouse their husbands' desire and copulate, becoming pregnant and giving birth there, as it is stated: 'Under the apple tree I aroused thee' (Song of Songs 8: 5).[2]

Nehama Leibowitz endorses Rashi's reading. She explains "the same instinct or impulse which can lead man to perversions, filth and destruction can also lead him to creativity, the building of a house and the continuity of the nation."[3]

Female desire functioned just that way in the beginning of the long eighteenth century. It led to creativity and creation, and it played its part in the defining of a nation and of a people. Reconfigured and sublimated by mid-century stabilities, women nevertheless continued to speak, as we always have and as we always will. We have known since the beginning of time that the arousal of desire in others is a means, not an end. We too seek transcendence—sometimes in the birth of a child, sometimes in the expression of a thought, sometimes in the face of a lover who opens our eyes to the potential divinity in us all. As Behn, Manley, Haywood, their

---

1   Quoted by Nehama Leibowitz, *New Studies in Shemot (Exodus)*, vol. 2, p. 692.
2   Ibid., vol. 2, p. 694.
3   Ibid.

literary progeny, and their paradigmatic foremothers realized, desire can certainly be debased into lust and venality, but without it there is no possibility of love—human or divine—at all.[4]

4   This is *my* last word, but attention to women of the past continues. Of particular interest are two works of scholarship relevant to this study—*The Torah: A Women's Commentary*, edited by Dr. Tamara Cohn-Eskenazi and Rabbi Andrea Weiss, and *Esther Through the Centuries* by Jo Carruthers, both scheduled to appear after my book goes to press.

Works Cited

Addison, Joseph and Richard Steele, *The Spectator*, ed. Donald F. Bond (5 vols, Oxford: Clarendon Press, 1965).

——, *The Tatler,* ed. Donald F. Bond (3 vols, Oxford: Clarendon Press, 1987).

Allen, Robert J., *The Clubs of Augustan London* (Cambridge: Harvard University Press, 1933).

Alliston, April, *Virtue's Faults: Correspondences in Eighteenth-Century British and French Women's Fiction* (Stanford: Stanford University Press, 1996).

Alter, Robert, *The Art of Biblical Narrative* (New York: Basic Books, 1981).

——, *The Five Books of Moses: A Translation with Commentary* (New York: W. W. Norton, 2004).

Anderson, G.K., "Popular Survivals of the Wandering Jew in England," in Galit Hasan-Rokem and Alan Dundes (eds), *The Wandering Jew: Essays in the Interpretation of a Christian Legend* (Bloomington: Indiana University Press, 1986), pp. 76–104.

Armstrong, Nancy, *Desire and Domestic Fiction: A Political History of the Novel* (New York and Oxford: Oxford University Press, 1987).

[Astell, Mary], *Bart'lemy Fair: Or, an Enquiry after Wit* (London: R. Wilkin, 1709).

Ballaster, Ros, *Seductive Forms: Women's Amatory Fiction from 1684 to 1740* (Oxford: Clarendon Press, 1982).

Barash, Carol L., "Gender, Authority and the 'Life' of an Eighteenth-Century Woman Writer: Delarivière Manley's *Adventures of Rivella*," *Women's Studies International Forum* 10:2 (1987): 165–69.

Barbauld, Anna Letitia, "On the Origin and Progress of Novel-Writing," *Anna Letitia Barbauld: Selected Poetry and Prose*, ed. William McCarthy and Elizabeth Kraft, Broadview Literary Texts (Peterborough, Ontario: Broadview Press, 2002), pp. 377–417.

Barchas, Janine, with Gordon D. Fulton, *The Annotations in Lady Bradshaigh's Copy of Clarissa*, English Literary Studies, University of Victoria (Victoria: ELS, 1998).

Barker Benfield, G. J., *The Culture of Sensibility: Sex and Society in Eighteenth-Century Britain* (Chicago: University of Chicago Press, 1996).

Bédoyère, Guy de la, headnote to *Sylva*, in *The Writings of John Evelyn* (Woodbridge, Suffolk, UK: Boydell Press, 1995).

Behn, Aphra, "The Golden Age: A Paraphrase on a Translation out of French," in *Poetry*, vol. 1 of *The Works of Aphra Behn*, ed. Janet Todd (7 vols, Columbus: Ohio State University Press, 1992), pp. 30–5.

——, "The History of the Nun," in *The Fair Jilt and Other Short Stories*, vol. 3 of *The Works of Aphra Behn*, ed. Janet Todd (7 vols, Columbus: Ohio State University Press, 1995), pp. 205–58.

——, *Love Letters Between a Nobleman and His Sister*, vol. 2 of *The Works of Aphra Behn*, ed. Janet Todd (7 vols, Columbus: Ohio State University Press, 1995).

——, *The Rover*, in *The Plays 1671–1677*, vol. 5 of *The Works of Aphra Behn*, ed. Janet Todd (7 vols, Columbus: Ohio State University Press, 1996), pp. 445–521.

Black, Joel, "Taking the Sex Out of Sexuality," in David H. J. Larmour, Paul Allen Miller, and Charles Platter (eds), *Rethinking Sexuality: Foucault and Classical Antiquity* (Princeton: Princeton University Press, 1998), pp. 42–60.

Bloch, Ariel and Chana Bloch, *The Song of Songs: A New Translation* (Berkeley: University of California Press, 1995).

Brelich, Mario, *The Holy Embrace*, trans. John Shepley (Chicago: Northwestern University Press, 1994).

Brophy, Brigid, review of *Fanny Hill*, *New Statesman* (15 November 1963), p. 710.

Buell, Lawrence, "Introduction: In Pursuit of Ethics," *PMLA* 114 (1999): 7–19.

Burney, Frances, *Evelina, or the History of a Young Lady's Entrance into the World*, ed. Edward A. Bloom and Lillian D. Bloom, Oxford World's Classics (Oxford: Oxford University Press, 2002).

——, *The Wanderer; or Female Difficulties*, ed. Margaret Anne Doody, Robert L. Mack, and Peter Sabor, Oxford World's Classics (Oxford: Oxford University Press, 1990).

Bysshe, Edward, *The Art of English Poetry*, 1702, ed. R. C. Alston, English Linguistics 1500–1800: A Collection of Facsimile Reprints 75 (Menston UK: The Scolar Press, 1968).

Canfield, J. Douglas, *Word as Bond in English Literature from the Middle Ages to the Restoration* (Philadelphia: University of Pennsylvania Press, 1989).

Castle, Terry, *Clarissa's Ciphers: Meaning and Disruption in Richardson's "Clarissa"* (Ithaca, NY: Cornell University Press, 1982).

——, *Masquerade and Civilization: The Carnivalesque in Eighteenth-Century English Culture and Fiction* (Stanford: Stanford University Press, 1986).

Chalier, Catherine, "Ethics and the Feminine," in Robert Bernasconi and Simon Critchley (eds), *Re-Reading Levinas* (Bloomington: Indiana University Press, 1991), pp. 119–29.

Colley, Linda, *Britons: Forging the Nation, 1707–1837* (New Haven and London: Yale University Press, 1992).

Congreve, William, *The Way of the World*, ed. Kathleen M. Lynch, Regents Restoration Drama Series (Lincoln: University of Nebraska Press, 1965).

Critchley, Simon, "'BOIS'–Derrida's Final Word on Levinas," in Robert Bernasconi and Simon Critchley (eds), *Re-reading Levinas* (Bloomington: Indiana University Press, 1991), pp. 162–89.

Critical Remarks on Sir Charles Grandison, Clarissa, And Pamela, Enquiring Whether they have a Tendency to corrupt or improve the Public Taste and Morals, by a Lover of Virtue (London: J. Dowse, 1754).

Crone, Patricia and Michael Cook, *Hagarism: The Making of the Islamic World* (Cambridge: Cambridge University Press, 1977).

Cusset, Catherine, "Editor's Preface: The Lesson of Libertinage," *Yale French Studies*, issue 94, *Libertinage and Modernity* (1998): 1–14.

David, Gail, *Female Heroism in the Pastoral* (New York: Garland Publishing, 1991).

Defoe, Daniel, *Robinson Crusoe*, ed. John Richetti (New York: Penguin, 2004).

Derrida, Jacques, "At this very moment in this work here I am," trans. Ruben Berezdivin, in Robert Bernasconi and Simon Critchley (eds), *Re-reading Levinas* (Bloomington, Indiana: Indiana University Press, 1991), pp. 11–48.

Dieckmann, Liselotte, *Hieroglyphics: The History of a Literary Symbol* (St. Louis: Washington University Press, 1970).

Doody, Margaret Anne, "The Gnostic Clarissa," *Eighteenth-Century Fiction* 11 (1998): 49–78.

———, *The True Story of the Novel* (New Brunswick: Rutgers University Press, 1996).

Doppelt, Gerald, "Can Traditional Ethical Theory Meet the Challenge of Feminism, Multiculturalism, and Environmentalism," *The Journal of Ethics* 6 (2002): 383–405.

Dryden, John, *Absalom and Achitophel: A Poem*, in *The Poetical Works of Dryden*, ed. George R. Noyes, Cambridge Edition of the Poets (New York: Houghton Mifflin, 1909), pp. 108–22.

———, "Astraea Redux: A Poem on the Happy Restoration and Return of his Sacred Majesty Charles the Second" in *The Poetical Works of Dryden*, pp. 7–11.

———, "The First Pastoral, or, Tityrus and Meliboeus," in *The Poetical Works of Dryden*, pp. 421–3.

Dufourmantelle, Anne, *Of Hospitality: Anne Dufourmantelle invites Jacques Derrida to Respond*, trans. Rachel Bowlby, Cultural Memory in the Present, gen. eds, Mieke Bal and Hent de Vries (Stanford: Stanford University Press, 2000).

Edelman-Young, Diana Pérez, "Cloistering and Fragmentation: The (Re)construction of Female Subjectivity in Elizabeth Inchbald's *A Simple Story* and Mary Shelley's *Mathilda*," unpublished M.A. thesis (Athens: University of Georgia, 1997).

Ellis, Markman, *The Politics of Sensibility: Race, Gender and Commerce in the Sentimental Novel*, Cambridge Studies in Romanticism, gen. eds Marilyn Butler and James Chandler (Cambridge: Cambridge University Press, 1996).

Empson, William, *Some Versions of Pastoral* (New York: New Directions, 1974).

Etherege, George, *The Man of Mode*, ed. William B. Carnochan, Regents Restoration Drama Series (Lincoln: University of Nebraska Press, 1966).

Etz Hayim: Torah and Commentary (New York: Rabbinical Assembly of the United Synagogue of Conservative Judaism, 2001).

Evelyn, John, *Sylva*, in *The Writings of John Evelyn* (Woodbridge, Suffolk, UK: Boydell Press, 1995).

Fabian, Bernhard, "English Books and Their German Readers," in Paul Korshin (ed.) *The Widening Circle: Essays on the Circulation of Literature in Eighteenth-Century Europe* (Philadelphia: University of Pennsylvania Press, 1976), pp. 119–96.

Fielding, Sarah. *The Adventures of David Simple and The Adventures of David Simple, Volume the Last*, ed. Peter Sabor, Eighteenth-Century Novels by Women, gen. ed. Isobel Grundy (Lexington, KY: University Press of Kentucky, 1998).

———, *The Cry: A New Dramatic Fable* (3 vols, London: R & J Dodsley, 1754).

——, *The History of the Countess of Dellwyn* (2 vols, London: A. Millar, 1759).

——, *The Lives of Cleopatra and Octavia* (London: printed for the author, 1757).

——, *Remarks on Clarissa, Addressed to the Author Occasioned by Some Critical Conversation on the Characters and Conduct of that Work* (London: J. Robinson, 1749).

Fletcher, Lorraine, *Charlotte Smith: A Critical Biography* (London: Macmillan, 1998).

Fox, Michael V., *The Song of Songs and the Ancient Egyptian Love Songs* (Madison: University of Wisconsin Press, 1985).

Foxhall, Lin, "Pandora Unbound: A Feminist Critique of Foucault's *History of Sexuality*," in David H. J. Larmour, Paul Allen Miller, and Charles Platter (eds), *Rethinking Sexuality: Foucault and Classical Antiquity* (Princeton: Princeton University Press, 1998), pp. 122–37.

Frankiel, Tamar, *The Voice of Sarah: Feminine Spirituality and Traditional Judaism* (New York: Biblio Press, 1990).

Friedman, Richard Elliott, *Commentary on the Torah* (New York: HarperCollins, 2001).

——, *The Hidden Face of God* (New York: HarperCollins, 1995).

Frymer-Kensky, Tikva, *Reading the Women of the Bible: A New Interpretation of their Stories* (New York: Schocken Books, 2002).

Gallagher, Catherine, *Nobody's Story: The Vanishing Acts of Women Writers in the Marketplace, 1670–1820* (Berkeley: University of California Press, 1994).

Gardiner, Judith Kegan, "The First English Novel: Aphra Behn's *Love Letters*, the Canon and Women's Tastes," *Tulsa Studies in Women's Literature* 8 (1989): 201–22.

Gellman, Jerome, *Abraham! Abraham! Kierkegaard and the Hasidim on the Binding of Isaac* (London: Ashgate, 2003).

Gibson, Margaret, "Guiltless Credit and the Moral Economy of Salvation," *j-spot: Journal of Social and Political Thought*, online edition, 1 (2001) http://www.yorku.ca/jspot/3/mgibson.htm (accessed 11/28/2003).

Gilbert, Sandra M. and Susan Gubar, *Madwoman in the Attic: The Woman Writer and the Nineteenth-Century Literary Imagination* (New Haven: Yale University Press, 1979).

Glikson, Yvonne, "Wandering Jew," *Encyclopaedia Judaica*, CD-Rom edition, 2006.

Godwin, William, *Political Justice*, ed. H.S. Salt (London: Swan Sonnenschein, 1890).

Goldgar, Bertrand A., *Walpole and the Wits: the Relation of Politics to Literature, 1722–1742* (Lincoln and London: University of Nebraska Press, 1976).

Hagar in the Desert, 4th ed. (Worcester, Mass: Isaiah Thomas, 1785).

Hardin, Richard F., *Love in a Green Shade: Idyllic Romances Ancient to Modern* (Lincoln: University of Nebraska Press, 2000).

Harman, Claire, *Fanny Burney: A Biography* (London: HarperCollins, 2000).

Harris, Frances, *A Passion for Government: The Life of Sarah, Duchess of Marlborough* (Oxford: Clarendon, 1991).

Haywood, Eliza, *Anti-Pamela: Or, Feign'd Innocence Detected, in a Series of Syrena's Adventures* (London: J. Huggonson, 1741).

——, *The History of Miss Betsy Thoughtless*, ed. Christine Blouch, Broadview Literary Texts (Peterborough, Ontario: Broadview Press, 1998).

——, *Love in Excess; or the Fatal Enquiry*, ed. David Oakleaf, Broadview Literary Texts (Peterborough, Ontario: Broadview Press, 1994).

Hover-Gabler, Janet, *Dreaming Black/Writing White: The Hagar Myth in American Cultural History* (Lexington: The University Press of Kentucky, 2000).

Hume, David, *The History of England from the Invasion of Julius Caesar to the Revolution in 1688*. 1778 ed. (6 vols, Indianapolis: Liberty Fund, 1983).

Hunter, J. Paul, *Before Novels: The Cultural Contexts of Eighteenth-Century Fiction* (New York: W. W. Norton, 1990).

——, "Sleeping Beauties: Are Historical Aesthetics Worth Recovering?" *Eighteenth-Century Studies* 24 (2000): 1–20.

Hutchinson, Lucy, *Lucy Hutchinson's Translation of Lucretius: De rerum natura*, ed. Hugh de Quehen (London: Gerald Duckworth & Co., 1996).

Hutner, Heidi, "Revisioning the Female Body: Aphra Behn's *The Rover* Parts I and II," in Heidi Hutner (ed.), *Rereading Aphra Behn: History, Theory, and Criticism* (Charlottesville, VA: University Press of Virginia, 1993), pp.102–20.

Inchbald, Elizabeth, *A Simple Story*, ed. J.M.S. Tompkins, The World's Classics (Oxford: Oxford University Press, 1988).

Irigaray, Luce, *Elemental Passions*, trans. Joanne Collie and Judith Still (New York: Routledge, 1992).

——, *An Ethics of Sexual Difference*, trans. Carolyn Burke and Gillian C. Gill (Ithaca, N.Y.: Cornell University Press, 1984).

——, "Questions to Emmanuel Levinas: On the Divinity of Love," in Robert Bernasconi and Simon Critchley (eds), *Re-reading Levinas* (Bloomington: Indiana University Press, 1991), pp. 109–18.

Jewish Publication Society Hebrew-English Tanakh: The Traditional Hebrew Text and the New JPS Translation (Philadelphia: Jewish Publication Society, 1999).

Jewish Study Bible Featuring the Jewish Publication Society Tanakh Translation, ed. Adele Berlin and Marc Zvi Brettler (Oxford: Oxford University Press, 1985).

Jones, Christopher, *Radical Sensibility: Literature and Ideas in the 1790s* (London and New York: Routledge, 1993).

Keymer, Tom and Peter Sabor, eds. *The Pamela Controversy: Criticisms and Adaptations of Samuel Richardson's "Pamela" 1740–50* (6 vols, London: Pickering and Chatto, 2001).

Kierkegaard, Søren, *Fear and Trembling: Dialectical Lyric by Johannes de silentio*, trans. Alastair Hannay (London: Penguin, 1985).

Kraft, Elizabeth. *Character and Consciousness in Eighteenth-Century Comic Fiction* (Athens: University of Georgia, 1992).

——, "Encyclopedic Libertinism and 1798: Charlotte Smith's *The Young Philosopher*," *The Eighteenth-Century Novel: A Scholarly Annual*, 2 (2002): 239–72.

——, "Laurence Sterne and the Ethics of Sexual Difference: Chiasmic Narration and Double Desire," *Christianity and Literature*, 51 (2002): 363–85.

——, "Wit and *The Spectator*'s Ethics of Desire," *Studies in English Literature* 45 (2005): 625–46.

Kristeva, Julia, *Desire in Language: A Semiotic Approach to Literature and Art*, ed. Leon S. Roudiez, trans. Thomas Gora, Alice Jardine, and Leon S. Roudiez (New York: Columbia University Press, 1980).

——, *Tales of Love*, trans. Leon S. Roudiez (New York: Columbia University Press, 1987).

Kropf, C. R., "Libel and Satire in the Eighteenth Century," *Eighteenth-Century Studies*, 8 (1974): 153–68.

Lamb, Jonathan, "The Job Controversy, Sterne, and the Question of Allegory," *Eighteenth-Century Studies*, 24 (1990): 1–19.

Laquer, Thomas, *Making Sex: Body and Gender From the Greeks to Freud* (Cambridge: Harvard University Press, 1990).

Leibowitz, Nehama, *New Studies in Bereshit*, trans Aryeh Newman (Jerusalem: Maor Wallah Press, n.d.)

——, *New Studies in Shemot*, trans. Aryeh Newman (2 vols, Jerusalem: Eliner Library, 1996).

Levinas, Emmanuel, "Enigma and Phenomenon," in Adriaan T. Peperzak, Simon Critchley, and Robert Bernasconi (eds), *Emmanuel Levinas: Basic Philosophical Writings* (Bloomington: Indiana University Press, 1996), pp. 65–77.

——, "Ethics as First Philosophy," trans. Seán Hand and Michael Temple, in Seán Hand (ed.), *The Levinas Reader* (Oxford: Blackwell, 1989), pp. 75–87.

——, *Otherwise Than Being or Beyond Essence*, trans. Alphonso Lingis, Martinus Nijhoff Philosophy Texts, vol. 3 (The Hague, 1981).

——, *Totality and Infinity: An Essay on Exteriority*, trans. Alphonso Lingis (Pittsburgh: Duquesne University Press, 1969).

——, "Wholly Otherwise," in Robert Bernasoni and Simon Critchley (eds) *Re-reading Levinas* (Bloomington: Indiana University Press, 1991), pp. 3–10.

Locke, John, *An Essay Concerning Human Understanding*, ed. Peter H. Nidditch (Oxford: Clarendon Press, 1975).

Lucretius, *Lucy Hutchinson's translation of Lucretius De Rerum Natura*, ed. Hugh de Quehen (London: Gerald Duckworth and Co., 1996).

Maccoby, Hyam, "The Wandering Jew as Sacred Executioner" in Galit Hasan-Rokem and Alan Dundes (eds), *The Wandering Jew: Essays in the Interpretation of a Christian Legend* (Bloomington: Indiana University Press, 1986), pp. 236–60.

McCrea, Brian, *Impotent Fathers: Patriarchy and Demographic Crisis in the Eighteenth-Century Novel* (Newark: University of Delaware Press, 1998).

Mackie, Erin, *Market á la Mode: Fashion, Commodity, and Gender in "The Tatler" and "The Spectator"* (Baltimore: Johns Hopkins University Press, 1997).

Manley, Delarivier, *The Adventures of Rivella*, ed. Katherine Zelinsky, Broadview Literary Texts (Peterborough, Ontario: Broadview Press, 1999).

——, *Memoirs of Europe, Towards the Close of the Eighth Century* (London: John Morphew, 1710).

——, *New Atalantis*, ed. Rosalind Ballaster (London: Penguin, 1992).

Mellinkoff, Ruth "Sarah and Hagar: Laughter and Tears," in Michelle P. Brown and Scott McKendrick (eds), *Illuminating the Book: Makers and Interpreters. Essays in Honor of Janet Blackhouse*, The British Library Studies in Medieval Culture (London and Toronto: The British Library and University of Toronto Press, 1998), pp. 35–51.

Messenger, Ann, *Pastoral Tradition and the Female Talent: Studies in Augustan Poetry* (New York: AMS Press, 2001).

Mitchell, W.J.T., "Ekphrasis and the Other," in his *Picture Theory: Essays on Verbal and Visual Representation* (Chicago: University of Chicago Press, 1994), pp.151–81.

Müllenbrock, Heinz-Joachim, *The Culture of Contention: A Rhetorical Analysis of the Public Controversy about the Ending of the War of the Spanish Succession, 1710–1713* (München: Wilhelm Fink Verlag, 1997).

Nestor, Deborah J., "Virtue Rarely Rewarded: Ideological Subversion and Narrative Form in Haywood's Later Fiction," *Studies in English Literature* 34 (1994): 579–98.

New, Melvyn, "Sterne, Warburton, and the Burden of Exuberant Wit," *Eighteenth-Century Studies*, 15 (1982): 245–74.

Newton, Adam Zachary, *Narrative Ethics* (Cambridge: Harvard University Press, 1995).

Nussbaum, Felicity A., *The Brink of All We Hate: English Satires on Women, 1660–1750* (Lexington, KY: The University Press of Kentucky, 1984).

———, "Effeminacy and Femininity: Domestic Prose Satire and *David Simple*," *Eighteenth-Century Fiction* 11 (1999): 421–44.

———, *Torrid Zones: Maternity, Sexuality, and Empire in Eighteenth-Century English Narratives*. (Baltimore: Johns Hopkins, 1995).

Oakleaf, David, Introduction to Eliza Haywood's *Love in Excess; or the Fatal Enquiry*, Broadview Literary Texts (Peterborough, Ontario: Broadview Press, 1994), pp. 3–25.

———, "The Eloquence of Blood in Eliza Haywood's *Lasselia*," *Studies in English Literature* 39 (1999): 483–98.

"On the Toasting Glasses of the Kit-Cat Club" (1703), *A Select Collection of Poems with Notes Biographical and Historical*, ed. John Nichols (8 vols, London: J. Nichols, 1782; New York: Kraus Reprint, 1969), vol. 5, pp. 168–76.

Pagels, Elaine, *Adam, Eve and the Serpent* (New York: Vintage Books, 1988).

Pamela Censured: in a Letter to the Editor: Shewing that under the Specious Pretence of Cultivating the Principles of Virtue in the Minds of the Youth of both Sexes, the Most Artful and Alluring Amorous Ideas are convey'd (1741), rpt. in Keymer and Sabor (eds), *The Pamela Controversy: Criticisms and Adaptations of Samuel Richardson's "Pamela" 1740–50* (6 vols, London: Pickering and Chatto, 2001), vol. 2, pp. 13–78.

Patterson, Annabel, *Pastoral and Ideology: Virgil to Valéry* (Berkeley: University of California Press, 1987).

Pepys, Samuel, *The Diary of Samuel Pepys*, ed. Robert Latham and William Matthews (11 vols, London: Harper Collins, 1995).

Pettit, Alexander, "Adventures in Pornographic Places: Eliza Haywood's *Tea Table* and the Decentering of Moral Argument," *Papers on Language and Literature* 38 (2002): 244–69.

——, "*David Simple* and the Attenuation of 'Phallic Power,'" *Eighteenth-Century Fiction* 11 (1999):169–84.

Plaut, W. Gunther, ed, *The Torah: A Modern Commentary* (New York: Union of American Hebrew Congregations, 1981).

Pocock, J.G.A., *The Machiavellian Moment: Florentine Political Thought and the Atlantic Republican Tradition* (Princeton and London: Princeton University Press, 1975).

Polhemus, Robert M., *Lot's Daughters: Sex, Redemption, and Women's Quest for Authority* (Stanford: Stanford University Press, 2005).

Pollak, Ellen, *Incest and the English Novel, 1684–1814* (Baltimore: Johns Hopkins University Press, 2003).

Pope, Alexander, *The Dunciad Variorum*, in *The Poems of Alexander Pope*, a one-volume edition of the Twickenham text, ed. John Butt (New Haven: Yale University Press, 1963), pp. 317–459.

Review of *Miss Betsy Thoughtless*. *Monthly Review* 5 (October 1752): 393–94, reprinted as Appendix B in Eliza Haywood, *The History of Miss Betsy Thoughtless*, ed. Christine Blouch, Broadview Literary Texts (Peterborough, Ontario: Broadview Press, 1998).

Review of *The Young Philosopher*, *The Anti-Jacobin Review and Magazine*, 1 (1798): 187–90.

Richardson, Samuel, *Clarissa, or The History of a Young Lady*, ed. Angus Ross (Harmondsworth, Middlesex, England: Penguin Books, 1985).

——, *The Correspondence of Samuel Richardson, Author of Pamela, Clarissa, and Sir Charles Grandison*, ed. Anna Letitia Barbauld (6 vols, London: Richard Phillips, 1804).

——, *The History of Sir Charles Grandison*, ed. Jocelyn Harris, The World's Classics (Oxford: Oxford University Press, 1986).

Richlin, Amy, "Foucault's *History of Sexuality*: A Useful Theory for Women?" in David H. J. Larmour, Paul Allen Miller, and Charles Platter (eds), *Rethinking Sexuality: Foucault and Classical Antiquity* (Princeton: Princeton University Press, 1998), pp. 138–70.

Ross, Angus, Introduction to *Clarissa, or The History of a Young Lady* (Harmondsworth, Middlesex, England: Penguin Books, 1985).

Rousseau, Jean-Jacques, *Emile, or On Education*, trans. Allan Bloom (New York: Basic Books, 1979).

Schellenberg, Betty A., *The Conversational Circle: Rereading the English Novel, 1740–1775* (Lexington: The University Press of Kentucky, 1996).

Segal, Lynne, *Straight Sex: Rethinking the Politics of Pleasure* (Berkeley: University of California Press, 1994).

Shea, Stuart, "Subversive Didacticism in Eliza Haywood's *Betsy Thoughtless*," *Studies in English Literature* 42 (2002): 559–75.

Sinfield, Alan. "Lesbian and Gay Taxonomies," *Critical Inquiry* 29 (2002): 120–38.

Smith, Charlotte, *Minor Morals, Interspersed with Sketches of Natural History, Historical Anecdotes, and Original Stories* (2 vols, London: Sampson Low, 1798).

——, *The Young Philosopher*, ed. Elizabeth Kraft, Eighteenth-Century Novels by Women, gen. ed. Isobel Grundy (Lexington, KY: University Press of Kentucky, 1999).

The Soncino Chumash, ed. Rabbi Dr. A. Cohen and Rev. Rabbi A. J. Rosenberg (London: Soncino Press, Ltd, 1947).

Sorkin, David, "William Warburton: The Middle Way of 'Heroic Moderation,'" *Nederlands Archief voor Kerkgeschiedenis*, 82.2 (2002): 262–300.

Spacks, Patricia Meyer, *Desire and Truth: Functions of Plot in Eighteenth-Century English Novels* (Chicago: University of Chicago Press, 1990).

Spivak, Gayatri, "French Feminism Revisited," in Judith Butler and Joan W. Scott (eds), *Feminists Theorize the Political* (London: Routledge, 1992), pp. 54–85.

Steen, Francis F., "The Politics of Love: Propaganda and Structural Learning in Aphra Behn's *Love-Letters between a Nobleman and His Sister*," *Poetics Today* 23 (2002): 91–122.

Stone, Lawrence and Jeanne C. Fawtier Stone, *An Open Elite? England 1540–1880* (Oxford: Clarendon Press, 1984).

Thompson, Peggy, "Abuse and Atonement: The Passion of Clarissa Harlowe," *Eighteenth-Century Fiction* 11 (1999): 255–70.

Todd, Janet, "'The hot brute drudges on': Ambiguities of Desire in Aphra Behn's *Love-Letters Between a Nobleman and his Sister*," *Women's Writing* 1 (1994): 277–90.

——, *The Secret Life of Aphra Behn* (New Brunswick, New Jersey: Rutgers University Press, 1996).

The Torah: A Modern Commentary, ed. W. Gunther Plaut (New York: Union of American Hebrew Congregations, 1981).

Ty, Eleanor, *Unsex'd Revolutionaries: Five Women Novelists of the 1790s* (Toronto: University of Toronto Press, 1993).

Virgil, "The First Pastoral, or, Tityrus and Meliboeus," trans. John Dryden, in *The Poetical Works of Dryden*, ed. George R. Noyes, Cambridge Edition of the Poets (New York: Houghton Mifflin, 1909), pp. 421–3.

Wahl, Elizabeth, *Invisible Relations: Representations of Female Intimacy in the Age of Enlightenment* (Stanford: Stanford University Press, 1999).

Warburton, William, *The Divine Legation of Moses Demonstrated* (1741) (4 vols, New York: Garland, 1978).

Warner, William, "Formulating Fiction: Romancing the General Reader in Early Modern Britain," in Deidre Lynch and William B. Warner (eds), *Cultural Institutions of the Novel* (Durham: Duke University Press, 1996), pp. 279–305.

Webb, Stephen H., "The Rhetoric of Ethics as Excess: A Christian Theological Response to Emmanuel Levinas," *Modern Theology* 15 (1999): 1–16.

Wehrs, Donald R., "Eros, Ethics, Identity: Royalist Feminism and the Politics of Desire in Aphra Behn's *Love Letters*," *Studies in English Literature* 32 (1992): 461–78.

Welch, John W., "Introduction," in John W. Welch (ed.), *Chiasmus in Antiquity: Structures, Analyses, Exegesis* (Gerstenberg: Verlag, 1981), pp. 9–16.

Wheeler, Roxann, *The Complexion of Race: Categories of Difference in Eighteenth-Century British Culture* (Philadelphia: University of Pennsylvania Press, 2000).

Whelan, Kevin, "Reinterpreting the 1798 Rebellion in County Wexford," in Daire Keogh and Nicholas Furlong (eds), *The Mighty Wave: The 1798 Rebellion in Wexford* (Dublin: Four Courts Press, 1996).

Willan, Leonard, *Astraea, or, True Love's Myrrour, A Pastoral* (London: R. White for Henry Cripps and Lodowick Lloyd, 1651).

Woolf, Virginia, *A Room of One's Own* (San Diego: Harcourt Brace and Co., 1929).

Wollstonecraft, Mary, *Vindication of the Rights of Woman*, ed. Miriam Brody (London: Penguin, 1982).

Yates, Frances, *Astraea: The Imperial Theme in the Sixteenth Century* (1975; rpt. London: Pimlico, 1993).

Zelinsky, Katherine, ed., *Adventures of Rivella* by Delarivier Manley, Broadview Literary Texts (Peterborough, Ontario: Broadview Press, 1999).

Index

Aaron, 103–4

Abigail, 25n40, 71

Abraham: 15–16, 16–20, 22, 23, 27n49, 35, 98, 133–7, 144, 148, 154, 159, 162–5, 170; in Islam, 136; in midrash, 136

Absalom, 48

Absalom and Achitophel (Dryden), 48n32

Act of Settlement, 4, 151

Adam, 34, 117

Addison, Joseph: 115, 127n52; and libertinism, 128–30; and Kit Cat Club, 128–9; on wit, 115, 126–30

Adventures of Rivella (Manley): 83–6; Albemarle lawsuit in, 85–6; and desire, 84–6; hieroglyphics in, 83, 85; interpretation in 84–5

Ahasuerus, 76–9, 77n14, 81

Akiba ben Joseph, 39

Albemarle, second duke of, 85–6

Allegory: 87–96; reading of Adam, Eve, and the serpent as, 117

Alliston, April, 3n3

Alter, Robert, 21, 24n35, 25–6, 25n40, 97, 163n8

Anderson, G. K., 150n40

Anne (queen of England), 5, 63, 65–6, 68

Anti-Jacobin Review, 142

Anti-Pamela: Or, Feign'd Innocence Detected (Haywood), 106–7, 108–9

Ariosto, Ludovico, 6

Armstrong, Nancy, 8–9, 8n12, 10

Astell, Mary: 129n56, *Bart'lemy Fair: Or an Enquiry after Wit*, 128–9

Astraea (Justice): 59–72; and Elizabeth I, 60; and female desire, 60; and the Golden Age, 59; as Aphra Behn's "code name," 59, 60, 61n17; as emblem of imperial revival, 59; in Dryden's poetry, 59; in *L'Astree* (D'Urfe), 60–61; in *New Atalantis* (Manley), 61, 63–5, 70–72, 73

Astraea, or, True Love's Myrrour (Willan), dedicatory preface to, 61

Austen, Jane: 10; *Persuasion*, 101

Bacon, Francis, on hieroglyphics, 74n5

Ballaster, Ros, 9–10, 51n1, 51n2, 64n21

Barak, 53–5, 54n7, 56

Barash, Carol L., 86n29

Barbauld, Anna Letitia, 7–8

Barchas, Janine, 111, 111n26, 113

Barker-Benfield, G. J., 119

"Bartleby the Scrivener" (Melville), 6

Bart'lemy Fair: Or an Enquiry after Wit (Astell), 128–9

Bathsheba, 25n40

Behn, Aphra: 4, 4n4, 9, 10, 11, 23, 33, 34, 34n4, 37n11, 51, 52, 56–9, 61, 61n17, 87, 89, 90, 91, 114, 167, 178, 179; "The Golden Age," 60; "History of the Nun," 56–9; *Love Letters Between a Nobleman and his Sister* (Behn), 35–50, 61, 65, 101; *The Rover*, 23n33; "To the Fair Clarinda, who made Love to me, imagin'd more than Woman," 4n4

Berkeley, Henrietta, 35, 40, 43, 46, 47

Betsy Thoughtless (Haywood): allegory in 93–4; Betsy as complex signifier in, 95; hieroglyphics in, 94–5; women as ciphers in, 95–6

Bezalel, 179

Black, Joel, 2n1

Bible: books of, *see under* individual books; foundational status of, 23, 23n33, 30; King James translation, 28n52; personages in, *see under* individual names; Richardson's heroines and, 116–17; women's voices in, 15, 34–5

Bloch, Ariel and Chana Bloch, 28n52, 35n8, 38

Boaz, 25n40, 159